MW00988005

SABR and SABR LIBOR Market Models in Practice

Applied Quantitative Finance series

Applied Quantitative Finance is a new series developed to bring readers the very latest market tested tools, techniques and developments in quantitative finance. Written for practitioners who need to understand how things work 'on the floor', the series will deliver the most cutting-edge applications in areas such as asset pricing, risk management and financial derivatives. Although written with practitioners in mind, this series will also appeal to researchers and students who want to see how quantitative finance is applied in practice.

Also available

Marc Henrard
INTEREST RATE MODELLING IN THE MULTI-CURVE FRAMEWORK
Foundations, Evolution and Implementation

Chris Kenyon, Roland Stamm
DISCOUNTING, LIBOR, CVA AND FUNDING
Interest Rate and Credit Pricing

Leo Krippner
ZERO LOWER BOUND TERM STRUCTURE MODELLING
A Practitioner's Guide

Adil Reghai
QUANTITATIVE FINANCE
Back to Basic Principles

Ignacio Ruiz
XVA DESKS: A NEW ERA FOR RISK MANAGEMENT
Understanding, Building and Managing Counterparty and Funding Risk

SABR and SABR LIBOR Market Models in Practice

With Examples Implemented in Python

Christian Crispoldi

Gérald Wigger

Peter Larkin

© Christian Crispoldi, Gérald Wigger and Peter Larkin 2015

All rights reserved. No reproduction, copy or transmission of this publication may be made without written permission.

No portion of this publication may be reproduced, copied or transmitted save with written permission or in accordance with the provisions of the Copyright, Designs and Patents Act 1988, or under the terms of any licence permitting limited copying issued by the Copyright Licensing Agency, Saffron House, 6–10 Kirby Street, London EC1N 8TS.

Any person who does any unauthorized act in relation to this publication may be liable to criminal prosecution and civil claims for damages.

The authors have asserted their rights to be identified as the authors of this work in accordance with the Copyright, Designs and Patents Act 1988.

First published 2015 by
PALGRAVE MACMILLAN

Palgrave Macmillan in the UK is an imprint of Macmillan Publishers Limited, registered in England, company number 785998, of Houndmills, Basingstoke, Hampshire RG21 6XS.

Palgrave Macmillan in the US is a division of St Martin's Press LLC, 175 Fifth Avenue, New York, NY 10010.

Palgrave Macmillan is the global academic imprint of the above companies and has companies and representatives throughout the world.

Palgrave® and Macmillan® are registered trademarks in the United States, the United Kingdom, Europe and other countries

ISBN: 978–1–137–37863–7

This book is printed on paper suitable for recycling and made from fully managed and sustained forest sources. Logging, pulping and manufacturing processes are expected to conform to the environmental regulations of the country of origin.

A catalogue record for this book is available from the British Library.

A catalog record for this book is available from the Library of Congress.

To Pamela and Stefano

To Charlie, Vincent and Emilia

To Shanti and Ella

Contents

List of Figures

List of Tables

Acknowledgments

We would like to thank Alexander Antonov, Michael Konikov and Michael Spector for the fruitful email exchange related to their SABR approximation. A special thanks also to Thomson Reuters for having provided us with the data used for our analysis.

List of Abbreviations

ATM	at the money
bps	basis point, 1bps=0.0001
CMS	constant maturity swap
CSA	credit support annex
CVA	credit value adjustment
FRA	forward rate agreement
HJM	Heath, Jarrow and Morton
IRS	interest rate swap
ITM	in the money
LIBOR	London interbank offered rate
LMM	LIBOR market model
OIS	overnight index swap
OTC	over-the-counter
OTM	out of the money
PDE	partial differential equation
PDF	probability density function
SABR	stochastic alpha-beta-rho model
SABR LMM	SABR LIBOR market model
SDE	stochastic differential equation
SMM	swap market model

List of Notations

T_k	Time T_k on the time grid
τ_k	Year fraction between T_k and T_{k+1}
C_x	Interest rate curve with tenor x. When $x = d$, we denote the discounting curve
$P_x(t, T_k)$	Value at time t of a zero-coupon bond with maturity T_k calculated on the curve with tenor x
$R(t, T_k)$	Spot rate at time t with maturity T_k
$r(t)$	Short rate at time t
$B_d(t)$	Value at time t of the bank account associated with the discounting curve C_d
$L(t, T_k)$	LIBOR rate at time t with maturity T_k
$F_x\left(t, T_{k-1}, T_k\right) \equiv F_{x,k}(t)$	FRA rate at time t, fixing at time T_{k-1} and maturing at time T_k calculated on the curve with tenor x
$f(t, T_k)$	Instantaneous forward rate at time t with maturity T_k
$S_{m,n}(t)$	Swap rate at time t associated with the IRS starting at T_m and ending at T_n
Blk	Black function for all Black related formulas
Norm	Normal model (Bachelier) function for all Normal model related formulas
$\sigma_k^B(y)$	Black implied volatility for a caplet/floorlet with strike y, expiry T_{k-1} and paying at T_k
$\sigma_k^N(y)$	Normal implied volatility for a caplet/floorlet with strike y, expiry T_{k-1} and paying at T_k
$\tilde{\sigma}_n^B(y)$	Black volatility for a cap/floor with maturity T_n and strike y
$\mathbf{FRA}(t, T_k, y)$	Value at time t of a forward rate agreement with agreed rate y and maturity at T_k
$\mathbf{FRA_{OIS}}(t, T_k, y)$	Value at time t of an OIS forward rate agreement with agreed rate y and maturity at T_k
$\mathbf{EDF}(t, T_k)$	Value at time t of a Eurodollar futures contract with maturity at T_k
$\mathbf{OISSwap_r}(t, T_m, T_n, y)$	Value at time t of a receiver swap (where the floating leg pays OIS) starting at T_m with maturity T_n and fixed rate y

$\text{OISSwap}_p\left(t, T_m, T_n, y\right)$ Value at time t of a payer swap (where the floating leg receives OIS) starting at T_m with maturity T_n and fixed rate y

$\text{IRS}_r\left(t, T_m, T_n, y\right)$ Value at time t of a receiver swap (where the floating leg pays LIBOR) starting at T_m with maturity T_n and fixed rate y

$\text{IRS}_p\left(t, T_m, T_n, y\right)$ Value at time t of a payer swap (where the floating leg receives LIBOR) starting at T_m with maturity T_n and fixed rate y

$A_{d,m,n}(t)$ Value at time t of the annuity, associated with the discounting curve C_d, for the swap starting at T_m and ending at T_n

$\text{TBasis}\left(t, T_m, T_n, basis\right)$ Value at time t of a basis swap between T_m and T_n

$\text{RS}(t, T_m, T_n, y)$ Value at time t of a receiver swaption with expiry at T_m. The underlying swap starts at T_m and ends at T_n with fixed rate y

$\text{PS}(t, T_m, T_n, y)$ Value at time t of a payer swaption with expiry at T_m. The underlying swap starts at T_m and ends at T_n with fixed rate y

$G_{m,n}(t)$ Value at time t of the cash annuity for the swap starting at T_m and ending at T_n

$\text{Cpl}\left(t, T_{k-1}, T_k, y\right)$ Value at time t of a caplet with strike y, expiry T_{k-1} and paying at T_k

$\text{Cap}\left(t, T_n, y\right)$ Value at time t of a cap with strike y and maturity T_n

$\text{Fll}\left(t, T_{k-1}, T_k, y\right)$ Value at time t of a floorlet with strike y, expiry T_{k-1} and paying at T_k

$\text{Floor}\left(t, T_n, y\right)$ Value at time t of a floor with strike y and maturity T_n

y_{ATM} At the money strike

$\mathbb{P}$ Real world measure

$\mathbb{Q}^k$ Risk neutral forward measure associated with the numeraire $P_d\left(t, T_k\right)$

$\mathbb{E}^k[\cdot]$ Expectation under the risk neutral forward measure associated with the numeraire $P_d\left(t, T_k\right)$

$\mathbb{Q}^N$ Risk neutral terminal measure associated with the numeraire $P_d\left(t, T_N\right)$ (last bond on the time grid)

$\mathbb{Q}^B$ Risk neutral spot measure associated with the numeraire $B_d(t)$

$\mathbb{E}^B[\cdot]$ Expectation under the risk neutral spot measure associated with the numeraire $B_d(t)$

$\mathbb{Q}^{m,n}$	Risk neutral swap measure associated with the numeraire $A_{d,m,n}(t)$
$\mathbb{E}^{m,n}[\cdot]$	Expectation under the risk neutral swap measure associated with the numeraire $A_{d,m,n}(t)$
$\mathcal{F}_t$	Filtration up to time t
$Num(t)$	General numeraire at time t
$M(t)$	Radon-Nikodym derivative at time t
$dW(t)$	Brownian motion
$dW_k(t)$	Brownian motion under the T_k-forward measure $\mathbb{Q}^k$
$dW_{m,n}(t)$	Brownian motion under the swap measure $\mathbb{Q}^{m,n}$
α_k	SABR model volatility associated with the forward F_k
β_k	Exponent of the forward rate F_k in the SABR model
v_k	SABR model volatility of α_k
ρ_k	Correlation factor between the SABR processes α_k and F_k
n_{sim}	Number of Monte Carlo simulations
n_{step}	Number of Monte Carlo time steps

1 | Introduction

Dubium sapientiae initium.

René Descartes

1.1 Who should read this book

In the last two decades an extensive selection of books on interest rate or equity derivatives modelling became available through various publishers. We therefore take the opportunity to say a few words on the main texts out there and how our work complements the current literature.

On the interest rate derivatives side, probably the most sophisticated book to date is the collection *Interest Rate Modeling I, II, III* by Andersen and Piterbarg (2010). Split into volumes I, II and III, it is a comprehensive piece of work, covering not only standard techniques but also discussing more complex topics such as the Markovian projection. Another book, which has become a standard reading for quantitative analysts working on interest rate derivatives is *Interest Rate Models – Theory and Practice: With Smile, Inflation and Credit* by Brigo and Mercurio (2006). It is strongly recommended for those seeking an applied practical approach, both for those with enough mathematics for a thorough understanding, yet without being off-putting for less mathematically minded readers. However, both these titles provide a limited overview of the SABR model, and although the first one covers term structure models with stochastic volatility, neither provide materials related to the SABR LIBOR Market Model (SABR LMM).

A third book, which completes the interest rate modelling spectrum is *The SABR/LIBOR Market Model: Pricing, Calibration and Hedging for Complex Interest-Rate Derivatives*, Rebonato et al. (2009). This publication covers very thoroughly the SABR LMM. It is however addressed to a seasoned public with very good foundations in the interest rate derivatives market.

A common factor of the three titles mentioned is that they all show a great depth of mathematical details but lack code examples or implementation 'recipes'. As a reminder, a large part of a typical quantitative analyst job is implementing models, adjusting calibration procedures, perfecting calendar grids. It is worth mentioning at this point that there are books showing code snippets, such as the great review of stochastic volatility by Lewis (2000), but the use of the coding language and the snippets remain rather impractical.

We aim to bridge the gap between the understanding of the models from a conceptual and mathematical perspective and the actual implementation by supplementing our review of the interest rate theory with working code. We do this by providing clear, specific, code examples for interest rate modelling written in Python. The code should bring the equations to life and lift the reader's understanding of models to a higher and clearer level. The mathematical complexity and model sophistication presented targets mainly new entry quants and risk managers. We emphasize however that the book can add value to any quantitative analyst who is interested in understanding the major concepts and the application of the LIBOR Market Model, the SABR model and the combined SABR LMM.

1.2 Outline

The main goal of this book is to teach the reader a practical and useful approach to modelling interest rates. In particular, we will go into detail on the stochastic alpha-beta-rho (SABR) model and the SABR LMM. By providing a clear coverage of these two models, together with their implementation, the reader will be able to add a wide tool set to her or his skills, in an enjoyable and stimulating way.

Besides the obvious application by exotic trading desks in pricing and hedging vanilla (SABR), complex and path-dependent derivatives (SABR LMM), these models could be also used by hedge funds speculating on the volatility space, mortgage traders arbitraging prepayment models or insurance companies managing the embedded optionalities in life insurance policies.

Throughout the book we will present examples and tests performed on real market data, sourced from Thomson Reuters Eikon, and collected in the period June–December 2013. The reference markets are CHF and EUR. The former has been chosen because it is particularly challenging from a modelling point of view. It has in fact been characterized by negative rates and very high implied volatility. The latter has been chosen due to its leading role in the interest rate derivatives space, where most exotic and structured instruments, along with a very high volume of vanilla products, are traded.

We introduce in Chapter 3 the mathematical foundation for the following chapters and define the basic financial instruments and their valuation in a deterministic world. Throughout the book, all valuations will be proposed in a multiple curve framework. This now almost standard curve setup emerged shortly after the 2007–2008 financial crisis when most derivatives required collateral to be posted. In short, cash flows in this framework are discounted using a curve that replicates the costs of collateral funding, that is an appropriate overnight risk free curve, and forwards are projected using a LIBOR projection replicating an unsecured funding.

To facilitate the entrance into the modelling of derivatives, we will be introducing the reader, in Chapter 4, to simplistic approaches needed for the pricing of caps, floors and swaptions.

Following this rather extensive introduction, we dedicate ourselves to the most popular stochastic volatility model for interest rates, the SABR model, in Chapter 5. The SABR model was first introduced to a wider audience by Hagan, Kumar, Lesniewski and Woodward in Hagan et al. (2002). In this model, the forward (LIBOR or swap) rate is modelled stochastically with a stochastic volatility process. The model is widely used for vanilla pricing and interpolation in the rates derivatives world due to closed form approximations that have been refined further in recent years. Perhaps due to its simplicity and the intuitive nature by which one can interpret its parameters, the model has caught the imagination of many academics and practitioners. This has resulted in many solutions, usable or not usable in practice. The model will be crucial later in the book when we cover the SABR LMM: a LIBOR Market Model with a stochastic volatility process for each forward rate.

In Chapter 6 we provide an analysis of the LIBOR Market Model (LMM). We will also cover in this chapter newer topics such as how one can use adjoint methods to compute Greeks in a quick way, and we will also spend time discussing how one calibrates correlation and volatility in this modelling setting. On reading this chapter and working through the provided code, the reader will be in a good position to understand the material related to the SABR LMM. We explain two approaches known in the literature and explicitly show our implementation of one of them in Chapter 7.

1.3 Python, NumPy and SciPy

Typically a large part of the day to day work of a quantitative analyst is to implement a model and integrate this into the pricing environment. Understanding the model and writing its complete set of dynamics is certainly one part of the job, but an arguably equally important and rewarding step is coding it. The readers of this book will come from many backgrounds, some very mathematically oriented and others perhaps have a computer science background, and so by providing the reader with the equations and code examples, both communities will be able to take something from the book. Python (see, e.g., Martelli 2006) is widely used in banking, often as a

Table 1.1 Python functions list

Python function name	Reference
black	Table 4.1
computeFirstDerivative	Table 4.6
computeSecondDerivative	Table 4.7
haganLogNormalApprox	Table 5.1
computeSABRDelta	Table 5.2
computeSABRVega	Table 5.3
drawTwoRandomNumbers	Table 5.4
simulateSABRMonteCarloEuler	Table 5.5
simulateSABRMonteCarloMilstein	Table 5.10
generateParametricCorrelationMatrix	Table 6.4
getCapletVolatility	Table 6.6
getInstantaneousVolatility	Table 6.7
reduceRank	Table 6.8
drawRandomNumbers	Table 6.10
simulateSABRLMM	Table 7.7

language for interfacing data feeds to a system or as an API to the pricing/risk library developed in C++. The advantages of providing examples in Python are multifold. It is easy to read for someone who already has some experience programming in other languages, offers object oriented structures, is open source, and has several excellent and well developed numerical libraries, notably SciPy and NumPy (see Jones et al. 2001–). Python also has the graphing capabilities comparable with R or Matlab, thanks to the matplotlib library (see Hunter 2007), which has been employed to produce most of the charts appearing in this book.

We will present a series of Python functions (Table 1.1) throughout the book, many of which will be used and referenced within more complex code examples in later chapters. The code presented should not be considered the unique, most efficient or fastest implementation available to solve the problem at hand. We rather focus on trying to convey an easy to grasp and propaedeutic solution.

2 | Interest Rate Derivatives Markets

2.1 Interest rates

There are today, many different interest rates, and since this can be confusing for newcomers to the area, we will spend some time discussing the various types; we will concentrate only on a small number of them, which will form the building blocks for the derivatives markets. The money market has become the predominant source for providing liquidity funding for financial institutions, and allows them to manage their operational cash requirements up to a time horizon of one year. Various instruments exist, such as deposits, certificates of deposits, commercial papers, bills and repurchase agreements. To learn more about all these short-term instruments, the reader is referred to Choudhry (2010).

A major component of the money market is called the overnight market, which involves the shortest possible term loan. The money is lent overnight, so that they have to be repaid at the start of the next business day. The amount to be repaid is equal to the amount borrowed plus a small interest on top. The money is literally attributed to the other party the same day and withdrawn, including the payable interest, the next day. Given the short period of the loan, the interest rate charged in the overnight market, known as the overnight rate, is, generally speaking, the lowest rate at which banks lend money.

We will discuss shortly why this type of interest rate has been brought to direct relevance for the pricing of a wide range of products, and how it plays an important role in the multiple curve (also known as the dual curve) framework. In this book we will refer to the overnight rate as the uncollateralized rate for overnight borrowing. As a concrete example, the EONIA, that is the European Overnight Index Average, is the average of all unsecured lending transactions between contributing panel banks in the Euro countries from the target day to the next banking day. The average is calculated by the European Central Bank and is quoted using the day count convention ACT/360 up to three decimal places. In the United States, the Fed Fund rate, or better the daily effective federal funds rate, is a volume-weighted average of rates on trades between the major market participants.

Table 2.1 Overnight rates in major currencies

Currency	Rate	Effective name
EUR	EONIA	Euro OverNight Index Average
USD	Fed Fund	US Federal Reserve Overnight rate
GBP	SONIA	Sterling OverNight Index Average
JPY	TONAR	Tokyo OverNight Average Rate
CHF	SARON	Swiss Average Rate OverNight

The rate is calculated by the Federal Reserve Bank of New York using data provided by the brokers. The day count convention is ACT/365. Some examples of currencies with an established overnight market are shown in Table 2.1

Another possibility for short-term cash-flow exchange is by going one day further; this is called the tomorrow-against-next-day, or tom-next, business, abbreviated T/N. In this case, money is exchanged the following day and returned the day after with the additional agreed upon interest. Extending this by another day brings us to the spot-against-next-day, or spot-next, business, abbreviated as S/N. Here money is exchanged at the spot date (often just called "spot"), which is delayed by zero to two days, depending on the market; for CHF and EUR, it is two days and the money is returned the day after with the agreed upon interest rate. The next iteration up brings us to another class of short dated contracts, referred to as call money. This is usually a bank deposit that can be called every two days. The duration of the call money can therefore be as short as two days, but is typically longer (with durations up to two months or more with an initial non-call period).

The most prominent of all rates however is probably the spot LIBOR (London Interbank Offered Rate) rate L. LIBOR denotes the short-term rate at which the major investment banks can borrow money unsecured from each other for a short period of time. Therefore, the important time points defining the LIBOR rate (which is settled at spot) are the actual date t and the time to maturity T, which can vary from overnight to one year. To illustrate the contract, we pay the notional at spot and receive the notional plus the LIBOR rate earned in return. The rate is annualized through the year fraction specified according to the day count convention (for most LIBOR rates this is ACT/360).

2.2 What you need for trading: ISDAs, netting agreements and CSAs

In order to trade over-the-counter derivatives, a contract needs to be drawn up between the two parties. These contracts have been standardized under the name of a service agreement called an ISDA master agreement.[1] We will not go into details here on the ISDA master agreements but feel we should highlight the necessity and the benefits of using them.

One of the successes of the ISDA master agreement has been the ability to net exposures of different trades. Netting allows parties to calculate their financial exposure under over-the-counter (OTC) transactions on a netted basis (i.e., a party calculates the difference it owes to the counterparty minus what the counterparty owes to it), so that, under the ISDA master agreement, only the net cash is exchanged. Depending on the usage, there are three different types of netting: "close-out netting", "netting for novation" and "payment netting". The close-out netting is probably the most common and covers the case of a bankruptcy where all trades are netted and a net balance is calculated. These calculations are made on a mark-to-market basis, meaning they reflect the current position of each transaction. In cases of bankruptcy, this reduces the claims from the insolvent company by all market values that the surviving company owns. Furthermore, if the market value of all transactions is positive to the surviving party, only a claim from the solvent to the insolvent party results. The payment netting mechanism, used by Clearstream and Euroclear, allows the automatic calculation of the overall position and hence only a single amount is exchanged between the trading counterparties. Most counterparties also agree to net all amounts due on a single day regardless of whether amounts are due under a single or multiple transactions.

The credit support annex (CSA) is an optional addition to the ISDA master agreement but is widely used between counterparties. The CSA regulates credit support in the form of collateral for derivative transactions and defines the terms or rules under which collateral is posted or transferred between swap counterparties to mitigate the credit risk arising from "in the money" derivative positions. The CSA also defines the types of collateral that may be used and the treatment of collateral by the secured party. Under a CSA, the counterparties agree that collateral is to be provided by one party if the exposure of the other to it exceeds an agreed amount.

In summary, one could say the master agreement has a strong influence on how day count and business day conventions are defined and standardized, the cash flows are calculated, etc., and the CSA has a great impact on collateral requirements and trading operations, and perhaps most importantly in the context of this book, on the valuation of derivatives and in particular on their discounting (see Chapter 3).

2.3 The evolution of complex derivatives trading

Up to the 1980s, the primary use of interest rate derivatives was to reduce the balance sheet risk of large companies. Balance sheet risk arises when a party funds, with a given term structure in a given currency, but holds assets with a different term structure and/or a different currency.

As an example, consider a regional bank that provides funding in the local markets through credit lending. The bank's asset side has a long duration due predominantly to (amortizing) fixed rate mortgages, but on the other hand, it might have a debt structure that is altogether different due to its funding in the capital markets. If this is not correctly managed, it could lead to a mismatch in cash flows and to a potentially significant interest rate risk.

Those corporations exposed to an undesired interest rate exposure make use of basic instruments such as forward rate agreements, Eurodollar futures (EDF), swaps, caps/floors and swaptions to reduce the residual risk. These instruments (which will be formally introduced in Chapter 3) are called vanilla instruments (as no exotic optionality is embedded in them) and form the basic building blocks of modern interest rate derivatives markets. On the investment banking side, the related trading activities are referred to these days as the "flow" business. These trades/contracts are usually of a bespoke nature so are typically executed OTC, rather than being settled on an exchange.

Moving into the 1990s/2000s, and particularly after the start of the millennium, there was a marked increase in tailor-made complex product structures. Building on top of the simpler products like swaps and caps/floors or swaptions, features were added such as path-dependency and callability, creating such products as range accruals, Targeted Accrual Redemption Notes (TARNs), snowballs, etc. These instruments were subsequently packaged into highly leveraged and highly complex structured bond issuances. Progressing in time a little further, speculative hedge fund managers jumped on the bandwagon using these complex derivatives to get positions on various parts of the yield curve or the volatility surface. In spite of the changes in the complexity of products, portfolio immunization risk, through the use of simple instruments, remained a large portion of the business.

To cater for the huge surge in both product variety and trading activity, technology and model complexity grew in sync. Naturally, derivatives technology and the models used became focused on pricing and risk managing structured products, efficiently and accurately. The dependence of products on many points of the volatility surface as well as of the term structure were important drivers to replace the short rate models (briefly reviewed in Chapter 6) by sophisticated multi-factor term structure models and models that incorporated the skewed distribution of the underlying rates (see Chapters 6 and 7). This was not only driven by academic work but the interconnection between academia and practitioners helped to create many mathematically interesting problems and realistic implementable solutions.

2.4 The effects of the financial credit crisis

Until the middle of 2008, large banks were continuing to grow, new structured products were created on an almost daily basis, and margins grew exorbitantly high. In 2008, several extraordinary events occurred: Bear Stearns was integrated into JP Morgan Chase and Lehman Brothers filed for Chapter 11 bankruptcy protection. The financial system almost collapsed. The meltdown of the system was not however due to the bankruptcy of any particular institution but because of a dry-up in market liquidity, partly brought on by interbank mistrust.

During the financial crisis, the regulators feared that the larger financial institutions were working at extremely high leverages and had insufficient liquid assets to continue operating. Subsequent to this concern, the Basel Committee introduced adaptations to the standards for banking, under the name of Basel III. This regulation increased the capital from roughly 8% of risk-weighted assets at some institutes to the required 19% target for large (too big to fail) institutions for after 2016.

Along with Basel III, new regulations were then introduced, namely the Dodd-Frank Act and the European Markets Infrastructure Regulation. These regulations resulted in wholesale changes to how OTC derivatives are settled, collateralized and reported. In particular, to reduce counterparty credit risk, the amount of collateral held against all OTC derivative transactions had to be increased dramatically.

Under these new regulations, most banks and broker dealers will fall under one of two regulatory designations – Swap Dealers (SDs) or Major Swap Participants (MSPs). Most large banks are expected to identify themselves as SDs and other institutions that trade swaps in the greatest volumes (smaller banks and broker dealers, insurance companies, large hedge funds and the like) will be classified as MSPs. For trades between SDs and MSPs, the counterparties must collect initial and variation margin for each trade, and this must be held with an independent third-party custodian and cannot be re-hypothecated. However, hedging swaps or other derivatives that mitigate balance sheet risks of non-financial institutions trading with a financial institution will be exempted. In this case, the financial institution is not required to collect a margin for each trade but is required to enter into a CSA. These changes increased the operational complexity rather quickly and collateral optimization has become a strategic priority for some institutes, who also need to consider that the supply of high grade collateral can vary.

The movement to clear trades or at least have a sufficient CSA in place has actually changed the valuation of derivatives. For those derivatives that are not migrated to a clearing facility, or where no collateral is posted, the credit risk becomes an important part of the price. This pricing though is not as simple as one might expect: if a party enters an uncollateralized swap with a counterparty, the latter is always at risk of losing the market value of the derivative if the former defaults. One can develop further arguments and quickly convince oneself that counterparty risk with respect to derivatives with a counterparty is a portfolio phenomenon. Larger financial institutions calculate this as the credit value adjustment (CVA). There are many other valuation adjustments which have cropped up in the last couple of years and we refer the reader to Cesari et al. (2009) and Kenyon and Stamm (2012) for more details.

So what happened to the structured products? Nobody wanted to buy any opaque products anymore, the structured products market came almost to an abrupt end, and in some markets, volatility trading almost disappeared. So why is there still a need for complex models? Well, the answer to this question is rather long, but in essence quite a few products survived, with payoffs that are path-dependent or complex functions of the entire volatility surface. This obviously includes well-known exotic LIBOR products or insurance riders in variable annuities, to name only a few prominent examples.

Note

1. An ISDA master agreement is part of a framework of documents, designed to enable over-the-counter derivatives to be documented fully and flexibly. The framework consists of a master agreement, a schedule, confirmations, definition booklets and possibly a credit support annex. Using this agreement, the terms for each transaction do not need to be redefined and apply automatically as described in the documents.

3 | Interest Rate Notions

In this chapter we will lay the conceptual foundations on which to develop more advanced topics later in the book. Along with some fundamental quantities (zero-coupon bond, short rate, bank account, etc.) and concepts (measures and associated numeraires), we will be reviewing several basic instruments used for yield curve as well as volatility trading. We will also be presenting an introduction related to the fundamental curves needed for trading/risk-managing interest rate derivatives.

Although we will dedicate a good portion of this chapter to the description of the multiple curve framework, we will provide what can be considered a simple overview of the topic. For a broader discussion on the subject, the interested reader is referred to Bianchetti (2010), Bianchetti and Carlicchi (2012), Henrard (2014) and Mercurio (2009).

3.1 Interest rate basics

When working with interest rate products, it is convenient to introduce a time grid (see Appendix A.1 for more details on this topic) representing when their corresponding cash flows happen. This is usually measured in years T_k and is defined as

$$0 = T_0 < T_1 < \cdots < T_N. \tag{3.1}$$

We will be alternatively referring to the first point on the grid as $t = 0$ or $t = T_0$.
The interval between two consecutive grid points

$$\tau_k = T_k - T_{k-1}, \tag{3.2}$$

represents a quantity known as the year fraction (sometimes also referred to as the rolling period).

After having defined the time grid on which our cash flows will take place, we can start introducing a set of basic quantities that will be used throughout the rest of the book.

A zero-coupon bond price is given by

$$P(t, T_k) = \frac{1}{1 + (T_k - t) L(t, T_k)}, \tag{3.3}$$

where $L(t, T_k)$ is the LIBOR rate (Section 2.1) at which banks borrow funds at t for the T_k maturity.

A zero-coupon bond is a fundamental quantity as it can be used to discount future cash flows to the present: for this reason we will also refer to it as the discount factor.

The continuously compounded spot rate is given by

$$R(t, T_k) = -\frac{ln(P(t, T_k))}{T_k - t}, \tag{3.4}$$

hence the zero-coupon bond can be also expressed as

$$P(t, T_k) = e^{-R(t, T_k)(T_k - t)}. \tag{3.5}$$

The short rate $r(t)$ is defined as the following limit

$$r(t) = \lim_{\Delta t \to 0} R(t, t + \Delta t).$$

To represent how interest accrues on a continuous basis we introduce the bank account (also known as the cash account)

$$B(t) = e^{\left(\int_0^t r(s) ds\right)}. \tag{3.6}$$

The bank accounts $B(t)$ and $B(T_k)$ allow us to rewrite the zero-coupon bond expression in terms of the short rate as

$$P(t, T_k) = \frac{B(t)}{B(T_k)} = e^{\left(-\int_t^{T_k} r(s) ds\right)}. \tag{3.7}$$

3.2 The multiple curve framework

There are two curves that are at the base of interest rate trading: the discount and the forward (also known as the projection) curve. As we will see extensively in the rest of the book, the former is used to discount future values to the present, while the latter is used to obtain a quantity on which all derivatives (under more or less complicated forms) depend: the FRA rate $F_k(t)$, which is the expected value at time t of the LIBOR rate $L(T_{k-1}, T_k)$, that is

$$F_k(t) \equiv F(t, T_{k-1}, T_k) = \mathbb{E}^k [L(T_{k-1}, T_k)],$$

with $\mathbb{E}^k$ being the expectation under the T_k-forward measure (see Section 3.3.2 for a discussion on various useful measures when modelling interest rate derivatives).

Prior to the credit crunch that started in 2007, interbank transactions did not account for credit risk. For example financing a period of six months was the same as financing twice for three months, that is, the following no-arbitrage argument held:

$$(1 + \tau_{3m} L(0, 3m)) (1 + \tau_{3m} F(0, 3m, 6m)) = 1 + \tau_{6m} L(0, 6m). \tag{3.8}$$

As a result it was possible, and customary, to obtain the forward curves, for different tenor lengths, using the above relationship. Moreover, the interbank market players were considered safe and the LIBOR rate was a proxy for the risk-free rate. Hence, the same curve was used for discounting of cash flows and rates projection. Such a set-up is commonly known as single curve framework.

However, starting from the summer of 2007, banks became more and more aware of counterparty risk, which led to the appearance of a basis spread between LIBOR rates with different underlying tenors. Short rate tenors became more appealing than longer ones (i.e., Equation (3.8) did not hold anymore) due to the shorter period in which the lending party is fully exposed to the counterparty default risk. The most apparent example of what has just been described was reflected in the LIBOR-OIS spread divergence observed after 2007 (Figure 3.1). Where an overnight index swap (OIS) is a daily collateralized trade (Section 3.2.1) it is perceived by the market as the best proxy to a credit risk free transaction.

The insurgence in counterparty risk awareness led many organizations to start attaching collateral agreements, with daily margin calls, to OTC trades.

These collateralized trades have to be discounted, to avoid arbitrage, using the rate earned on the posted margins (see, e.g., Mercurio 2010). The best candidate for this purpose is the overnight rate (Table 2.1), which represents an average of the

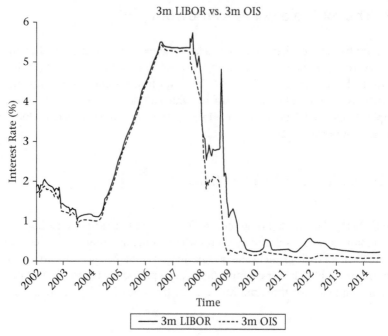

Figure 3.1 Historical time series for the *3m* LIBOR rate and the *3m* OIS rate

rates charged in the overnight interbank market, and can be effectively considered a risk free rate.

As a consequence banks had to change the whole curve paradigm by:

- Building a curve C_x for every underlying tenor x (see e.g., Bianchetti 2010) in which they are interested to trade. Each of these curves has to be built exclusively with underlying instruments sharing all the same tenor. Only in this way will it be possible to take into account the credit risk embedded in each tenor length.
- Adopting different discounting curves C_d according to the type of transaction (collateralized/uncollateralized).

We should at this point introduce a tenor dependent notation for all the quantities connected to the C_x curves (such as $F_{x,k}(t), P_x(t, T_k)$). In the same fashion we should also use $F_{d,k}(t), P_d(t, T_k)$, etc. for the quantities associated with the C_d curves. For the sake of readability we will however omit the subscript x, considering it to be implicitly present. This is also justified from the fact that we will always, unless explicitly mentioned, work under the same tenor x. In particular in all our real data examples, involving CHF and EUR, we will be considering $x = 6m$, as this is the standard tenor length in both markets.

The second simplification which we make is related to the C_d curve. As the majority of interest rate vanilla derivatives (caps/floors, swaptions, etc.) are nowadays collateralized, we can safely assume the OIS curve to be the most popular discounting curve C_d among market players. For this reason we will be employing it as our standard discounting curve.

Summarizing, we will be using:

- $F_k(t), P(t, T_k)$, etc. to represent quantities computed from the C_{6m} curve.
- $F_{d,k}(t), P_d(t, T_k)$, etc. to represent quantities computed from the C_d (OIS) curve.

All our results will be however valid for any choice of C_x and C_d curves.

3.2.1 The OIS curve

We define the OIS rate $r_{OIS}(t, T_k)$ as the following geometric sum

$$r_{OIS}(t, T_k) = \frac{360}{n} \left(\prod_{j=t}^{T_k - 1d} \left(1 + \frac{r_{ON,j}}{360} \right) - 1 \right), \tag{3.9}$$

where $r_{ON,j}$ is the overnight rate (e.g., EONIA) from time T_j to $T_j + 1d$.

The zero-coupon bond associated with $r_{OIS}(t, T_k)$ is

$$P_d(t, T_k) = e^{-\int_t^{T_k} r_{OIS}(s, s+1d) ds}$$
$$= e^{-r_{OIS}(t, T_k)(T_k - t)}. \tag{3.10}$$

In several markets, such as the United States, the European Union or the United Kingdom, the central banks set, at their periodic meetings, a short-term borrowing rate. This rate does not change in-between meeting dates. OIS forward rate agreements (OIS FRAs) are used to take a view on where this rate will be fixed at the next meeting date.

An OIS FRA struck at time t gives to its holder at maturity T_k an interest rate payment for the period $T_k - T_{k-1}$ with fixed rate y against a reference rate over the same period. Its value at time t is given by

$$\text{FRA}_{OIS}(t, T_k, y) = P_d(t, T_k) \tau_k (y - F_{d,k}(t)). \tag{3.11}$$

The quantity which makes this contract fair is the FRA OIS rate which is defined as

$$F_{d,k}(t) = \frac{1}{\tau_k} \left(\frac{P_d(t, T_{k-1})}{P_d(t, T_k)} - 1 \right). \tag{3.12}$$

In an OIS swap a series of fixed cash flows is exchanged against a series of floating cash flows. Only the net cash flow is settled and the notionals are not exchanged. In an OIS swap transaction the fixed leg is given by

$$\text{Fixed}_{\text{OIS}}\left(t, T_m, T_n, y\right) = y \sum_{k=m+1}^{n} \tau_k P_d(t, T_k). \tag{3.13}$$

The OIS swap floating leg compounds the overnight rate

$$\text{Floating}_{\text{OIS}}\left(t, T_m, T_n\right) = \sum_{k=m+1}^{n} P_d\left(t, T_k\right) \tau_j F_{d,k}(t),$$

which, after substituting $F_{d,k}(t)$ with Equation (3.12), gives

$$\text{Floating}_{\text{OIS}}\left(t, T_m, T_n\right) = \sum_{k=m+1}^{n} P_d\left(t, T_{k-1}\right) - P_d\left(t, T_k\right)$$
$$= P_d(t, T_m) - P_d(t, T_n). \tag{3.14}$$

We can now combine these two legs into a receiver OIS swap (i.e., a swap where we receive the fixed coupon)

$$\text{OISSwap}_{\text{r}}\left(t, T_m, T_n, y\right) = \text{Fixed}_{\text{OIS}}\left(t, T_m, T_n, y\right) - \text{Floating}_{\text{OIS}}\left(t, T_m, T_n\right)$$
$$= y \sum_{k=m+1}^{n} \tau_k P_d\left(t, T_k\right) - \left(P_d\left(t, T_m\right) - P_d\left(t, T_n\right)\right). \tag{3.15}$$

Following the same reasoning we can construct a payer OIS swap (where we pay the fixed coupon)

$$\text{OISSwap}_{p}\left(t, T_m, T_n, y\right) = -y \sum_{k=m+1}^{n} \tau_k P_d\left(t, T_k\right) + \left(P_d\left(t, T_m\right) - P_d\left(t, T_n\right)\right).$$

$$\tag{3.16}$$

It is interesting to note how, for the OIS based products just introduced, discounting factors $P_d\left(t, T_k\right)$ and forwards $F_{d,k}(t)$ are computed on the same curve $\mathcal{C}_d$; we are effectively working in a single curve framework.

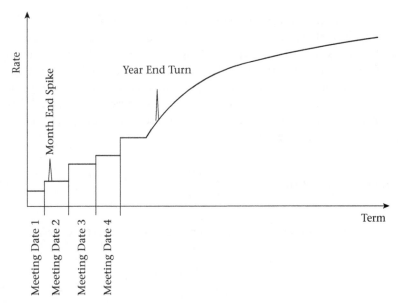

Figure 3.2 Prototypical OIS curve

The OIS curve construction usually starts by using the current publication of the overnight rate (see Table 2.1) as the first tenor. The short end of the curve can be constructed using short-term OIS swaps or OIS FRAs maturing on central banks' meeting dates. Finally the long end of the curve is usually constructed using long-term OIS swaps.

Some institutes account also for month/year end effects or any other extraordinary adjustments, such as, for example, those resulting from tax dates. These adjustments, which reflect the sharp and temporally local decrease in liquidity, affect the curve under the form of steps and/or turns. A step is like a short step-wise function that increases the rate over a period of time. Turns and spikes at month/year end, or at certain events where traders tend to close their books, make short term financing more expensive and increase the rates locally. There is however no market quote for the height or the duration of these spikes and therefore it is at a trader's discretion to set these according to her/his willingness to lend money.

A prototypical OIS curve is displayed in Figure 3.2.

3.2.2 The forward curve

In this section we will provide more details related to the instruments used for the construction of any x tenor forward curve. We have seen, in Section 3.2.1, how an OIS FRA is defined. We will now introduce a LIBOR FRA (which we will simply refer to as a forward rate agreement or FRA). In a FRA two parties agree on the rate for an uncollateralized financing between T_{k-1} and T_k. The cash flow is exchanged at the beginning of the period, that is, T_{k-1}. As it is an uncollateralized financing the cash flow is the same as that paid in arrears (i.e., at the end of the period) but discounted using the funded discount rate. The funded discount factor reads as $(1 + \tau_k F_k(t))^{-1}$. As a FRA is, in most cases, a collateralized trade, its cash flows at T_{k-1} are discounted to time t using the risk free discount factor $P_d(t, T_{k-1})$. Hence, the value of a FRA at time t is

$$\mathbf{FRA}\left(t, T_k, y\right) = P_d(t, T_{k-1}) \frac{\tau_k \left(y - F_k(t)\right)}{1 + \tau_k F_k(t)}. \tag{3.17}$$

The value which makes this contract fair is the FRA rate $F_k(t)$ defined as

$$F_k(t) = \frac{1}{\tau_k} \left(\frac{P\left(t, T_{k-1}\right)}{P\left(t, T_k\right)} - 1 \right). \tag{3.18}$$

We will alternatively refer to this quantity also as the forward LIBOR rate or forward (interest) rate. At time $t = T_{k-1}$ the LIBOR rate and the FRA rate coincide, that is

$$L\left(T_{k-1}, T_k\right) = F_k(T_{k-1}). \tag{3.19}$$

An interest rate swap (IRS) is a financial product that allows the exchange of fixed and floating cash flows. Corporate treasury departments wanting to hedge their liabilities or alter the portfolio's duration dominate the swaps market. So, if the semi-annual coupon bonds dominate the bond market, then the treasuries will face a six months tenor risk and a fairly long duration. In order to reduce the long maturity risk from the bonds, the treasuries can swap the fixed against the floating rate and reduce the duration mismatch of their balance sheets. This will result in a very short duration risk that is easier to manage.

Standard IRSs in CHF and EUR pay semi-annual LIBOR against an annual coupon (i.e., the time grid is semi-annually spaced). The cash flows for this IRS can be seen in Figure 3.3.

The market value of a receiver IRS is calculated as the market value of a fixed leg minus the market value of a floating leg. Although in practice these two legs have different payment frequencies, we will assume them, throughout the rest of the book, to be the same. This will help keeping the notation lighter and clearer. Summarized the market value of the receiver swap at time t is given by

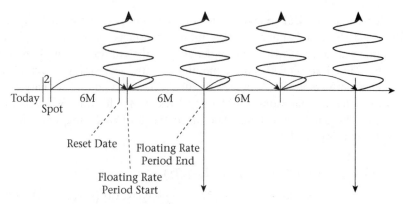

Figure 3.3 Interest rate swap cash flows

$$\mathbf{IRS_r}\left(t, T_m, T_n, y\right) = y A_{d,m,n}(t) - \sum_{k=m+1}^{n} \tau_k F_k(t) P_d\left(t, T_k\right), \tag{3.20}$$

where

$$A_{d,m,n}(t) = \sum_{k=m+1}^{n} \tau_k P_d\left(t, T_k\right), \tag{3.21}$$

is known as the annuity or annuity factor. The value of y which makes the IRS fair at time t is called the swap rate, and it is defined as

$$y = S_{m,n}(t) = \frac{\sum_{k=m+1}^{n} \tau_k F_k(t) P_d\left(t, T_k\right)}{\sum_{k=m+1}^{n} \tau_k P_d\left(t, T_k\right)}. \tag{3.22}$$

Analogously we can define a payer IRS as a contract paying the fixed leg and receiving the floating leg. Its value at time t is given by

$$\mathbf{IRS_p}\left(t, T_m, T_n, y\right) = -y A_{d,m,n}(t) + \sum_{k=m+1}^{n} \tau_k F_k(t) P_d\left(t, T_k\right). \tag{3.23}$$

The instruments just introduced are the basic ingredients to use to build the forward curve. The short term of the curve is composed of the spot LIBOR rate $L(t, T_k)$ at time $t = 0$ and of the FRAs, while the long end is composed of IRSs. Depending on the market in which we are focusing, it is also possible to add, at the short end, deposits or futures.

Particularly in the USD market, EDF contracts are used due to high liquidity. EDFs are cash settled money market futures contracts traded at the Chicago Mercantile Exchange (CME). The underlying of the contract is the Eurodollar Interbank Time Deposit with a three-month maturity (hence this product inherits the three-month credit risk, Labuszewski 2013). The most liquid EDF have expiry on IMM (International Monetary Market) dates in March, June, September and December. The date is set such that it occurs on the third Wednesday of the month. The EDF value is given by

$$
\begin{aligned}
\mathbf{EDF}\left(t, T_k\right) &= 100 - 100 \cdot fut\left(t, T_{k-1}, T_k\right) \\
&= 100 - 100 \cdot \left(F\left(t, T_{k-1}, T_k\right) + \text{convexity}\left(t, T_{k-1}, T_k\right)\right), \quad (3.24)
\end{aligned}
$$

where $fut\left(t, T_{k-1}, T_k\right)$ is a futures rate, which can be decomposed into a forward rate and a convexity adjustment convexity $\left(t, T_{k-1}, T_k\right)$. The future convexity can be calculated using a Hull-White model, as we outline in Equation (6.13).

It is important to note, by looking at the equations introduced in this section, how FRAs and IRSs need to be discounted using the zero-coupon bond $P_d\left(t, T_k\right)$ obtained from the OIS curve. Hence, before building a forward curve it is important to have a discounting curve in place. This multiple curve construction methodology is quite involved; we refer the interested reader to Henrard (2014).

3.2.3 Constructing tenor curves from tenor basis swaps

We have introduced in Section 3.2.2 the basic instruments needed to build a forward curve related to a particular tenor x. There are however particular tenors for which these instruments are not traded or for which they lack liquidity.[1] In this situation we would need to resort to tenor basis swaps.

A tenor basis swap is an instrument where two LIBOR streams, with different underlying tenor, are exchanged, as depicted in Figure 3.4. As we have previously mentioned, the longer the tenor, the more credit spread is inherent in the rate. Hence, these two cash flows cannot have the same value. In order to make the swap fair, a spread is paid by the party paying the shorter leg.

The value at time t of the tenor basis swap receiving the flat LIBOR stream is

$$
\begin{aligned}
\mathbf{TBasis}\left(t, T_m, T_n, basis\right) = &\sum_{k=m+1}^{n} \tau_k F_{x,k}(t) P_d(t, T_k) \\
&- \sum_{j=m+1}^{n} \tau_j \left(F_{z,j}(t) + basis\right) P_d(t, T_j), \quad (3.25)
\end{aligned}
$$

where *basis* is the aforementioned spread.

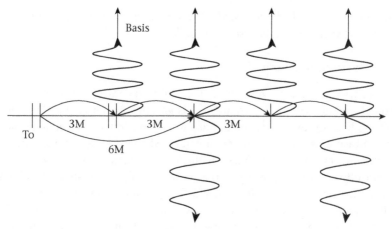

Figure 3.4 Cash flow of a tenor basis swap paying 6m LIBOR and receiving 3m LIBOR

We observe that we have now three curves involved in Equation (3.25): the discounting curve $\mathcal{C}_d$, the curve $\mathcal{C}_x$, used to calculate the forwards of the receiving leg, and the curve $\mathcal{C}_z$, used to calculate the forwards of the paying leg.

3.3 Interest rate valuations and measures

After having introduced the cardinal instruments used to build the fundamental curves employed in the interest rate market, we will review four of the most useful measures (and associated numeraires) for what concerns interest rate derivative valuations.

It is a very well known result (see, e.g., Shreve 2008, Brigo and Mercurio 2006) that the present value of a security is the conditional expectation of its discounted terminal value under the risk neutral probability, with respect to the filtration $\mathcal{F}_t$. For any measure $\mathbb{Q}$, associated to a numeraire Num, the valuation of any payoff $V(T)$ paid at time T is defined according to

$$V(t) = Num_t \mathbb{E}\left[\frac{V(T)}{Num_T}|\mathcal{F}_t\right]. \tag{3.26}$$

With this in mind we will present in what follows the spot, terminal, forward and swap measures, all of them associated with the discount curve $\mathcal{C}_d$. The latter condition will be implicitly assumed, unless otherwise stated and whenever these measures are employed in the rest of the book.

3.3.1 The spot measure

Often we wish to choose a numeraire that can be extended to arbitrary horizons by compounding. The cash account $B(t)$ is an obvious candidate. However, the corresponding continuously compounded numeraire (often referred to as the risk neutral measure) is cumbersome and unnatural when working with a discrete tenor structure. An analogy can be made with physics, where finding a solution to a problem often involves working in the most natural coordinates, which benefit the structure of the problem. If we change from a continuously compounded cash account to a discretely compounded one, we will be able to compound to different tenor points in a natural way. At time T_0 we invest one unit of currency of the account in $\frac{1}{P_d(T_0,T_1)}$, yielding at time T_1

$$\frac{1}{P_d(T_0, T_1)} = 1 + \tau_1 F_{d,1}(T_0).$$

Reinvesting this amount at time T_1 in T_2—the maturity zero-coupon bond yields at time T_2

$$\frac{1}{P_d(T_0, T_1)} \frac{1}{P_d(T_1, T_2)} = \left(1 + \tau_1 F_{d,1}(T_0)\right)\left(1 + \tau_2 F_{d,2}(T_1)\right).$$

Repeating this strategy at each future date in the tenor structure results in a price process $B_d(t)$, where $B_d(T_0) = 1$ and

$$B_d(t) = P_d(t, T_i) \prod_{k=1}^{i} \left(1 + \tau_k F_{d,k}(T_{k-1})\right), \quad T_{i-1} < t \le T_i.$$

We can think of $B_d(t)$ as being a discrete version of the cash account previously mentioned (where d indicates that it has been obtained from the C_d discounting curve). $B_d(t)$ will tend towards the cash account as the time spacing of the tenor structure gets smaller. The measure associated with $B_d(t)$ is called the spot measure. We denote it by $\mathbb{Q}^B$ while $\mathbb{E}^B[\cdot]$ is the expectation under this measure. We therefore have under the spot measure

$$V(t) = \mathbb{E}^B\left[\frac{B_d(t)}{B_d(T)} V(T)\right], \tag{3.27}$$

where

$$\frac{B_d(t)}{B_d(T)} = \frac{P_d(t, T_i)}{P_d(T, T_j)} \prod_{k=i+1}^{j} \left(1 + \tau_k F_{d,k}(T_{k-1})\right)^{-1}, \quad T_{i-1} < t \le T_i, \quad T_{j-1} < T \le T_j.$$

The spot measure can in many ways be thought of as a discrete version of the risk neutral measure. One advantage with working with this measure, when pricing derivatives using Monte Carlo techniques, is that the numeraire asset $B_d(t)$ will remain alive throughout the span of tenors, so we are able to value products which mature at any date. This is a useful property when dealing with products with early exercise features. Also, when working with a long time grid where most cash flows appear early, this measure introduces low simulation variance.

3.3.2 The terminal and forward measures

The terminal measure $\mathbb{Q}^N$ corresponds to picking a zero-coupon bond $P_d(t, T_N)$ terminating at the last tenor of the time grid, T_N, as the numeraire asset. One advantage of this measure is that it is certain to remain alive throughout the entire Monte Carlo simulation.

Following the same lines as in the spot measure, we can consider a security with payoff $V(T)$ paid at a date $T \le T_N$. Its value at time t is given by

$$V(t) = P_d(t, T_N) \mathbb{E}^N \left[\frac{V(T)}{P_d(T, T_N)} \right], \quad t \le T \le T_N. \tag{3.28}$$

The term in brackets $\frac{V(T)}{P_d(T, T_N)}$ represents the value at time T_N of investing $V(T)$ at time T in zero-coupon bonds expiring at time T_N. If we wish to relate the terminal and spot measures $\mathbb{Q}^N$ and $\mathbb{Q}^B$ respectively, we note that

$$P_d(T, T_N) \mathbb{E}^N \left[\frac{B_d(T_N)}{B_d(T)} \right] = B_d(T) \mathbb{E}^B \left[\frac{B_d(T_N)}{B_d(T) B_d(T_N)} \right] = 1.$$

Using this relationship, together with the tower law, that is, $\mathbb{E}\left[\mathbb{E}[X \mid \mathcal{F}_s] \mid \mathcal{F}_t\right] = \mathbb{E}[X \mid \mathcal{F}_t]$ for all $\mathcal{F}_s > \mathcal{F}_t$, we can rewrite Equation (3.28) as

$$\begin{aligned} V(t) &= P_d(t, T_N) \mathbb{E}^N \left[\frac{V(T)}{P_d(T, T_N)} \right] \\ &= P_d(t, T_N) \mathbb{E}^N \left[V(T) \mathbb{E}_T^N \left[\frac{B_d(T_N)}{B_d(T)} \right] \right] \\ &= P_d(t, T_N) \mathbb{E}^N \left[V(T) \frac{B_d(T_N)}{B_d(T)} \right], \end{aligned}$$

which is in agreement with Equation (3.27).

In the case where the numeraire expires before the security, we can consider, at the numeraire expiry, investing the security in the spot measure numeraire asset. For such reasons often it is useful to define a hybrid numeraire $H_d(t, T)$ which is composed of different numeraire assets depending on which part of the tenor structure we are in; for example, we could initially purchase zero-coupon bonds maturing at time T, then at this time, invest the cash into the spot measure numeraire

$$H_d(t, T) = \begin{cases} P_d(t, T), & t \le T \\ B_d(t)/B_d(T), & t > T. \end{cases}$$

Taking as the numeraire a zero-coupon bond maturing at a time point T_k has an associated measure called the forward measure for maturity T_k, or the T_k-forward measure, and which is represented as $\mathbb{Q}^k$.

3.3.3 The swap measure

When we are interested in pricing interest rate derivatives on swap rates (such as swaptions) we will find that it is also convenient to use the annuity factor, $A_{d,m.n}$, defined in Equation (3.21), as the numeraire. This stems from the fact that, as observed in Equation (3.22), the swap rate is in fact simply a linear combination of traded assets, more specifically, zero-coupon bonds. The measure $\mathbb{Q}^{m,n}$ induced by this numeraire is referred to as the swap measure. Under this measure, we are able to price products using

$$V(t) = A_{d,m,n}(t)\mathbb{E}^{m,n}\left[\frac{V(T)}{A_{d,m,n}(T)}\right],$$

where $\mathbb{E}^{m,n}[\cdot]$ denotes the expectation under $\mathbb{Q}^{m,n}$. The forward swap rate under this measure is a martingale.

3.4 Volatility trading

Volatility trading can be many things; in our context we refer to any instrument which has vega sensitivity (i.e., its value changes if either the swaption volatility or the cap volatility surfaces change). These instruments can be further separated into vanillas and exotics. Vanilla instruments usually consist of caps, floors and (European) swaptions. Some desks/institutions also include, among the vanilla products, constant maturity swaps (CMS) and CMS caps/floors (see, e.g., Hagan 2003 for more details on these products). Under exotic instruments we can assume everything else, such as callables, snowballs and TARNs (see, e.g., Brigo and Mercurio 2006 for more details on these products).

In this section we will introduce a subset of the aforementioned vanilla derivatives: caps/floors (along with caplets/floorlets) and swaptions. These are, what we believe, the pillars of volatility trading, and which form the basis for the calibration of any model used to price more or less complicated products.

3.4.1 Caps, floors – caplets, floorlets

Caps and floors are mainly used for tail risk management by banks, asset managers and insurance companies. A cap is a series of options on a LIBOR rate. Each option is called a caplet.

A caplet is a call option with expiry T_{k-1} and strike y on the forward rate $F_k(T_{k-1})$ paying at T_k. Its payoff is given by

$$\tau_k \left(F_k \left(T_{k-1} \right) - y \right)^+, \tag{3.29}$$

where the operator $(...)^+$ is the maximum of the expression inside the brackets or 0.

Aggregating a series of caplets (where the end date of a caplet is just the start date of the next one) with the same strike y we form a cap

$$\sum_{k=i+1}^{n} \tau_k \left(F_k \left(T_{k-1} \right) - y \right)^+. \tag{3.30}$$

A floorlet is a put option with expiry T_{k-1} and strike y on the forward rate $F_k(T_k)$, paying at T_k. Its payoff is given by

$$\tau_k \left(y - F_k \left(T_{k-1} \right) \right)^+. \tag{3.31}$$

A floor can be defined, similarly to a cap, as

$$\sum_{k=i+1}^{n} \tau_k \left(y - F_k \left(T_{k-1} \right) \right)^+. \tag{3.32}$$

The value of these instruments can be calculated through the expectation of the discounted payoff. Under the forward measure $\mathbb{Q}^k$ the value at time t of a caplet is given by

$$\mathbf{Cpl}\left(t, T_{k-1}, T_k, y \right) = P_d \left(t, T_k \right) \tau_k \mathbb{E}^k \left[\left(F_k(T_{k-1}) - y \right)^+ \right]. \tag{3.33}$$

This relationship can be easily extended to value floorlets, caps and floors.

3.4.2 Swaptions

A swaption is a contract granting a party the right to enter a swap in the future, with another counterparty. The swaption buyers consist predominantly of large corporations, banks, financial institutions and hedge funds. Corporations and banks use swaptions to manage interest rate risk arising from their core business or from their financing arrangements, mainly to protect against changes in interest rates. Hedge funds and some asset managers use them for speculation purposes or as a risk-diversifying asset. Major investment and commercial banks make markets in swaptions in the major currencies, and these banks trade among themselves in the swaption interbank market. The market making banks typically manage large portfolios of swaptions that they have written with various counterparties over-the-counter.

There are two types of settlements for swaptions: cash or physical. As we will see later in this section, each settlement type influences the way in which the swaption is valued. Interestingly, in the EUR market, the majority of the swaption trades with cash settlement. Anyhow, in the rest of the book we will always refer to physically settled swaptions, unless specifically stated.

A European receiver swaption with physical settlement gives the right to enter at time T_m into a receiver IRS with strike y. Its payoff at time T_m is given by

$$\left(y A_{d,m,n}(T_m) - \sum_{k=m+1}^{n} \tau_k F_k(T_m) P_d(T_m, T_k) \right)^+, \tag{3.34}$$

which can be rewritten in terms of the swap rate $S_{m,n}(t)$ at T_m as

$$A_{d,m,n}(T_m) \left(y - S_{m,n}(T_m) \right)^+. \tag{3.35}$$

We observe that a receiver swaption is actually a put option on the swap rate. The receiver swaption helps to protect against lower interest rates. The value at time t, of a receiver swaption under the swap measure $\mathbb{Q}^{m,n}$ associated with the swap annuity numeraire $A_{d,m,n}$, is given by

$$\mathbf{RS}(t, T_m, T_n, y) = A_{d,m,n}(t) \mathbb{E}^{m,n} \left[\left(y - S_{m,n}(T_m) \right)^+ \right]. \tag{3.36}$$

On the other end, a European payer swaption gives the holder the right to enter at time T_m into a payer IRS with strike y. Its payoff at time T_m is given by

$$\left(\sum_{k=m+1}^{n} \tau_k F_k (T_m) P_d (T_m, T_k) - y A_{d,m,n} (T_m) \right)^+, \tag{3.37}$$

which can be rewritten in terms of the swap rate $S_{m,n}(t)$ at T_m as

$$A_{d,m,n}(T_m) \left(S_{m,n}(T_m) - y \right)^+. \tag{3.38}$$

Under the swap measure $\mathbb{Q}^{m,n}$ the receiver swaption value at time t is given by

$$\mathbf{PS}(t, T_m, T_n, y) = A_{d,m,n}(t) \mathbb{E}^{m,n} \left[\left(S_{m,n}(T_m) - y \right)^+ \right]. \tag{3.39}$$

The peculiarity of a cash settled swaption is an immediate payout at the option expiry or, more accurately, at the settlement date, which is shortly afterward. In order to calculate the cash amount, which will be used to settle the swaption, the market has introduced a shortcut which consists in discounting all future cash flows using the fixed swap rate $S_{m,n}(T_m)$.

The cash settled payer swaption (see Mercurio 2008 for a detailed overview on the subject) paying at T_m has payoff

$$G_{m,n}(T_m) \left(y - S_{m,n}(T_m) \right)^+,$$

where $G_{m,n}(T_m)$ is the cash annuity

$$G_{m,n}(T_m) = \sum_{j=m+1}^{n} \frac{\tau_j}{\left(1 + \tau_j S_{m,n}(T_m) \right)}. \tag{3.40}$$

The value at time t of the cash settled swaption under the swap measure $\mathbb{Q}^{m,n}$ is

$$\mathbf{PS}(t, T_m, T_n, y) = P_d(t, T_m) \mathbb{E}^{m,n} \left[G_{m,n}(T_m) \left(S_{m,n}(T_m) - y \right)^+ \right]. \tag{3.41}$$

Unfortunately the cash annuity is not a martingale under the $\mathbb{Q}^{m,n}$ measure, which leads to various complications in the valuation of this type of swaption.

There are two main ways to quote swaptions: in volatility or premium terms. We will expand on volatility quoting in Chapter 4. Regarding premium quoting,

Table 3.1 Quotes for EUR at the money swaptions in forward premium terms. The horizontal axis represents the tenor of the underlying swap, whereas the vertical axis represents the option expiry

	1y	2y	5y	7y	10y
1y	31.84	83.09	267.26	372.58	509.52
2y	69.82	154.12	417.26	565.71	765.03
3y	105.35	215.06	528.53	711.29	943.14
5y	152.88	293.88	688.59	919.75	1224.54
10y	193.56	369.67	868.27	1157.81	1550.2

we can distinguish between spot and forward premium quotes (see Table 3.1). In the former the premium is paid upfront. This method, hugely popular before the 2007–08 financial crisis, creates a large credit risk (for the swaption buyer) between the payment of the premium and the settlement date. However, as with the financial crisis, the credit risk awareness increases and, most of the major dealers moved to forward premium (paid at exercise date) type of contracts. Moreover in a forward premium the cash settled swaption value

$$\mathbb{E}^{m,n}\left[G_{m,n}(T_m)\left(S_{m,n}(T_m) - y\right)^+\right],$$

depends solely on the forward swap rate, independent of any discounting.

Note

1. For CHF, a typical example tenor for which this applies is $x = 3m$, as there are hardly any quotes and nearly no trades on three-month swaps.

4 | Vanilla Models

We have defined, in Section 3.4, how the value of caps/floors (as well as caplets/floorlets) depends on the future distribution of $F_k(t)$ under the T_k-forward measure $\mathbb{Q}^k$ associated with the numeraire $P_d(t, T_k)$. Equivalently, the swaption value depends on the future distribution of $S_{m,n}(t)$ under the swap measure $\mathbb{Q}^{m,n}$ associated with the numeraire $A_{d,m,n}(t)$.

To find the price of these instruments, it is necessary to define the distribution of the associated forward rate $(F_k(t)$ or $S_{m,n}(t))$ under its respective measure. We will see in the rest of the book how this task can be accomplished under different assumptions. In this chapter we introduce the two most basic modelling assumptions for the underlying processes, a lognormal and a normal distribution.

4.1 Lognormal Black model

The first assumption of the lognormal Black model (Black 1976) is that the dynamics of the forward $F_k(t)$ can be explained by a simple lognormal diffusion. The increment between time steps in the forward interest rate $dF_k(t)$ is defined in continuous time by the following stochastic process

$$dF_k(t) = \sigma_k(t) F_k(t) dW_k(t), \tag{4.1}$$

where $\sigma_k(t)$ is the instantaneous lognormal volatility and the Wiener process $W_k(t)$ is defined under the forward measure $\mathbb{Q}^k$. We also introduce the Black implied volatility (often referred to as the lognormal implied volatility)

$$\sigma_k^B = \sqrt{\frac{1}{T_{k-1} - t} \int_t^{T_{k-1}} \sigma_k(u)^2 \, du}. \tag{4.2}$$

Equation (4.2) would suggest that a single Black implied volatility should be used to price options with the same expiry T_{k-1} but different strikes. In reality the market assigns different volatilities at different strikes (Table 4.2). To adjust for this shortcoming of the Black model, we introduce a strike dependence in the Black implied volatility, changing the notation to $\sigma_k^B(y)$.

The value at time t of a caplet with strike y, expiring at T_{k-1} and paying at T_k, under the lognormal Black model (often simply referred to as the Black model) is given by

$$\mathbf{Cpl}^{Blk}\left(t, T_{k-1}, T_k, y, \sigma_k^B(y)\right) = P_d(t, T_k)\,\tau_k \mathbf{Blk}\left(F_k(t), y, \sigma_k^B(y)\sqrt{T_{k-1}-t}, 1\right),$$

(4.3)

where

$$\mathbf{Blk}\left(F_k(t), y, \sigma_k^B(y)\sqrt{T_{k-1}-t}, \omega\right) = \left[F_k(t)\omega\Phi\left(\omega d_k^+\right) - y\omega\Phi\left(\omega d_k^-\right)\right]$$ (4.4)

is known as the Black formula (see, e.g., Brigo and Mercurio 2006 for a proof). The variables $d_k^\pm$ can be defined as

$$d_k^\pm = \frac{\ln\left(\frac{F_k(t)}{y}\right) \pm \frac{1}{2}\left(\sigma_k^B(y)\right)^2\left(T_{k-1}-t\right)}{\sigma_k^B(y)\sqrt{T_{k-1}-t}},$$

(4.5)

with

$$\omega = \pm 1 \quad (\text{caplet/floorlet}),$$

and Φ is the standard Gaussian cumulative distribution function. A Python code implementation of the Black formula is provided in Table 4.1.

The market however does not quote the Black implied volatility $\sigma_k^B(y)$ for each single caplet but rather the cap lognormal implied volatility $\tilde{\sigma}_n^B(y)$ (Table 4.2), which corresponds to the single implied volatility value used to value a cap with strike y and maturity T_n. The cap value at time t is

$$\mathbf{Cap}^{Blk}\left(t, T_n, y, \tilde{\sigma}_n^B(y)\right) = \sum_{k=i+1}^{n} P_d(t, T_k)\,\tau_k \mathbf{Blk}\left(F_k(t), y, \tilde{\sigma}_n^B(y)\sqrt{T_{k-1}-t}, 1\right).$$

(4.6)

We can consider the term $\tilde{\sigma}_n^B$ a market artefact to facilitate the trading of caps, where a unique value is used to value caplets with different expiries T_{k-1}. In reality, as we have seen in Equation (4.3), each of these caplets has assigned to it a different Black implied volatility $\sigma_k^B(y)$ which can be extracted from $\tilde{\sigma}_n^B(y)$ through a procedure called volatility stripping (see, e.g., Hagan and Konikov 2004). This allows us to rewrite Equation (4.6) as

$$\sum_{k=i+1}^{n} P_d(t, T_k)\, \tau_k \mathbf{Blk}\left(F_k(t), y, \sigma_k^B(y)\sqrt{T_{k-1}-t}, 1\right).$$

Analogously, the value at time t of a floorlet with strike y, expiring at T_{k-1} and paying at T_k can be computed as

$$\mathbf{Fll}^{Blk}\left(t, T_{k-1}, T_k, y, \sigma_k^B(y)\right) = P_d(t, T_k)\, \tau_k \mathbf{Blk}\left(F_k(t), y, \sigma_k^B(y)\sqrt{T_{k-1}-t}, -1\right).$$
(4.7)

The value at time t of a floor with strike y and maturity T_n is given by the sum of the floorlets, priced using the floor lognormal implied volatility $\tilde{\sigma}_n^B(y)$:

$$\mathbf{Floor}^{Blk}\left(t, T_n, y, \tilde{\sigma}_n^B(y)\right) = \sum_{k=i+1}^{n} P_d(t, T_k)\, \tau_k \mathbf{Blk}\left(F_k(t), y, \tilde{\sigma}_n^B(y)\sqrt{T_{k-1}-t}, -1\right),$$
(4.8)

or alternatively using a different Black implied volatility $\sigma_k^B(y)$ for each floorlet, that is

$$\sum_{k=i+1}^{n} P_d(t, T_k)\, \tau_k \mathbf{Blk}\left(F_k(t), y, \sigma_k^B(y)\sqrt{T_{k-1}-t}, -1\right).$$

The lognormal Black model can be easily extended and used to price swaptions, where we model the swap rate $S_{m,n}(t)$ under the swap measure $\mathbb{Q}^{m,n}$ associated with the numeraire $A_{d,m,n}(t)$

$$dS_{m,n}(t) = \sigma_{m,n}(t)S_{m,n}(t)dW_{m,n}(t).$$
(4.9)

We define the Black implied volatility as

$$\sigma_{m,n}^{B} = \sqrt{\frac{1}{T_m - t} \int_{t}^{T_m} \sigma_{m,n}(u)^2 \, du,}$$

and introduce a strike dependency, as we did for the caplet/floorlet case, changing the notation to $\sigma_{m,n}^{B}(y)$.

The value at time t of a payer swaption with strike y and expiring at T_m under the Black model is given by

$$\text{PS}^{Blk}\left(t, T_m, T_n, y, \sigma_{m,n}^{B}(y)\right) = A_{d,m,n}(t)\text{Blk}\left(S_{m,n}(t), y, \sigma_{m,n}^{B}(y)\sqrt{T_m - t}, 1\right).$$

$$(4.10)$$

Equivalently, the value at time t of a receiver swaption with strike y and expiring at T_m is

$$\text{RS}^{Blk}\left(t, T_m, T_n, y, \sigma_{m,n}^{B}(y)\right) = A_{d,m,n}(t)\text{Blk}\left(S_{m,n}(t), y, \sigma_{m,n}^{B}(y)\sqrt{T_m - t}, -1\right).$$

$$(4.11)$$

Table 4.1 Black formula – Python code

```python
from scipy.stats import norm
import math

def black(F_0, y, expiry, vol, isCall):
    '''
    Compute the Black formula.

    @var F_0: forward rate at time 0
    @var y: option strike
    @var expiry: option expiry (in years)
    @var vol: Black implied volatility
    @var isCall: True or False
    '''
    option_value = 0
    if expiry * vol == 0.0:
        if isCall:
            option_value = max(F_0 - y, 0.0)
        else:
```

```
                    option_value = max(y - F_0, 0.0)
        else:
            d1 = dPlusBlack(F_0 = F_0, y = y, expiry = expiry,
                            vol = vol)
            d2 = dMinusBlack(F_0 = F_0, y = y, expiry = expiry,
                             vol = vol)
            if isCall:
                option_value = (F_0 * norm.cdf(d1) - y *
                                norm.cdf(d2))
            else:
                option_value = (y * norm.cdf(-d2) - F_0 *
                                norm.cdf(-d1))

        return option_value


def dPlusBlack(F_0, y, expiry, vol):
    '''
    Compute the d+ term appearing in the Black formula.

    @var F_0: forward rate at time 0
    @var y: option strike
    @var expiry: option expiry (in years)
    @var vol: Black implied volatility
    '''
    d_plus = ((math.log(F_0 / y) + 0.5 * vol * vol * expiry)
              / vol / math.sqrt(expiry))

    return d_plus


def dMinusBlack(F_0, y, expiry, vol):
    '''
    Compute the d- term appearing in the Black formula.

    @var F_0: forward rate at time 0
    @var y: option strike
    @var expiry: option expiry (in years)
    @var vol: Black implied volatility
    '''
    d_minus = (dPlusBlack(F_0 = F_0, y = y, expiry = expiry,
                          vol = vol) - vol * math.sqrt(expiry))

    return d_minus
```

Most brokers quote caps/floors and swaptions using implied lognormal volatility based on the Black model. This is possible as a one to one relationship between the price and the volatility exists. Prior to the financial crisis these market quotes

Table 4.2 Quotes (%) for OIS discounted EUR caps/floors in lognormal implied volatility terms. The horizontal axis represents the option strike (%), whereas the vertical axis represents the option expiry. The 1y cap is usually composed of three-month (i.e., $\tau_k = 3m$) caplets instead of the standard six-month ones

	0.5	1	1.5	2	2.5	3	3.5	4	4.5	5
1y	94.34	96	98.26	100.45	102.53	104.45	106.23	107.84	109.31	110.65
2y	103.7	101.94	101.21	101	101.06	101.27	101.56	101.87	102.18	102.5
3y	87.79	75.97	69.91	67.76	67.35	67.61	68.1	68.67	69.27	69.86
4y	81.6	68.67	62.27	59.35	58.17	57.81	57.82	58.01	58.3	58.64
5y	78.96	66.13	60.04	56.73	54.71	53.44	52.64	52.14	51.85	51.71
6y	74.35	61.45	55.05	51.38	48.99	47.39	46.35	45.7	45.33	45.15
7y	69.69	57.95	51.44	47.59	45.03	43.28	42.13	41.42	41.02	40.83
8y	67.47	55.2	48.67	44.72	42.05	40.18	38.92	38.12	37.65	37.42
9y	64.95	53	46.5	42.53	39.82	37.86	36.47	35.54	34.96	34.63
10y	60.86	49.64	43.28	39.35	36.63	34.61	33.12	32.07	31.39	30.98

Table 4.3 Quotes (%) for OIS discounted EUR ATM swaptions in lognormal implied volatility terms. The horizontal axis represents the tenor of the underlying swap, whereas the vertical axis represents the option expiry

	1y	2y	5y	7y	10y
1y	87.53	65.26	46.20	37.83	31.08
2y	77.61	55.91	40.2	34.15	29.3
3y	56.75	45.3	35.06	31.03	27.67
5y	37.78	33.16	28.4	26.67	25.31
10y	23.13	22.17	21.84	21.76	21.7

implicitly used the classical LIBOR discounting. As the markets have moved toward the OIS dual curve framework, the quotations have altered into two subsets – volatilities that match the market prices of uncollateralized trades using LIBOR discounting and volatilities that match collateralized trades using OIS discounting. In Tables 4.2 and 4.3 we show (OIS discounted) quotes for caps/floors and at the money (ATM) swaptions, expressed in lognormal terms. For caps/floors the reference strike is reported on the horizontal axis, and is represented as an absolute function of the underlying forward rate, for example, if the 10y forward rate is 5%, the equivalent ATM strike will be also quoted as 5% .

4.2 Normal model

In 1900, Louis Bachelier, Bachelier (1900), proposed a continuous time model to describe the evolution of spot stock prices. In the forward adaptation of his model, the process driving $F_k(t)$ under the measure $\mathbb{Q}^k$ is a normal diffusion and the stochastic differential equation reads as

$$dF_k(t) = \sigma_k(t)dW_k(t),$$

(4.12)

where $\sigma_k(t)$ is the instantaneous normal volatility.

The distribution of the forward interest rate produced by this model is normal, therefore $F_k(t)$ can assume negative values. This feature allows us to price options also when the underlying goes into negative territory. Moreover, this model can assign a positive value to negative strike options. Both of these features (not present in the lognormal Black model of Section 4.1) have characterized several interest rate markets in recent years. This explains also why brokers have started quoting interest rate options in normal volatility terms (Tables 4.4 and 4.5) besides (or instead of) the lognormal volatility $\sigma_k^B(y)$ quotes.

The prices for caplets, floorlets and swaptions are obtained following an analogous procedure (integration of the expected values) as the one proposed for the Black model. In what follows we will simply show, leaving aside details, the pricing formulas, under the normal model, for the instruments introduced in Section 3.4.

The value at time t for a caplet with strike y, expiring at T_{k-1} and paying at T_k is

$$\mathbf{Cpl}^{\text{Norm}}\left(t, T_{k-1}, T_k, y, \sigma_k^N(y)\right) = P_d(t, T_k)\,\tau_k \mathbf{Norm}\left(F_k(t), y, \sigma_k^N(y)\sqrt{T_{k-1}-t}, +\right),$$

(4.13)

with $\mathbf{Norm}\left(F_k(t), y, \sigma_k^N(y)\sqrt{T_{k-1}-t}, \pm\right)$ known as the Bachelier formula

$$\mathbf{Norm}\left(F_k(t), y, \sigma_k^N(y)\sqrt{T_{k-1}-t}, \pm\right) = \sigma_k^N(y)\sqrt{T_{k-1}-t}\left(d_k^{\pm}\Phi\left(d_k^{\pm}\right) + \phi\left(d_k^{\pm}\right)\right),$$

(4.14)

where

$$d_k^{\pm} = \pm\frac{F_k(t) - y}{\sigma_k^N(y)\sqrt{T_{k-1}-t}},$$

(4.15)

while ϕ is the Gaussian probability density function and $\sigma_k^N(y)$ is a constant volatility (known as normal volatility) depending on the caplet expiry T_{k-1} and the strike y.

Table 4.4 Quotes (in basis points) for OIS discounted EUR caps/floors in normal implied volatility terms. The horizontal axis represents the option strike (%), whereas the vertical axis represents the option expiry

	0.5	1	1.5	2	2.5	3	3.5	4	4.5	5
1y	35.07	53.26	69.94	85.89	101.44	116.7	131.74	146.57	161.2	175.66
2y	43.19	63.44	80.81	96.8	111.95	126.53	140.67	154.43	167.89	181.1
3y	45.08	60.04	71.74	83.55	95.63	107.75	119.73	131.54	143.18	154.66
4y	56.85	73.82	87.3	99.79	111.78	123.38	134.65	145.63	156.37	166.91
5y	59.43	75.6	88.07	99.29	109.81	119.94	129.85	139.61	149.28	158.85
6y	60.63	75.54	86.53	96.19	105.05	113.56	121.97	130.42	138.95	147.51
7y	61.42	75.36	85.19	93.64	101.33	108.69	116.08	123.64	131.41	139.32
8y	62.01	75.19	84.08	91.6	98.37	104.8	111.28	118.01	125.03	132.29
9y	62.52	75.01	83.13	89.94	96.02	101.69	107.34	113.21	119.4	125.9
10y	62.98	74.37	81.31	87.04	92.11	96.76	101.3	106.06	111.18	116.69

Table 4.5 Quotes (in basis points) for OIS discounted EUR ATM swaptions in normal implied volatility terms. The horizontal axis represents the tenor of the underlying swap, whereas the vertical axis represents the option expiry

	1y	2y	5y	7y	10y
1y	38.57	50.61	69.91	71.64	72.46
2y	62.08	69.39	78.16	78.32	77.41
3y	77.27	80.12	82.43	81.72	80
5y	87.31	86.1	84.85	83.89	82.39
10y	79	77.99	76.95	76.12	75.05

Analogously, the value at time t of a floorlet with strike y, expiring at T_{k-1} and paying at T_k is given by

$$\text{Fll}^{\text{Norm}}\left(t, T_{k-1}, T_k, y, \sigma_k^N(y)\right) = P_d(t, T_k)\,\tau_k\text{Norm}\left(F_k(t), y, \sigma_k^N(y)\sqrt{T_{k-1} - t}, -\right).$$

(4.16)

The pricing formulas for caps and floors under the normal model can be easily obtained using the above relationship and following the same methodology reported in Section 4.1.

The normal model can be extended to the modelling of the forward swap rate under the swap measure $\mathbb{Q}^{m,n}$, where the following stochastic differential equation

$$dS_{m,n}(t) = \sigma_{m,n}(t)dW_{m,n}(t),$$

(4.17)

describes the evolution of the increments of $S_{m,n}(t)$.

Under this model, the value at time t of a payer swaption with strike y and expiring at T_m is given by

$$\mathbf{PS}^{\mathrm{Norm}}\left(t, T_m, T_n, y, \sigma^N_{m,n}(y)\right) = A_{d,m,n}(t)\mathbf{Norm}\left(S_{m,n}(t), y, \sigma^N_{m,n}(y)\sqrt{T_m - t}, +\right).$$

(4.18)

Equivalently, the value at time t of a receiver swaption with strike y and expiring at T_m is

$$\mathbf{RS}^{\mathrm{Norm}}\left(t, T_m, T_n, y, \sigma^N_{m,n}(y)\right) = A_{d,m,n}(t)\mathbf{Norm}\left(S_{m,n}(t), y, \sigma^N_{m,n}(y)\sqrt{T_m - t}, -\right).$$

(4.19)

4.3 Risk sensitivities

So far we have discussed the valuation of some basic interest rate derivatives such as caps/floors (as well as caplets/floorlets) and swaptions. In order to manage a book of derivatives, it is important to know, not only the value of the products therein included, but also to understand how the book value changes when the underlying risk factors and market data change. This information is given by the risk sensitivities, also known as the Greeks. Ideally, these sensitivities should be calculated as accurately and quickly as possible, so that the trader can hedge these risks with appropriate hedging trades, where necessary. Another widely used application of the Greeks is to explain the changes in the theoretical price (and/or profit and loss) by means of a Taylor expansion. For example, if we calculated a value V_{prev} and some short time later calculate a new value V_{new}, we may wish to attribute/explain the changes to particular changes in contingent parameters such as time t, underlying F, volatility σ, correlation ρ and other known parameters, that is we may have something like

$$V_{\mathrm{new}}(t_{\mathrm{new}}, F_{\mathrm{new}}, d_{\mathrm{new}}, \sigma_{\mathrm{new}}, \rho_{\mathrm{new}}, \ldots)$$

$$= V_{\mathrm{prev}} + \frac{\partial V_{\mathrm{prev}}}{\partial t}(t_{\mathrm{new}} - t_{\mathrm{prev}})$$

$$+ \frac{\partial V_{\mathrm{prev}}}{\partial F}(F_{\mathrm{new}} - F_{\mathrm{prev}}) + \frac{1}{2}\frac{\partial^2 V_{\mathrm{prev}}}{\partial F^2}(F_{\mathrm{new}} - F_{\mathrm{prev}})^2$$

$$+ \frac{\partial V_{\mathrm{prev}}}{\partial \sigma}(\sigma_{\mathrm{new}} - \sigma_{\mathrm{prev}}) + \frac{\partial V_{\mathrm{prev}}}{\partial \rho}(\rho_{\mathrm{new}} - \rho_{\mathrm{prev}}) + \cdots$$

The main risk sensitivities are delta, gamma, vega and theta. Depending on the type of product there might also be additional Greeks such as (vanna, volga, correlation delta). By including other cross-gamma terms we could improve the accuracy of the approximation. In what follows, we will introduce delta, gamma and vega for a caplet priced using the Black model. All the results can be easily extended to other vanilla products (swaptions for example) and other models, such as the Bachelier (normal) model.

4.3.1 Delta

Delta at time t is the first derivative of the caplet price with respect to the forward rate $F_k(t)$

$$\Delta(t) = \frac{\partial\left(P_d(t,T_k)\,\tau_k \mathbf{Blk}\left(F_k(t),y,\sigma_k^B(y)\sqrt{T_{k-1}-t},1\right)\right)}{\partial F_k(t)}$$

$$= P_d(t,T_k)\,\tau_k \frac{\partial \mathbf{Blk}\left(F_k(t),y,\sigma_k^B(y)\sqrt{T_{k-1}-t},1\right)}{\partial F_k(t)}$$

$$+ \frac{\partial P_d(t,T_k)}{\partial F_k(t)}\tau_k \mathbf{Blk}\left(F_k(t),y,\sigma_k^B(y)\sqrt{T_{k-1}-t},1\right),$$

in a multiple curve framework, such as the one in which we are working (Section 3.2). We have seen that the discount curve does not depend on the forward curve. This independency stems from the fact that the instruments used to build the former are different from the ones used to construct the latter. This translates into

$$\frac{\partial P_d(t,T_k)}{\partial F_k(t)} = 0,$$

and allows us to simplify the delta relationship even further to

$$\Delta(t) = P_d(t,T_k)\,\tau_k \Delta_{Blk}(t), \qquad (4.20)$$

where

$$\Delta_{Blk}(t) = \frac{\partial \mathbf{Blk}\left(F_k(t),y,\sigma_k^B(y)\sqrt{T_{k-1}-t},1\right)}{\partial F_k(t)}, \qquad (4.21)$$

is called Black delta and represents the change in $\mathrm{Blk}\left(F_k(t),y,\sigma_k^B(y)\sqrt{T_{k-1}-t},1\right)$ with respect to $F_k(t)$. Equation (4.20) is composed of a model independent term, $P_d(t,T_k)\,\tau_k$, as well as a model dependent term, $\Delta_{Blk}(t)$. It can therefore be used under different modelling assumptions, by simply changing the model dependent term.

4.3.2 Gamma

In general, most derivatives are not only linear but have higher order sensitivity to the underlying rate. The second order, or quadratic, term is called gamma and is given, at time t, by

$$\Gamma(t) = \frac{\partial^2 \left(P_d(t, T_k)\, \tau_k \mathbf{Blk}\left(F_k(t), y, \sigma_k^B(y)\sqrt{T_{k-1} - t}, 1\right)\right)}{\partial F_k^2(t)}$$

$$= P_d(t, T_k)\, \tau_k \frac{\partial^2 \mathbf{Blk}\left(F_k(t), y, \sigma_k^B(y)\sqrt{T_{k-1} - t}, 1\right)}{\partial F_k^2(t)}$$

$$+ \frac{\partial^2 P_d(t, T_k)}{\partial F_k^2(t)} \tau_k \mathbf{Blk}\left(F_k(t), y, \sigma_k^B(y)\sqrt{T_{k-1} - t}, 1\right)$$

$$+ 2\frac{\partial P_d(t, T_k)}{\partial F_k(t)} \tau_k \Delta_{Blk}(t),$$

which, considering the independence of the discounting curve from the forward curve, reduces to

$$\Gamma(t) = P_d(t, T_k)\, \tau_k \Gamma_{Black}(t),$$

where

$$\Gamma_{Black}(t) = \frac{\partial^2 \mathbf{Blk}\left(F_k(t), y, \sigma_k^B(y)\sqrt{T_{k-1} - t}, 1\right)}{\partial F_k^2(t)}, \qquad (4.22)$$

is called Black gamma.

4.3.3 Vega

Sensitivity to the volatility is called vega. At time t it is defined as follows

$$\mathcal{V}(t) = P_d(t, T_k)\, \tau_k \frac{\partial \mathbf{Blk}\left(F_k(t), y, \sigma_k^B(y)\sqrt{T_{k-1} - t}, 1\right)}{\partial \sigma_k^B(y)}$$

$$= P_d(t, T_k)\, \tau_k \mathcal{V}_{Blk}(t),$$

where we have introduced the Black vega

$$\mathcal{V}_{Blk}(t) = \frac{\partial \mathbf{Blk}\left(F_k(t), y, \sigma_k^B(y)\sqrt{T_{k-1} - t}, 1\right)}{\partial \sigma_k^B(y)}. \qquad (4.23)$$

4.3.4 Risk sensitivities computation

The risk sensitivities introduced in the previous section can be computed in various ways, such as closed analytic form, finite difference or using a Monte Carlo simulation. For the Black Greeks $\Delta_{Blk}, \Gamma_{Blk}, \mathcal{V}_{Blk}$ the most accurate and fast computation method is to use a closed form expression. However, as an analytical form is not available for every model, we will present in this section a more general methodology which can be used with a broad set of models: finite difference methods.

The computation of first-order risk sensitivities such as delta and vega can be carried out using three types of finite difference methods:

- Forward Difference

$$\frac{\partial V}{\partial u} = \frac{V(u + \Delta u) - V(u)}{\Delta u} + O(\Delta u),$$

- Backward Difference

$$\frac{\partial V}{\partial u} = \frac{V(u) - V(u - \Delta u)}{\Delta u} + O(\Delta u),$$

- Central Difference

$$\frac{\partial V}{\partial u} = \frac{V(u + \Delta u) - V(u - \Delta u)}{2\Delta u} + O((\Delta u)^2).$$

Here we have used $V(u)$ to indicate a function with respect to that which we want to compute the risk sensitivity, for example, a caplet pricing function such as Equation (4.4) or Equation (4.13). The quantity Δu corresponds to an infinitesimal bumping amount to be applied to the variable with respect to that which we want to compute the risk sensitivity ($F_k(0)$ for Black delta, σ_k^B for Black vega, etc.). When implementing a numerical algorithm to compute risk sensitivities, the quantity Δu has to be chosen according to the characteristics of the machine in use and of the programming language adopted (see, e.g., Glasserman 2003). For example, the risk sensitivity tests computed in Chapter 5 have been carried out using $\Delta u = 1E - 06$.

Among the three methods outlined above, the central difference one provides a greater accuracy (ibid.). In this light, we have decided to report the Python function (Table 4.6) which can be used to compute first-order sensitivities, and more generally first-order derivatives, for this method only.

Also the computation of second-order risk sensitivities such as gamma can be carried out using the same forward, backward and central difference. The greater accuracy of the latter holds true also in this case. Mathematically it can be expressed as

Table 4.6 First-order derivative of a function using central difference – Python code

```
def computeFirstDerivative(v_u_plus_du, v_u_minus_du, du):
    '''
    Compute the first derivatve of a function using
    central difference

    @var v_u_plus_du: is the value of the function
    computed for a positive bump amount du
    @var v_u_minus_du: is the value of the function
    computed for a negative bump amount du
    @var du: bump amount
    '''
    first_derivative = (v_u_plus_du - v_u_minus_du) / (2.0 * du)

    return first_derivative
```

Table 4.7 Second-order derivative of a function using central difference – Python code

```
def computeSecondDerivative(v_u, v_u_plus_du, v_u_minus_du, du):
    '''
    Compute the second derivatve of a function using
    central difference

    @var v_u: is the value of the function
    @var v_u_plus_du: is the value of the function
    computed for a positive bump amount du
    @var v_u_minus_du: is the value of the function
    computed for a negative bump amount du
    @var du: bump amount
    '''
    second_derivative = ((v_u_plus_du - 2.0*v_u + v_u_minus_du)/
                         (du * du))

    return second_derivative
```

$$\frac{\partial^2 V}{\partial u^2} = \frac{V(u + \Delta u) - 2V(u) + V(u - \Delta u)}{(\Delta u)^2} + O((\Delta u)^2).$$

In Table 4.7 we detail the Python function which can be used to compute second-order sensitivities, and more generally second-order derivatives, using central difference.

5 | SABR Model

5.1 Introduction

We have introduced in Chapter 4 the normal and lognormal models. They play an important role as they are intuitive, simple and their parameters can be adjusted quickly to obtain a price in agreement with the market. However, these simple models cannot be calibrated to more than one volatility per expiry. The authors of two papers, Derman and Kani (1994) and Dupire (1994), proposed a model, where the volatility is dependent on the current state of the underlying process. These so-called local volatility models could be calibrated, with some extra effort, to the entire volatility surface. One shortcoming of the local volatility models is that they predict a dynamic behaviour of the smile and the skew (the smile moves in the opposite direction as the underlying) that is different from what is observed in the market (where the smile moves in the same direction as the underlying).

It is a well known fact that models where the volatility of the underlying process is also a stochastic process, that is, in stochastic volatility models, would describe the smile dynamics observed in the market much better than local volatility models. But unfortunately, the calibration of these models is not straightforward. Hagan et al. (2002) proposed a new stochastic volatility model: SABR (stochastic-α-β-ρ) accompanied by a simple calibration formula. Since this breakthrough paper, the SABR model has gained widespread popularity across various asset classes, and has become the market standard in the interest rate vanilla market for pricing, for example, caps, floors and swaptions.

The SABR model is described by the following set of processes

$$dF_k(t) = \alpha_k(t)F_k(t)^{\beta_k}dW_{F_k}(t), \tag{5.1}$$

$$d\alpha_k(t) = \nu_k\alpha_k(t)dW_{\alpha_k}(t), \tag{5.2}$$

where $F_k(t)$ is the forward interest rate with maturity T_k (its notation at time $t = 0$ can be simplified to F_k), $\alpha_k(t)$ is the volatility (as for $F_k(t)$, at time $t = 0$ we will simply use α_k), β_k is the elasticity coefficient and v_k is the volatility of the volatility process.

The Wiener process $W_{F_k}(t)$ is related to the stochastic forward interest rate $F_k(t)$, while the Wiener process $W_{\alpha_k}(t)$ is related to the stochastic volatility $\alpha_k(t)$. These processes are correlated as

$$\mathbb{E}^k \left[dW_{F_k}(t) dW_{\alpha_k}(t) \right] = \rho_k dt, \qquad (5.3)$$

using a constant correlation factor ρ_k.

The success of the SABR model can be summarized in the following points:

- Each of the SABR parameters $\alpha_k, v_k, \beta_k, \rho_k$ has a direct and clear influence on the calibrated implied volatility smile. A detailed analysis of each of these model parameters is reported in Section 5.2.
- There exists an analytical formula, Equation (5.13), which returns the price of vanilla options (such as caplets, floorlets, swaptions) under the SABR model, in terms of a Black implied volatility. This is an excellent feature, as a trader or sales person can price a deal using the SABR model and communicate to the client the option price in market standard terms (i.e., quoted in $\sigma_k^B(y)$ units, see Section 3.4). Besides the equation for Black implied volatilities, Hagan et al. (2002) also provided an analytical approximation, Equation (5.16), for normal implied volatilities $\sigma_k^N(y)$. This formula has been less widely accepted, as in most markets brokers have been traditionally quoting deals in $\sigma_k^B(y)$ terms. However, due to economic reasons and partly due to governmental interventions in the years after the 2007–08 financial crisis, interest rates have been continuously low, forcing many brokers to quote in $\sigma_k^N(y)$ units.
- Equations (5.13) and (5.16) are, in general, able to provide a very good fit to the implied volatility smile quoted in the market. The computational simplicity allows the model to be naturally used as an interpolation scheme along the strike axis. Applying this interpolation mechanism, implied volatilities for illiquid strike options can be accurately and easily found.

A model which combines all these positive aspects is extremely appealing and not many other pricing models proposed in the last decades can claim such qualities. However, the SABR model and the Hagan et al. lognormal approximations are not without their flaws and various criticisms have been reported over the years (see, e.g., Antonov and Spector 2012, Doust 2012). In what follows we outline these potentially important pitfalls:

- The forward process, Equation (5.1), is not mean reverting; if we do a historical analysis of how the forward curve changes over the years, we can clearly see that forward interest rates tend to revert, in the long run, to a mean value. Equation

(5.1) does not capture this behaviour correctly unless a further mean reverting term is added to it.

- The SABR model assumes that each forward rate lives in a world of its own; it is therefore impossible to model more than one forward rate at the time. Furthermore, the parameters of the process are not time-dependent and can only be calibrated to a single expiry. This is comparable to the Black model, before it was extended by Brace et al. (1997) and Jamshidian (1997) to include all the forward rates under a single measure (Chapter 6). It should therefore not be used to price exotic products depending on more than one forward rate. To overcome this limitation, extended versions of the LIBOR Market Model, which include stochastic volatility à la SABR, have been developed by various practitioners (Chapter 7). As a consequence of this, the SABR (forward interest rate) model defined by Equations (5.1) and (5.2) should not even be used to price swaptions: as they depend on the joint evolution of several forward rates (Section 3.4). However, it is possible to define a SABR forward swap model as

$$dS_{m,n}(t) = \alpha_{m,n}(t)S_{m,n}(t)^{\beta_{m,n}}dW_{S_{m,n}}(t), \tag{5.4}$$

$$d\alpha_{m,n}(t) = v_{m,n}\alpha_{m,n}(t)dW_{\alpha_{m,n}}(t), \tag{5.5}$$

with

$$\mathbb{E}^{m,n}\left[dW_{S_{m,n}}(t)dW_{\alpha_{m,n}}(t)\right] = \rho_{m,n}dt, \tag{5.6}$$

where we model directly the forward swap rate $S_{m,n}(t)$ under the swap measure $\mathbb{Q}^{m,n}$.

- The Hagan et al. approximations suffer from two main problems: the risk neutral probability density function at low strikes can become negative, and the expansion methods become questionable as the condition $v_k^2 T_{k-1} \ll 1$ is not fulfilled. The effect of the former issue is that the option prices produced are arbitrageable (i.e., the option prices are no longer convex in the strike dimension), while the latter translates into an unreliable set of parameters $\alpha_k, v_k, \beta_k, \rho_k$ produced by calibrating to market quotes. Along with these two main issues, affecting any vanilla derivatives (caplets, floorlets, swaptions, etc.) priced and hedged using the SABR model, there is also a third issue which affects mainly CMS products. Under some conditions (Section 5.8.5) the Hagan et al. approximations return unreliable implied volatilities for very high strike options. These issues will be analysed in depth in Section 5.8. Plenty of research articles have been published about these drawbacks and how to try to resolve them (see, e.g., Henry-Labordere 2008, Obloj 2008, Paulot 2009, Doust 2012, Antonov et al. 2013). We will discuss one of the most promising proposed resolutions, together with its limitations, in Section 5.9.

In the remainder of the book, unless we specify otherwise, we will use the SABR (forward interest rate) model and its approximation formulas to simulate the forward interest rate $F_k(t)$. All the results and considerations presented will anyhow hold also for the SABR (forward swap) model defined by Equations (5.4) and (5.5).

5.2 SABR parameters

Let us analyse in details the impact which each of the SABR parameters has on the implied volatility smile.

5.2.1 The α_k parameter

The parameter α_k is the $t = 0$ value of the stochastic volatility process $\alpha_k(t)$. The effect of α_k is to move up or down the volatility smile with almost no effect on the shape of the smile (Figure 5.1). The value of α_k can be approximated, for options with a small time to expiry T_{k-1}, by

$$\alpha_k \approx \frac{\sigma_k^B(y_{ATM})}{F_k^{\beta_k-1}},$$

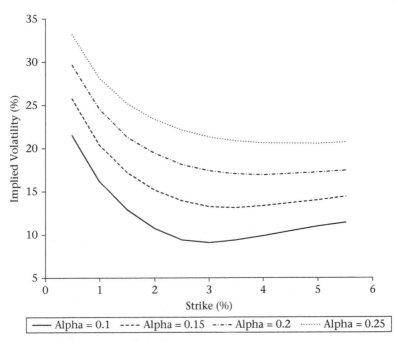

Figure 5.1 Effect of α_k on the smile level

where $\sigma_k^B(y_{ATM})$ is the lognormal Black implied volatility for the at the money strike y_{ATM}.

5.2.2 The β_k parameter

The constant elasticity of variance (CEV) parameter β_k is usually taken between 0 and 1. The reason behind this choice is that the SABR model is a martingale only if $0 \le \beta_k < 1$ or as long as $\rho_k \le 0$ for $\beta_k = 1$ (see, e.g., Henry-Labordere 2008).

The main effect of β_k is a change in the smile slope. In particular the slope gets more pronounced as β_k moves from 1 to 0 (Figure 5.2). The intuitive explanation of the change in the slope is the fact that the model switches from lognormal-like to normal-like behaviour when β_k is lowered. As β_k controls also the distribution of the forward rate $F_k(t)$, it could be chosen a priori to reflect a market view. In particular:

- $\beta_k = 0$. Equation (5.1) reduces to

$$dF_k(t) = \alpha_k(t)dW_{F_k}(t).$$

If $\alpha_k(t)$ is taken constant, the SABR model actually stops being a stochastic volatility model and corresponds to the normal model (Equation (4.12)); this

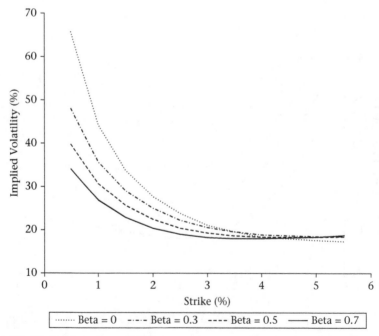

Figure 5.2 Effect of β_k on the smile slope

is the only case where the distribution of $F_k(t)$ is truly normal (for all the other choices of α_k, with $\beta_k = 0$, the actual distribution of $F_k(t)$ is not of normal type). For the particular case $\beta_k = 0$, $\rho_k = 0$ it is valuable to know that a closed form solution exists (see, e.g., Hagan et al. 2005) which can be used to obtain an exact price instead of an approximated one. The major feature of the choice $\beta_k = 0$ is to assign a probability mass to negative outcomes of $F_k(t)$ (Figure 5.3). The user needs to make, at this point, what we could consider a "philosophical" choice. Is it meaningful that the forward interest rate turns negative? A positive answer to this question might be justified by the recent appearance of negative rates in various economies.

- $0 < \beta_k < 1$. The SABR model becomes one of CEV type. For the particular case in which $\alpha_k(t)$ is taken constant and $\beta_k = 0.5$, Equation (5.1) reduces to

$$dF_k(t) = \alpha_k(t)\sqrt{F_k}dW_{F_k}(t),$$

which corresponds to a squared root CEV model (see Cox and Ross 1976). In order to avoid arbitrage with this choice of β_k exponent, it is necessary to set an absorbing boundary for $F_k(t)$ at zero (see, e.g, Andersen and Andreasen (2000)). For $0 < \beta_k < 1$ the forward interest rate cannot go into negative territory and whenever $F_k(t)$ reaches zero, it will stay at zero forever. The implication of this modelling choice is that a considerable mass function is assigned to the zero value. This mass is bigger, the lower F_k and the longer the forward maturity is (Figure 5.4). The no arbitrage restriction posed by CEV type models raises the question as to how they are able to represent (at least in some markets) the reality. One can argue that there is a limit to how much a forward rate can go negative, and usually this limit should not be too far from zero. Using a model with an absorbing boundary at zero can be seen as a real world approximation.

- $\beta_k = 1$. Equation (5.1) reduces to

$$dF_k(t) = \alpha_k(t)F_k dW_{F_k}(t).$$

If $\alpha_k(t)$ is taken as constant, the SABR model corresponds to the lognormal Black model (Equation (4.1)); this is the only case in which the distribution of the forward interest rate is truly lognormal. When $\alpha_k(t)$ is a stochastic quantity, the actual distribution of $F_k(t)$ is not lognormal (Figure 5.5). It is however true that with such a choice of β_k, $F_k(t)$ can, by definition, never change sign.

5.2.3 The v_k parameter

We denote with v_k the volatility of $\alpha_k(t)$; for this reason it is also known as volatility of volatility. The effect of v_k on the smile is to increase or decrease its curvature. In

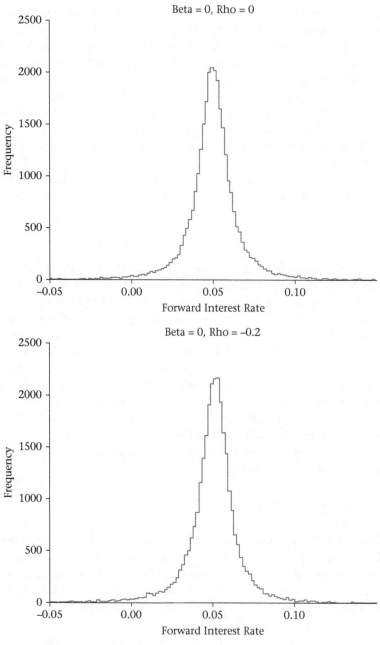

Figure 5.3 Distribution of $F_k(t)$ for $\beta_k = 0$, $F_k = 5\%$ and various choices of ρ_k

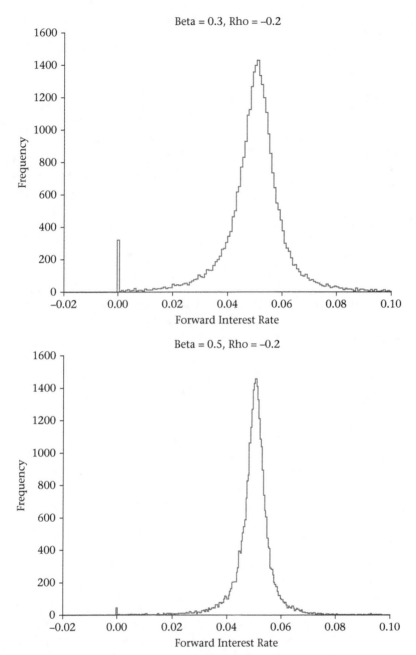

Figure 5.4 Distribution of $F_k(t)$ for various choices of β_k ($\rho_k = -0.2$ and $F_k = 5\%$). The spike at zero, present for $\beta_k = 0.3$ and $\beta_k = 0.5$, is the effect of the absorbing boundary

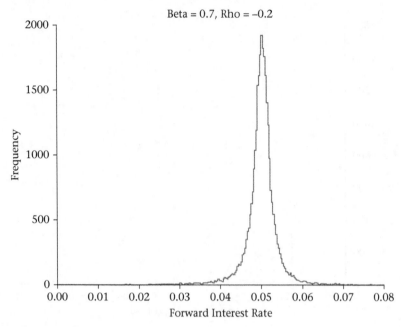

Figure 5.4 Continued

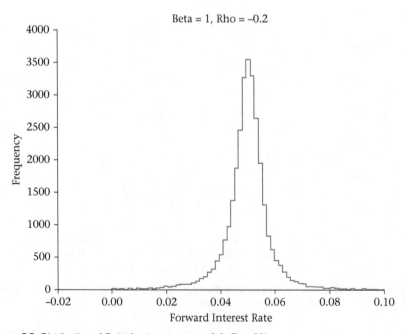

Figure 5.5 Distribution of $F_k(t)$ for $\beta_k = 1$, $\rho_k = -0.2$, $F_k = 5\%$

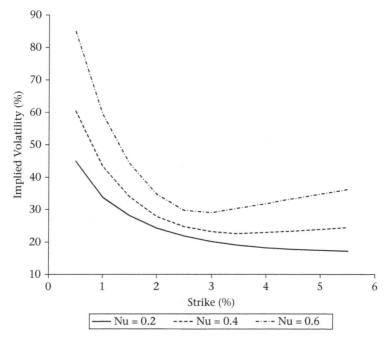

Figure 5.6 Effect of ν_k on the smile curvature

essence, an increase of ν_k makes the implied volatility increase for out of the money (OTM) and in the money (ITM) options, as can be seen in Figure 5.6.

5.2.4 The ρ_k parameter

As shown in Equation (5.3), ρ_k is the correlation between the Brownian motion governing the forward rate process and the Brownian motion governing the volatility process. It can take any value between -1 and 1. In many markets the sign of ρ_k is negative, which translates into an increasing volatility $\alpha_k(t)$ when the forward interest rate $F_k(t)$ decreases and vice versa.

The effect of ρ_k on the smile is similar to the one produced by β_k: the smile gets more and more steep as we move from 1 to -1. This effect can be seen in Figure 5.7.

5.3 PDE and Kolmogorov equations

Having described the SABR model parameters we are now in a position to introduce the Hagan et al. approximations for the implied volatilities. Before doing so, we briefly review the Kolmogorov equations, which are the fundamental mathematical tools used to find the expectation of a future payoff valued using a stochastic volatility model.

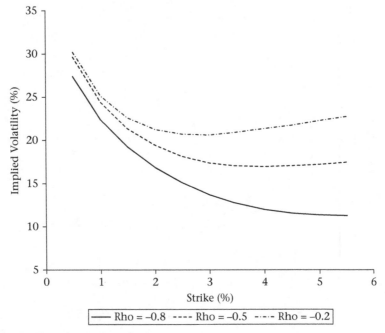

Figure 5.7 Effect of ρ_k on the smile slope

Let us focus on the expected value of a caplet (our results are equally valid for a floorlet) in the SABR model, which is defined as the expectation of the payoff under the T_k-forward measure conditional on the filtration generated by the observed processes, that is

$$\mathbb{E}^k \left[\left(F_k(T_{k-1}) - y \right)^+ \right] = \mathbb{E}^k \left[V \left(F_k(T_{k-1}), \alpha_k(T_{k-1}) \right) | \mathcal{F}_t \right],$$

where we have defined the payoff as the function $V \left(F_k(T_{k-1}), \alpha_k(T_{k-1}) \right)$ at expiry T_{k-1} and which depends on the terminal forward rate and implicitly also the volatility process.

The expectation can also be written as an integral over the payoff multiplied by the probability density p. The probability density p describes the probability that the diffusion processes $\{ F_k(s), \alpha_k(s) \}$ reach the forward rate F and the volatility α at time $T = T_{k-1}$ given the filtration at time t, that is, the state of the economy with current forward rate F_k and initial volatility α_k

$$p \left(t, F_k, \alpha_k; T_{k-1}, F, \alpha \right) dF d\alpha \qquad (5.7)$$
$$= Prob \left[F < F_k(T_{k-1}) < F + dF; \alpha < \alpha_k(T_{k-1}) < \alpha + d\alpha | F_k, \alpha_k \right].$$

Using this definition of the density function, we define the expectation as the integral over all future states folded with the payoff function

$$\mathbb{E}^k\left[\left(F_k(T_{k-1})-y\right)^+\right]=\int\int V(F,\alpha)\,p\left(T_{k-1},F,\alpha\right)dF\,d\alpha. \tag{5.8}$$

Now, let us expand the payoff using Itô's rule to obtain (see e.g., Karatzas and Shreve 1988)

$$V\left(F_k(T_{k-1}),\alpha_k(T_{k-1})\right)$$

$$= V(F_k(t),\alpha_k(t)) + \int_t^{T_{k-1}} \frac{1}{2}\alpha^2(s)F(s)^{2\beta_k}\frac{\partial^2 V(F,\alpha)}{\partial F^2}\,ds + \int_t^{T_{k-1}} \left(\frac{1}{2}v_k^2\alpha^2\frac{\partial^2 V(F,\alpha)}{\partial \alpha^2}\right.$$

$$\left. + \rho_k v_k\alpha^2(s)F(s)^{\beta_k}\frac{\partial^2 V(F,\alpha)}{\partial\alpha\partial F}\right)ds + \int_t^{T_{k-1}} \frac{\partial V(F,\alpha)}{\partial F}\alpha(s)F(s)^{\beta_k}dW_{F_k}(s)$$

$$+ \int_t^{T_{k-1}} \frac{\partial V(F,\alpha)}{\partial\alpha}v_k\alpha(s)dW_{\alpha_k}(s).$$

When inserting this expansion into Equation (5.8) one finds straight-away that the stochastic terms vanish due to the Itô isometry. Therefore we obtain

$$\mathbb{E}^k\left[\left(F_k(T_{k-1})-y\right)^+\right]= V(F_k,\alpha_k)$$

$$+ \frac{1}{2}\int\int\int_t^{T_{k-1}} \alpha^2(s)F(s)^{2\beta_k}\frac{\partial^2 V}{\partial F^2}p\left(T_{k-1},F,\alpha\right)ds\,dF\,d\alpha$$

$$+ \frac{1}{2}\int\int\int_t^{T_{k-1}} v_k^2\alpha^2(s)\frac{\partial^2 V}{\partial\alpha^2}p\left(T_{k-1},F,\alpha\right)ds\,dF\,d\alpha$$

$$+ \int\int\int_t^{T_{k-1}} \rho_k v_k\alpha^2(s)F(s)^{\beta_k}\frac{\partial^2 V}{\partial\alpha\partial F}p\left(T_{k-1},F,\alpha\right)ds\,dF\,d\alpha. \tag{5.9}$$

Now, let us differentiate this equation with respect to the expiry $T = T_{k-1}$. We observe from Equation (5.8) that only the probability density (and not the payoff function) depends on T, therefore the left-hand side can also be written using the derivative of the probability density. Hence both sides equate to

$$\int\int V(F,\alpha)\frac{\partial p\left(T_{k-1},F,\alpha\right)}{\partial T}\,dFd\alpha = \frac{1}{2}\int\int \alpha^2 F^{2\beta_k}\frac{\partial^2 V}{\partial F^2}p\left(T_{k-1},F,\alpha\right)dF\,d\alpha$$

$$+\frac{1}{2}\int\int v_k^2\alpha^2\frac{\partial^2 V}{\partial\alpha^2}p\left(T_{k-1},F,\alpha\right)dF\,d\alpha$$

$$+\int\int \rho_k v_k\alpha^2 F^{\beta_k}\frac{\partial^2 V}{\partial\alpha\partial F}p\left(T_{k-1},F,\alpha\right)dF\,d\alpha.$$

(5.10)

Integrating by parts twice the right-hand side and neglecting any boundary terms (which can be found to be zero), the equation turns out to be a solution of a partial differential equation (PDE) called the Fokker-Planck or forward Kolmogorov equation (see, e.g. Karatzas and Shreve 1988)

$$\frac{\partial p}{\partial T} = \frac{1}{2}\frac{\partial^2\alpha^2 F^{2\beta_k}p}{\partial F^2}+\frac{1}{2}v_k^2\frac{\partial^2\alpha^2 p}{\partial\alpha^2}+\rho_k v_k\frac{\partial^2\alpha^2 F^{\beta_k}p}{\partial\alpha\partial F},$$

(5.11)

with the boundary conditions

$$p=\delta(F-F_k)\delta(\alpha-\alpha_k),$$

at $T=T_{k-1}=t$.

Moreover, applying the Feynman-Kac theorem (ibid.) to the option forward value we obtain the backward Kolmogorov equation

$$-\frac{\partial p}{\partial t} = \frac{1}{2}\frac{\partial^2\alpha^2 F^{2\beta}p}{\partial F^2}+\frac{1}{2}v_k^2\frac{\partial^2\alpha^2 p}{\partial\alpha^2}+\rho_k v_k\frac{\partial^2\alpha^2 F^{\beta}p}{\partial\alpha\partial F}.$$

(5.12)

We therefore observe from Equations (5.11) and (5.12) that the solution to the PDE is time-homogeneous and therefore can transform to the time to expiry variable $\theta=T_{k-1}-t$. The PDE for the variable θ is

$$\frac{\partial p}{\partial\theta} = \frac{1}{2}\frac{\partial^2\alpha^2 F^{2\beta}p}{\partial F^2}+\frac{1}{2}v_k^2\frac{\partial^2\alpha^2 p}{\partial\alpha^2}+\rho_k v_k\frac{\partial^2\alpha^2 F^{\beta}p}{\partial\alpha\partial F}.$$

This PDE can be solved not only by Monte Carlo simulation via the Feynman-Kac theorem (see, e.g. Glasserman 2003) but also traditionally by using a finite difference scheme such as Crank-Nicolson (1996). These methods however turn out to be very time consuming and cannot be used for calibration. Therefore we have to resort to using analytical or asymptotical methods as we will show in Section 5.4.

5.4 Hagan et al. approximations

Hagan et al. proposed two different approximation formulas to swiftly compute plain vanilla option prices in the SABR model: one which returns the lognormal Black implied volatility $\sigma_k^B(y)$, Equation (5.13), and one which returns the normal implied volatility $\sigma_k^N(y)$, Equation (5.16).

Hagan et al. (2002) determine prices for European options under a SABR-like model using a technique called singular perturbation theory (which is of great use in solid state physics, quantum optics and many other sciences). These prices can then be used to calculate an approximate closed-form algebraic formula for the implied volatility. The start of the perturbation approach consists in forcing a small volatility expansion, that is, both the volatility process α as well as the volatility of volatility ν are replaced by small term equivalents $\varepsilon\alpha$ and $\varepsilon\nu$, where ε is a small number. The authors obtain the density function p satisfying the forward Kolmogorov equation (Equation 5.11) as a function of time, the underlying forward and volatility. To solve the PDE, the density is integrated over the terminal volatility to yield a function

$$P\left(t, F_k, \alpha_k, y, T\right) = \int_{-\infty}^{\infty} p\left(t, F_k, \alpha_k, T_{k-1}, y, \alpha\right) d\alpha,$$

which simplifies the forward pricing formula to

$$V\left(t, F_k, \alpha_k\right) = \left[F_k - y\right]^+ + \frac{1}{2}\varepsilon^2 y^{2\beta} \int_0^{T_{k-1}} P\left(t, F_k, \alpha_k, T_{k-1}, y\right) dT,$$

where the function P satisfies the backward Kolmogorov equation (Equation 5.12). Unfortunately, a closed form solution for this equation does not exist and there are no numerical methods which can be easily adopted to solve it. Hence the authors make a series of variable transformations and remove any terms in various expansion approximations higher than second order. The variable transformations are not so straightforward and the approximations for readers not familiar with quantum wave theory are hard to follow. We therefore refer the interested reader for a detailed derivation and proofs to the appendix in Hagan et al. (2002).

We report in this section these approximating solutions for the implied volatilities, including some special cases. In Section 5.5.1 we present some calibration tests, for both types of approximation formulas, done on real market data. An analysis of the limitations of these approximations is reported in Section 5.8.

Before introducing Hagan et al. equations, a couple of remarks might be in order. As the approximation formulas return an implied volatility value, they can be employed to price either caplets or floorlets. It is in fact a well known result for a deterministic volatility model, given by the call-put parity (see, e.g., Shreve 2008), that the implied volatility for a call (caplet) or a put (floorlet) option, which share the same underlying $F_k(t)$, strike y and expiry T_{k-1}, is the same. It is therefore just a matter of plugging the implied volatility obtained (by the approximation formulas) into the Black or normal pricing formula, respectively Equations (4.4) and (4.14), to get the desired expected value.

5.4.1 Lognormal approximation

The approximation formula which returns the lognormal Black implied volatility $\sigma_k^B(y)$ at time $t = 0$ for a caplet/floorlet maturing at time T_{k-1} with strike y is

$$
\sigma_k^B(y) = \frac{\alpha_k}{(yF_k)^{\left(\frac{1-\beta_k}{2}\right)} \left[1 + \frac{(1-\beta_k)^2}{24} \ln^2\left(\frac{F_k}{y}\right) + \frac{(1-\beta_k)^4}{1920} \ln^4\left(\frac{F_k}{y}\right) + \cdots\right]}
$$
$$
\cdot \left(\frac{z_k}{\xi(z_k)}\right)
$$
$$
\cdot \left[1 + \frac{(1-\beta_k)^2}{24} \frac{\alpha_k^2}{(yF_k)^{(1-\beta_k)}} T_{k-1}\right.
$$
$$
\left. + \frac{1}{4} \frac{\alpha_k \beta_k \rho_k \nu_k}{(yF_k)^{\left(\frac{1-\beta_k}{2}\right)}} T_{k-1} + \frac{2 - 3\rho_k^2}{24} \nu_k^2 T_{k-1} + \cdots\right],
\tag{5.13}
$$

where

$$
z_k = \frac{\nu_k}{\alpha_k} (yF_k)^{\left(\frac{1-\beta_k}{2}\right)} \ln\left(\frac{F_k}{y}\right),
$$
$$
\xi(z_k) = \ln\left(\frac{\sqrt{1 - 2\rho_k z_k + z_k^2} + z_k - \rho_k}{1 - \rho_k}\right).
$$

We provide below the special case related to ATM options, for which $y = F_k$:

$$\sigma_k^B(y) = \frac{\alpha_k}{F_k^{(1-\beta_k)}}$$

$$\cdot \left[1 + \frac{(1-\beta_k)^2}{24} \frac{\alpha_k^2}{F_k^{(2-2\beta_k)}} T_{k-1} \right.$$

$$+ \frac{1}{4} \frac{\rho_k \beta_k \nu_k \alpha_k}{F_k^{(1-\beta_k)}} T_{k-1} + \left. \frac{2-3\rho_k^2}{24} \nu_k^2 T_{k-1} + \cdots \right]. \qquad (5.14)$$

When β_k is taken as equal to zero, the Hagan et al. lognormal approximation becomes

$$\sigma_k^B(y) = \alpha_k \frac{\ln\left(\frac{F_k}{y}\right)}{F_k - y} \left(\frac{z_k}{\xi(z_k)} \right)$$

$$\cdot \left[1 + \left(\frac{\alpha_k^2}{24yF_k} + \frac{2-3\rho_k^2}{24} \nu_k^2 \right) T_{k-1} + \cdots \right], \qquad (5.15)$$

where

$$z_k = \frac{\nu_k}{\alpha_k} \sqrt{yF_k} \ln\left(\frac{F_k}{y}\right),$$

$$\xi(z_k) = \ln\left(\frac{\sqrt{1 - 2\rho_k z_k + z_k^2} + z_k - \rho_k}{1 - \rho_k} \right).$$

When β_k is taken as equal to one, the Hagan et al. lognormal approximation becomes

$$\sigma_k^B(y) = \alpha_k \left(\frac{z_k}{\xi(z_k)} \right) \left[1 + \left(\frac{\alpha_k \rho_k \nu_k}{4} + \frac{2-3\rho_k^2}{24} \nu_k^2 \right) T_{k-1} + \cdots \right],$$

where

$$z_k = \frac{\nu_k}{\alpha_k} \ln\left(\frac{F_k}{y}\right),$$

$$\xi(z_k) = \ln\left(\frac{\sqrt{1 - 2\rho_k z_k + z_k^2} + z_k - \rho_k}{1 - \rho_k} \right).$$

The Python code to generate $\sigma_k^B(y)$ using the Hagan et al. lognormal approximation is reported in Table 5.1.

Table 5.1 Hagan et al. lognormal approximation – Python code

```python
import math

def haganLogNormalApprox(y, expiry, F_0, alpha_0, beta,
nu, rho):
    '''
    Function which returns the Black implied volatility,
    computed using the Hagan et al. lognormal
    approximation.

    @var y: option strike
    @var expiry: option expiry (in years)
    @var F_0: forward interest rate
    @var alpha_0: SABR Alpha at t=0
    @var beta: SABR Beta
    @var rho: SABR Rho
    @var nu: SABR Nu
    '''
    one_beta = 1.0 - beta
    one_betasqr = one_beta * one_beta
    if F_0 != y:
        fK = F_0 * y
        fK_beta = math.pow(fK, one_beta / 2.0)
        log_fK = math.log(F_0 / y)
        z = nu / alpha_0 * fK_beta * log_fK
        x = math.log((math.sqrt(1.0 - 2.0 * rho *
                    z + z * z) + z - rho) / (1 - rho))
        sigma_1 = (alpha_0 / fK_beta / (1.0 + one_betasqr /
                    24.0 * log_fK * log_fK +
                    math.pow(one_beta * log_fK, 4) / 1920.0) *
                    (z / x))
        sigma_exp = (one_betasqr / 24.0 * alpha_0 * alpha_0 /
                    fK_beta / fK_beta + 0.25 * rho * beta *
                    nu * alpha_0 / fK_beta +
                    (2.0 - 3.0 * rho * rho) / 24.0 * nu * nu)
        sigma = sigma_1 * ( 1.0 + sigma_exp * expiry)
    else:
        f_beta = math.pow(F_0, one_beta)
        f_two_beta = math.pow(F_0, (2.0 - 2.0 * beta))
        sigma = ((alpha_0 / f_beta) * (1.0 +
                ((one_betasqr / 24.0) *
                (alpha_0 * alpha_0 / f_two_beta) +
                (0.25 * rho * beta * nu * alpha_0 / f_beta) +
                (2.0 - 3.0 * rho * rho) /
                24.0 * nu * nu) * expiry))

    return sigma
```

5.4.2 Normal approximation

The approximation formula which returns the normal implied volatility $\sigma_k^N(y)$ at time $t = 0$ for a caplet/floorlet maturing at time T_{k-1} with strike y is

$$\sigma_k^N(y) = \alpha_k \left(y F_k\right)^{\left(\frac{\beta_k}{2}\right)} \frac{1 + \frac{1}{24} \ln^2\left(\frac{F_k}{y}\right) + \frac{1}{1920} \ln^4\left(\frac{F_k}{y}\right) + \cdots}{1 + \frac{(1-\beta_k)^2}{24} \ln^2\left(\frac{F_k}{y}\right) + \frac{(1-\beta_k)^4}{1920} \ln^4\left(\frac{F_k}{y}\right) + \cdots}$$

$$\cdot \left(\frac{z_k}{\xi(z_k)}\right)$$

$$\cdot \left[1 + \frac{-\beta_k(2-\beta_k)}{24} \frac{\alpha_k^2}{(y F_k)^{(1-\beta_k)}} T_{k-1} \right.$$

$$\left. + \frac{1}{4} \frac{\alpha_k \beta_k \rho_k v_k}{(y F_k)^{\left(\frac{1-\beta_k}{2}\right)}} T_{k-1} + \frac{2-3\rho_k^2}{24} v_k^2 T_{k-1} + \cdots \right], \tag{5.16}$$

where

$$z_k = \frac{v_k}{\alpha_k} \left(y F_k\right)^{\left(\frac{1-\beta_k}{2}\right)} \ln\left(\frac{F_k}{y}\right),$$

$$\xi(z_k) = \ln\left(\frac{\sqrt{1 - 2\rho_k z_k + z_k^2} + z_k - \rho_k}{1 - \rho_k}\right)$$

and $+\ldots$ are higher order terms which should not affect the final result.

When β_k is taken as equal to zero, the Hagan et al. normal approximation becomes[1]

$$\sigma_k^N(y) = \alpha_k \left(1 + \frac{2 - 3\rho_k^2}{24} v_k^2 T_{k-1} + \cdots \right) \left(\frac{z_k}{\xi(z_k)}\right), \tag{5.17}$$

where

$$z_k = \frac{v_k}{\alpha_k} \sqrt{y F_k} \ln\left(\frac{F_k}{y}\right),$$

$$\xi(z_k) = \ln\left(\frac{\sqrt{1 - 2\rho_k z_k + z_k^2} + z_k - \rho_k}{1 - \rho_k}\right).$$

When β_k is taken as equal to one, the Hagan et al. normal approximation becomes

$$\sigma_k^N(y) = \alpha_k \frac{F_k - y}{\ln\left(\frac{F_k}{y}\right)} \left(\frac{z_k}{\xi(z_k)}\right)$$

$$\cdot \left[1 + \left(-\frac{\alpha_k^2}{24} + \frac{\alpha_k \rho_k v_k}{4} + \frac{2 - 3\rho_k^2}{24} v_k^2\right) T_{k-1} + \cdots\right], \qquad (5.18)$$

where

$$z_k = \frac{v_k}{\alpha_k} \ln\left(\frac{F_k}{y}\right),$$

$$\xi(z_k) = \ln\left(\frac{\sqrt{1 - 2\rho_k z_k + z_k^2} + z_k - \rho_k}{1 - \rho_k}\right).$$

5.5 SABR calibration in practice

Equation (5.13) gives us a way of recovering the Black implied volatility from a set of parameters $\alpha_k, v_k, \beta_k, \rho_k$ and a few other known quantities such as the current forward rate $F_k(t)$, the time to expiry T_{k-1} and the strike y. The parameters $\alpha_k, v_k, \beta_k, \rho_k$ – or more usually a subset of them, as we will see later – are chosen by a calibration procedure, which consists in matching the market implied volatility $\sigma_k^{B-MKT}(y)$ (of a caplet/floorlet) to the Black volatility $\sigma_k^B(y)$ calculated using the Hagan et al. lognormal approximation for a specific strike y and time to expiry T_{k-1}. The optimization of the parameters is done by minimizing the sum of squared errors

$$\sum_{y \in Y} \left(\sigma_k^{B-MKT}(y) - \sigma_k^B(y)\right)^2, \qquad (5.19)$$

where Y represents the set of strikes to be employed in the calibration.

The minimization exercise can be performed by employing one of the many functions, such as *fmin_powell, fmin_tnc* available in the *numpy.optimize* package (see Jones et al. 2001–). The set of parameters $\alpha_k, v_k, \beta_k, \rho_k$ which minimizes Equation (5.19), for a particular expiry T_{k-1}, are then used to price any other deal which has the same expiry. Obviously the parameters $\alpha_k, v_k, \beta_k, \rho_k$ will have to be recalibrated with a frequency which depends on how fast the smile shape changes in the particular market in which we are active. For instruments with expiry between those that are quoted in the market, either the implied volatilities or the SABR parameters can be interpolated. Often the interpolation occurs between the implied volatilities, but we found that carefully doing otherwise would result in minor deviations around the ATM strike.

Although we have so far illustrated only the calibration procedure pertaining to the Black implied volatilities, the same process is valid, and can be easily extended, to the normal volatility $\sigma_k^N(t)$ case. We would simply need to adopt the Hagan et al. normal approximation, Equation (5.16), instead of the lognormal one.

As seen in Section 5.2, the parameters β_k and ρ_k produce a very similar effect on the skew. For this reason only one of them is usually calibrated, keeping the other fixed. If we decide to keep β_k fixed, its value could be chosen a priori according to our own market view (Section 5.2.2). If alternatively we decide to keep ρ_k fixed, its value could be chosen so that we could benefit from a simplified model set-up. This feature becomes extremely beneficial when the numerical complexity of the model chosen could turn into a major setback, such as for the SABR LMM case (Section 7.3.4).

5.5.1 Hagan et al. approximation calibration tests: fixed β_k

We report in this section a series of calibration tests that we have performed with the 4 December 2013 market data for CHF. We have elected the caplets/floorlets with expiry $T_{k-1} = 14.5y$ as our subject test. The calibration has been performed keeping β_k fixed and calibrating α_k, ν_k, ρ_k. We tested both the Hagan et al. lognormal approximation (results shown in Figures 5.8, 5.9 and 5.10), as well as the Hagan et al. normal approximation (results shown in Figures 5.11, 5.12 and 5.13).

The aim of the tests is to quantify the calibration quality of the Hagan approximations, and how this would be influenced by the particular β_k chosen. We have repeated the calibration exercise using:

$$\beta_k = 0,$$
$$\beta_k = 0.3,$$
$$\beta_k = 0.5,$$
$$\beta_k = 0.7,$$
$$\beta_k = 1.$$

As largely anticipated in this chapter, all approximations provide excellent fit to market quotes. The best performance seems to be given by the choice $\beta_k = 0.3$, while the worst one is given by $\beta_k = 0$. Although we report, for obvious capacity reasons, only results for a particular day, the outcome for the same tests carried out on the period June–December 2013 is not very much different, and it leads always

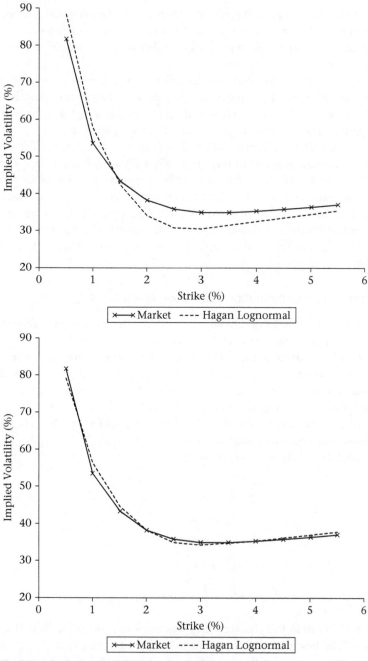

Figure 5.8 Hagan et al. lognormal approximation calibration to 4 December 2013 CHF market data, with $\beta_k = 0$ (top) and $\beta_k = 0.3$ (bottom). For both tests $T_{k-1} = 14.5y$

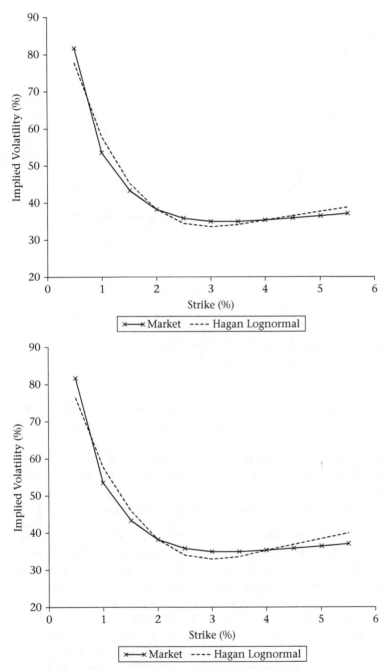

Figure 5.9 Hagan et al. lognormal approximation calibration to 4 December 2013 CHF market data, with $\beta_k = 0.5$ (top) and $\beta_k = 0.7$ (bottom). For both tests $T_{k-1} = 14.5y$

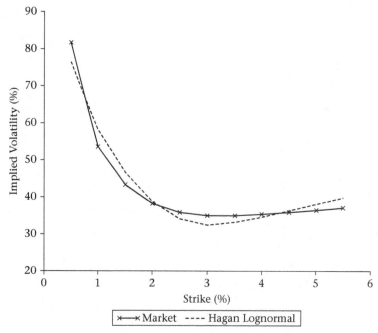

Figure 5.10 Hagan et al. lognormal approximation calibration to 4 December 2013 CHF market data, with $\beta_k = 1$, $T_{k-1} = 14.5y$

to similar conclusions. Also the caplet expiry T_{k-1} does not seem to influence too much the calibration results: using a β_k value in the range 0.3–0.5 generally leads to the best fit.

A concluding word on the market: similar outcomes, for the same period analysed, have also been observed for EUR (although not reported here).

5.5.2 Hagan et al. approximation calibration tests: fixed ρ_k

To be able to provide an all-round and comprehensive spectrum of tests, we also present an assessment for the calibration case in which ρ_k is kept fixed and α_k, β_k, ν_k are chosen by the minimization algorithm. From our time series of data spanning June–December 2013, we have picked three testing dates, spaced a month apart from each other: 15 July 2013, 15 August 2013 and 16 September 2013. The caplet expiry tested has been, as for the fixed β_k case, $T_{k-1} = 14.5y$.

We have tested the case $\rho_k = 0$ as it will be useful when working with the SABR LMM (Section 7.3.4). Even when keeping ρ_k fixed, the Hagan et al. lognormal approximation (we do not report the results for the Hagan et al. normal approximation in this occurrence) provides excellent calibration performance. The results, for CHF and EUR, are reported in Figures 5.14, 5.15 and 5.16.

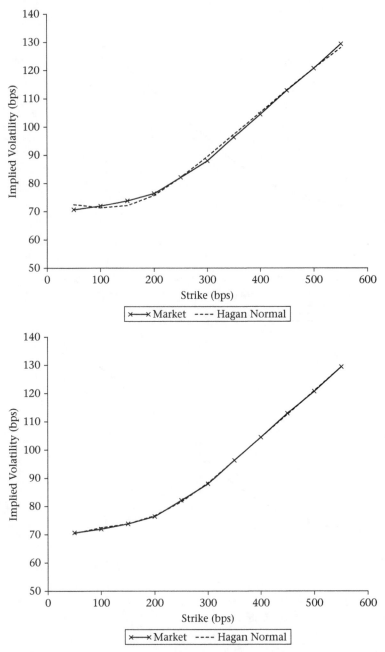

Figure 5.11 Hagan et al. normal approximation calibration to 4 December 2013 CHF market data, with $\beta_k = 0$ (top) and $\beta_k = 0.3$ (bottom). For both tests $T_{k-1} = 14.5y$

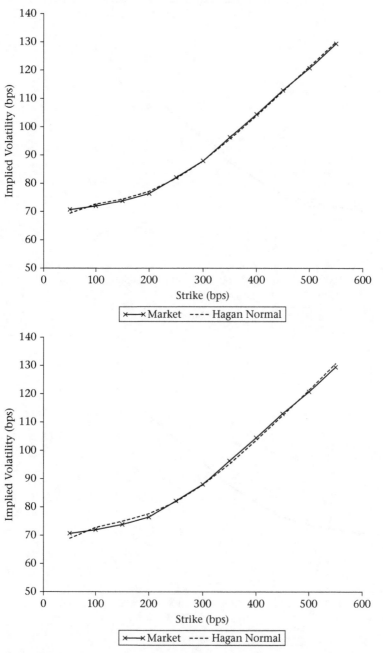

Figure 5.12 Hagan et al. normal approximation calibration to 4 December 2013 CHF market data, with $\beta_k = 0.5$ (top) and $\beta_k = 0.7$ (bottom). For both tests $T_{k-1} = 14.5y$

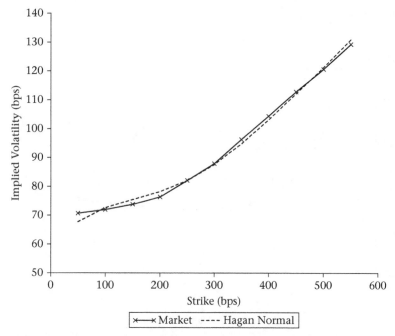

Figure 5.13 Hagan et al. normal approximation calibration to 4 December 2013 CHF market data, with $\beta_k = 1$, $T_{k-1} = 14.5y$

5.6 Risk sensitivities

We have introduced a set of risk sensitivities under the Black model in Section 4.3. We will now see how the definition of these quantities changes under the SABR model, and how they relate to their Black model equivalents. The SABR model, being characterized by a large number of parameters, allows us also to specify new risk types and their corresponding Greeks.

In our examples the reference option, for which we are computing sensitivities, is a caplet valued at $t = 0$. However, the sensitivity computations can be easily extended to other types of plain vanilla interest rate options priced under the SABR model, such as floorlets, swaptions.

For more exotic products, depending on the evolution of multiple forward rates, for example, CMS spread options or any callable's payoff profile, the sensitivity computation technique described here cannot be applied, the reason being that the SABR model is too simplistic to correctly price these products. We will see in Chapters 6 and 7 that for such products we need to resort to a term structure model such as the LIBOR Market Model or the SABR LMM. For a discussion on how to compute risk sensitivities for the LIBOR Market Model, see Section 6.6.

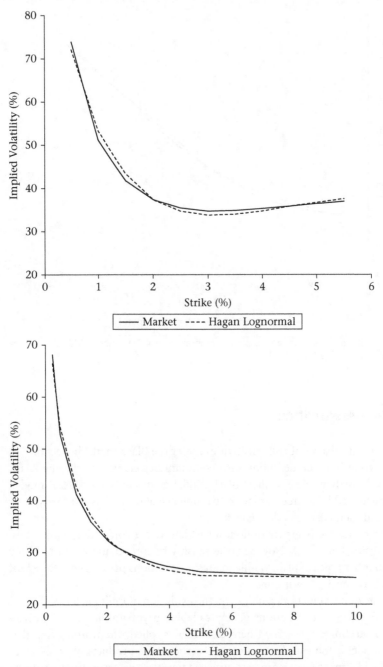

Figure 5.14 Hagan et al. lognormal approximation calibration to 15 July 2013 market data: CHF (top) and EUR (bottom). For both tests: $T_{k-1} = 14.5y$, $\rho_k = 0$

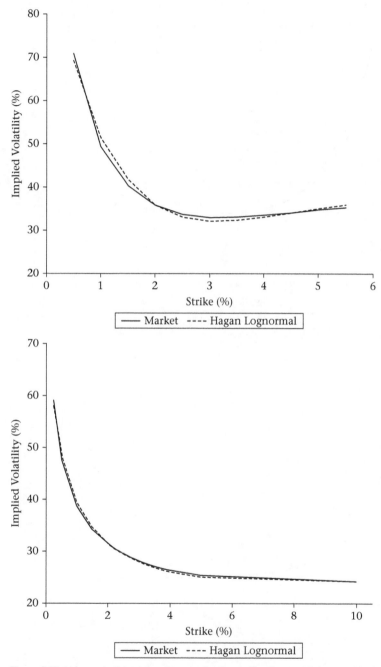

Figure 5.15 Hagan et al. lognormal approximation calibration to 15 August 2013 market data: CHF (top) and EUR (bottom). For both tests: $T_{k-1} = 14.5y$, $\rho_k = 0$

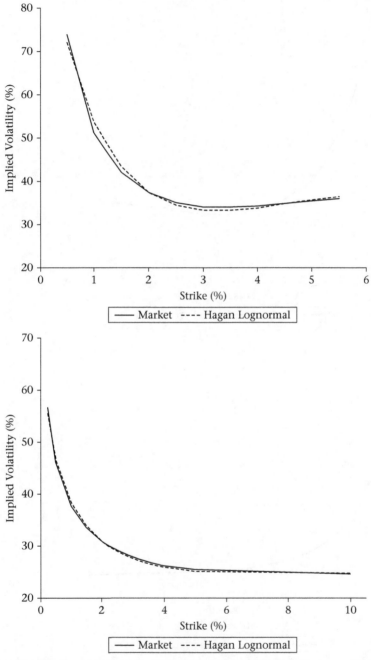

Figure 5.16 Hagan et al. lognormal approximation calibration to 16 September 2013 market data: CHF (top) and EUR (bottom). For both tests: $T_{k-1} = 14.5y$, $\rho_k = 0$

5.6.1 SABR delta and SABR gamma

SABR delta, Δ_{SABR}, is the first derivative of the SABR option price with respect to the forward rate F_k at time $t = 0$. Bartlett (2006) proposes that since F_k and α_k are correlated, when F_k changes, there is a change in α_k as well. This relationship can be represented as follows

$$
\begin{aligned}
F_k &\rightarrow F_k + \partial F_k, \\
\alpha_k &\rightarrow \alpha_k + \lambda_{F_k} \alpha_k,
\end{aligned}
$$

where $\lambda_{F_k} \alpha_k$ is the average change in α_k caused by the change in F_k. The author finds that

$$
\lambda_{F_k} \alpha_k = \frac{\rho_k \nu_k}{F_k^{\beta_k}} \partial F_k,
$$

and that SABR delta equals

$$
\Delta_{SABR} = \Delta_{Blk} + \mathcal{V}_{Blk} \cdot \left(\frac{\partial \sigma_k^B(y)}{\partial F_k} + \frac{\partial \sigma_k^B(y)}{\partial \alpha_k} \frac{\rho_k \nu_k}{F_k^{\beta_k}} \right),
$$

which shows how the SABR delta can be expressed in terms of Black delta Δ_{Blk} (Equation (4.21)), Black vega $\mathcal{V}_{Blk}$ (Equation (4.23)) and an additional term: $\frac{\partial \sigma_k^B(y)}{\partial F_k} + \frac{\partial \sigma_k^B(y)}{\partial \alpha_k} \frac{\rho_k \nu_k}{F_k^{\beta_k}}$. The numerical computation of Δ_{SABR} does not require one to actually perform such a complicated derivative; the SABR delta can be computed by reverting to finite difference methods (Section 4.3.4), as shown in the Python code reported in Table 5.2. A visual comparison of SABR delta versus Black delta is shown in Figure 5.17.

SABR gamma, Γ_{SABR}, is the second derivative of the SABR option price with respect to the forward rate F_k at time $t = 0$. It can be obtained following the same reasoning proposed by Bartlett for the SABR delta case. Numerically its computation is very much like the code reported in Table 5.2 for SABR delta, with the major difference being the need to use a second-order finite difference method, such as the one introduced in Table 4.7. A visual comparison of SABR gamma versus Black gamma is reported in Figure 5.17.

5.6.2 SABR vega

Vega in the SABR model (SABR vega), $\mathcal{V}_{SABR}$, is given by the change of the SABR option price due to an infinitesimal change in α_k (since α_k is a measure of the

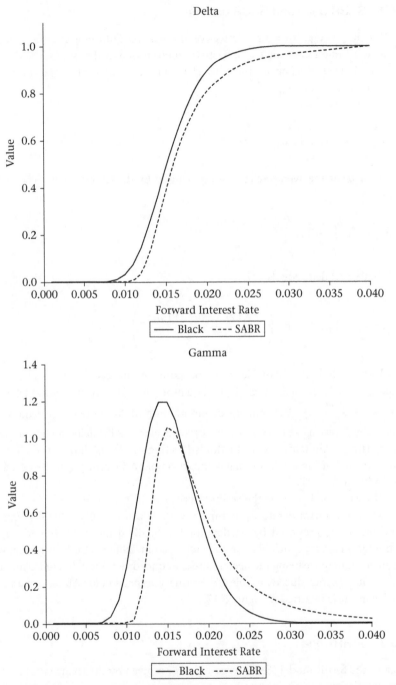

Figure 5.17 Comparison of risk sensitivities computed under the SABR and Black (where applicable) model. All the numerical tests have been performed with the following set of parameters: $T_{k-1} = 5y$, $y = 0.0156$, $\alpha_k = 0.1$, $\beta_k = 1$, $\rho_k = -0.8$ $v_k = 0.25$

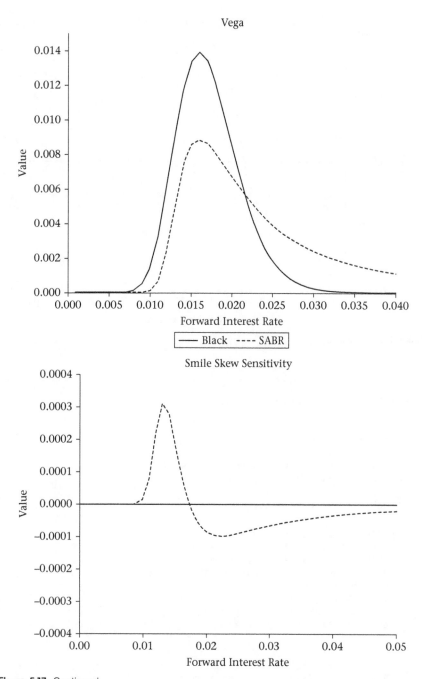

Figure 5.17 Continued

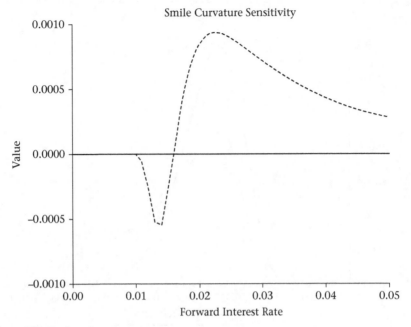

Figure 5.17 Continued

Table 5.2 SABR delta computation – Python code

```python
import math

def computeSABRDelta(y, expiry, F_0, alpha_0, beta,
rho, nu, isCall):
    '''
    Compute the SABR delta.

    @var y: option strike
    @var expiry: option expiry (in years)
    @var F_0: forward interest rate
    @var alpha_0: SABR Alpha at t=0
    @var beta: SABR Beta
    @var rho: SABR Rho
    @var nu: SABR Nu
    @var isCall: True or False
    '''
    small_figure = 1e-6
    F_0_plus_h = F_0 + small_figure
    avg_alpha = (alpha_0 + (rho * nu /
                math.pow(F_0, beta)) * small_figure)
```

```
vol = haganLogNormalApprox (y, expiry, F_0_plus_h, avg_alpha,
                            beta, nu, rho)
px_f_plus_h = black(F_0_plus_h, y, expiry, vol, isCall)

F_0_minus_h = F_0 - small_figure
avg_alpha = (alpha_0 + (rho * nu /
                math.pow(F_0, beta)) * (-small_figure))
vol = haganLogNormalApprox (y, expiry, F_0_minus_h,
                            avg_alpha, beta,
                            nu, rho)
px_f_minus_h = black(F_0_minus_h, y, expiry, vol, isCall)

sabr_delta = computeFirstDerivative (px_f_plus_h, px_f_minus_h,
                            small_figure)

return sabr_delta
```

volatility level, see Section 5.2.1). Bartlett (2006) proposes a rationale analogous to the one presented in the derivation of Δ_{SABR}. Since F_k and α_k are correlated, when α_k changes, there is a change in F_k as well. This relationship can be expressed as follows

$$
\begin{aligned}
\alpha_k &\rightarrow \alpha_k + \partial\alpha_k, \\
F_k &\rightarrow F_k + \lambda_{\alpha_k} F_k,
\end{aligned}
$$

where $\lambda_{\alpha_k} F_k$ is the average change in F_k caused by the change in α_k. Bartlett finds that

$$
\lambda_{\alpha_k} F_k = \frac{\rho_k F_k^{\beta_k}}{\nu_k} \partial\alpha_k,
$$

and that SABR vega equals

$$
\mathcal{V}_{\text{SABR}} = \mathcal{V}_{\text{Blk}} \cdot \left(\frac{\partial \sigma_k^B(y)}{\partial \alpha_k} + \frac{\partial \sigma_k^B(y)}{\partial F_k} \frac{\rho_k F_k^{\beta_k}}{\nu_k} \right). \tag{5.20}
$$

Equation (5.20) shows how SABR vega equals Black vega multiplied by an additional term: $\frac{\partial \sigma_k^B(y)}{\partial \alpha_k} + \frac{\partial \sigma_k^B(y)}{\partial F_k} \frac{\rho_k F_k^{\beta_k}}{\nu_k}$. The Python code to compute SABR vega is presented in Table 5.3 and a visual comparison of SABR vega versus Black vega is shown in Figure 5.17.

Table 5.3 SABR vega computation – Python code

```python
import math

def computeSABRVega (y, expiry, F_0, alpha_0, beta,
rho, nu, isCall):
    '''
    Compute the SABR vega.

    @var y: option strike
    @var expiry: option expiry (in years)
    @var F_0: forward interest rate
    @var alpha_0: SABR Alpha at t=0
    @var beta: SABR Beta
    @var rho: SABR Rho
    @var nu: SABR Nu
    @var isCall: True or False
    '''
    small_figure = 1e-6
    alpha_plus_h = alpha_0 + small_figure
    avg_F = (F_0 + (rho * math.pow(F_0, beta)
                 / nu) * small_figure)
    vol = haganLogNormalApprox (y, expiry, avg_F, alpha_plus_h,
                                    beta, nu, rho)
    px_a_plus_h = black(F_0, y, expiry, vol, isCall)

    alpha_minus_h = alpha_0 - small_figure
    avg_F = (F_0 + (rho * math.pow(F_0, beta)
                 / nu) * (-small_figure))
    vol = haganLogNormalApprox (y, expiry, avg_F, alpha_minus_h,
                                    beta, nu, rho)
    px_a_minus_h = black(F_0, y, expiry, vol, isCall)

    sabr_vega = computeFirstDerivative (px_a_plus_h, px_a_minus_h,
                                            small_figure)

    return sabr_vega
```

5.6.3 Smile skew and smile curvature sensitivities

One of the major drawbacks related to the Black model is its assumption that the volatility is a fixed quantity, flat across all the strikes belonging to a particular expiry. Such a simplification does not allow one to capture the risks associated with a change in the volatility smile shape. The SABR model, on the contrary, allowing the volatility to be stochastic, allows us to define two additional risk sensitivities, which are not available under the Black model: smile skew and smile curvature sensitivity. The first one represents the risk of a change in the volatility smile skewness. It can be expressed as the amount at which the Black price changes due to an infinitesimal change of ρ_k (as seen in Section 5.2.4 ρ_k controls the smile skew)

$$\frac{\partial_{\text{Blk}}\left(F_k, y, \sigma_k^B\left(y\right)\sqrt{T_{k-1}}, 1\right)}{\partial \rho_k}.$$ (5.21)

Hagan et al. (2002) proposed expressing the above quantity as

$$V_{\text{Blk}}\frac{\partial \sigma_k^B\left(y\right)}{\partial \rho_k},$$ (5.22)

which shows how the smile skew sensitivity simply equals the Black vega, V_{Blk}, scaled by a factor: $\frac{\partial \sigma_k^B(y)}{\partial \rho_k}$. Numerical results for the sensitivity to the smile skew are shown in Figure 5.17. The SABR smile skew sensitivity is sometimes also referred to as vanna. A Greek typically used in the FX market, which represents the first derivative of vega with respect to the forward rate, is

$$\frac{\partial V_{\text{SABR}}}{\partial F_k}.$$

We prefer however to keep these two quantities distinct as, although providing a similar risk profile, they are indeed different. As a result a trader/risk manager might be interested in working with both.

Smile curvature sensitivity (also known as volga) represents the risk of a change in the volatility smile curvature. It can be expressed as the amount at which the Black price changes due to an infinitesimal change of v_k (this is the parameter controlling the smile curvature, see Section 5.2.3):

$$\frac{\partial_{\text{Blk}}\left(F_k, y, \sigma_k^B\left(y\right)\sqrt{T_{k-1}}, 1\right)}{\partial v_k}.$$ (5.23)

The above quantity was firstly represented in Hagan et al. (2002) as

$$V_{\text{Blk}}\frac{\partial \sigma_k^B\left(y\right)}{\partial v_k}.$$ (5.24)

Numerical results for the sensitivity to the smile curvature are reported in Figure 5.17.

5.7 Monte Carlo simulation schemes for SABR

After having introduced the analytical formulas developed by Hagan et al. for the SABR model and having analysed their performances in terms of calibration fitting, we would like to introduce a tool which can be used to investigate, if and how, they are able to correctly approximate the evolution of the processes described by Equations (5.1) and (5.2). The benchmark method which can be used to accomplish such a comparison is a Monte Carlo algorithm, where the SABR processes are simulated.

We will introduce in this section various Monte Carlo schemes which can be used to simulate the SABR processes. We try to focus on finding a reliable and numerically stable technique. The actual numerical tests which compare Hagan et al. approximations versus Monte Carlo will be reported later in Section 5.8.4.

Furthermore, gaining confidence with the various Monte Carlo schemes and their computational performances is of paramount importance for tackling numerically the SABR LMM (Chapter 7). As we will see in the rest of this section, creating a stable and fast simulation scheme for the SABR model is not trivial and requires an extensive amount of analysis.

In general, the tools presented here can be extended and adopted for any stochastic volatility model and can be used as a basis on which to analyse, develop and introduce new modelling techniques. The code examples provided are based on the Python libraries NumPy and SciPy, which give the possibility to quickly create pricing prototypes. We must however emphasize that Monte Carlo scheme performances are heavily affected by the choice of programming language (Python, C++, Java, etc.) as well as from the particular technological platform (parallel computing, GPUs, etc.) in use. We will not go into details for what concerns these more technically oriented features as they are beyond the scope of our work.

5.7.1 Monte Carlo standard error

Before presenting various Monte Carlo schemes and simulation techniques, we want to introduce a quantity which can help us to compare the various numerical tests carried out: the Monte Carlo standard error. Let us first of all introduce the standard Monte Carlo average estimator $\bar{F}_k$ as

$$\bar{F}_k = \frac{1}{n_{\text{sim}}} \sum_{i=1}^{n_{\text{sim}}} F_k^i(T_{k-1}),$$

where n_{sim} is the total number of paths simulated and $F_k^i(T_{k-1})$ is the forward interest rate $F_k(T_{k-1})$ outcome generated by the $i-th$ simulation. The quantity

$$\varsigma^2_{n_{\text{sim}}} = \frac{1}{n_{\text{sim}} - 1} \sum_{i=1}^{n_{\text{sim}}} \left(F_k^i(T_{k-1}) - \bar{F}_k \right)^2$$

is used to determine the Monte Carlo standard error

$$\text{StdErr} = \frac{\varsigma_{n_{\text{sim}}}}{\sqrt{n_{\text{sim}}}}. \tag{5.25}$$

This quantity can be used as an approximation for the Monte Carlo variance. The lower the standard error the better the accuracy of the tested Monte Carlo scheme.

5.7.2 Pseudo random numbers

The standard Python and SciPy default random number generator is the Mersenne Twister, which is a pseudo-random number generator developed by Makoto Matsumoto and Takuji Nishimura (1998). The values obtained from a pseudo-random sequence are not random, but completely deterministic.

The advantage of using pseudo-random numbers is the possibility to reproduce the same results, by simply reusing the same "seed". This is a very helpful property when running the type of tests we will be showing in the rest of the book.

5.7.3 Generating correlated random numbers

The Monte Carlo simulation of correlated Brownian motions requires the generation of correlated normal random numbers. To create these random variables one usually makes use of a Gaussian copula approach that benefits from the Cholesky decomposition of the correlation matrix. This method is often chosen due to its enhanced performance compared to other decomposition techniques. We will review this technique briefly (the interested reader is referred to Glasserman 2003, where this subject is reviewed with a greater amount of detail), and show how to apply it numerically using Python.

The Cholesky decomposition of a symmetric positive definite matrix M is given by

$$M = LL^{\dagger},$$

where L is a lower triangular matrix and $L^{\dagger}$ is its conjugate transpose. If we consider M as the correlation matrix characterizing our random processes, and u a vector of uncorrelated Gaussian random numbers, the matrix product Lu produces a vector of Gaussian random numbers with correlation described by M.

As seen in Section 5.2.4, the Brownian motions governing the $F_k(t)$ and $\alpha_k(t)$ processes are correlated by a constant correlation factor ρ_k. This translates numerically into the need to generate correlated random numbers used to simulate the process random paths. The correlation matrix M which relates F_k and α_k is defined as

	F_k	α_k
F_k	1	ρ_k
α_k	ρ_k	1

and the lower triangular matrix given by its Cholesky decomposition is

$$L = \begin{bmatrix} 1 & 0 \\ \rho_k & \sqrt{1 - \rho_k^2} \end{bmatrix}.$$

If we have at our disposal two uncorrelated random numbers Z_1 and Y_1, with normal distribution $N(0, 1)$, by computing

$$\begin{bmatrix} 1 & 0 \\ \rho_k & \sqrt{1 - \rho_k^2} \end{bmatrix} \begin{bmatrix} Z_1 \\ Y_1 \end{bmatrix},$$

we can transform them into two correlated (with correlation factor ρ_k) random numbers X_1, X_2 defined as

$$
\begin{aligned}
X_1 &= Z_1, \\
X_2 &= Z_1 \rho_k + Y_1 \sqrt{1 - \rho_k^2}.
\end{aligned}
$$

The Python code to generate X_1, X_2 is reported in Table 5.4. As an alternative to the code proposed, we could have also used the NumPy function *numpy.linalg.cholesky* to compute the Cholesky decomposition of the SABR correlation matrix M defined above.

Table 5.4 Draw two correlated random numbers – Python code

```
import random
# Seed the random number generator
random.seed()
import math

def drawTwoRandomNumbers(rho):
    '''
    Draw a pair of correlated random numbers.
```

```
@var rho: SABR Rho
'''
rand_list = []
z1 = random.gauss(0,1)
y1 = random.gauss(0,1)
rand_list.append(z1)
term1 = z1 * rho
term2 = (y1 *
     math.pow((1.0 - math.pow(rho, 2.0)), 0.5))
x2 = term1 + term2
rand_list.append(x2)

return rand_list
```

5.7.4 Euler scheme

The set of Equations (5.1) and (5.2) can be modelled using Monte Carlo simulations, where a discrete time approximation is used for both processes. The most basic discretization technique is the Euler scheme. Under this scheme the SABR processes can be rewritten as

$$\widehat{F}_k(t_{i+1}) = \widehat{F}_k(t_i) + \widehat{\alpha}_k(t_i)\widehat{F}_k(t_i)^{\beta_k}\,\Delta W_{\widehat{F}_k}(t_{i+1}), \qquad (5.26)$$

$$\widehat{\alpha}_k(t_{i+1}) = \widehat{\alpha}_k(t_i) + \nu_k\widehat{\alpha}_k(t_i)\,\Delta W_{\widehat{\alpha}_k}(t_{i+1}), \qquad (5.27)$$

where $\widehat{F}_k$ and $\widehat{\alpha}_k$ are the discrete versions of F_k and α_k respectively.[2]

The idea behind this scheme is that the sample path used to simulate the random process is divided into many steps. For example a path from $t = 0$ to $t = T_{k-1}$ can be divided into n_{step} time steps, generating a time partition $0 = t_0 < t_1 < \cdots < t_{n_{step}} = T_{k-1}$. When simulating the SABR model using the Euler scheme, we will be drawing, at each time step $i = 0, \ldots, n_{step}$, two random numbers $Z(t_{i+1}), Y(t_{i+1})$ (with normal distribution $N(0,1)$), and use them to simulate two different paths: one for the forward interest rate process $F_k(t)$ and one for the stochastic volatility process $\alpha_k(t)$. The Wiener increments $\Delta W_{\widehat{F}_k}(t_{i+1})$, $\Delta W_{\widehat{\alpha}_k}(t_{i+1})$ can be approximated through the scaled random walk (see, e.g., Capinski and Zastawniak 2011), and correlated by applying the Cholesky decomposition introduced in Section 5.7.3, as

$$\Delta W_{\widehat{F}_k}(t_{i+1}) = \sqrt{t_{i+1} - t_i}Z(t_{i+1}),$$

$$\Delta W_{\widehat{\alpha}_k}(t_{i+1}) = \sqrt{t_{i+1} - t_i}\left(\rho_k Z(t_{i+1}) + \sqrt{1 - \rho_k^2}Y(t_{i+1})\right). \qquad (5.28)$$

After substituting them in Equations (5.29) and (5.30) we obtain

$$\widehat{F}_k(t_{i+1}) = \widehat{F}_k(t_i) + \widehat{\alpha}_k(t_i)\widehat{F}_k(t_i)^{\beta_k} Z(t_{i+1})\sqrt{t_{i+1} - t_i}, \tag{5.29}$$

$$\widehat{\alpha}_k(t_{i+1}) = \widehat{\alpha}_k(t_i) + \nu_k\widehat{\alpha}_k(t_i)\left(\rho_k Z(t_{i+1}) + \sqrt{1-\rho_k^2}Y(t_{i+1})\right)\sqrt{t_{i+1} - t_i}. \tag{5.30}$$

As mentioned in Section 5.2, a zero absorbing boundary for the forward process must be implemented when $0 < \beta_k < 1$. We have implemented a very simple numerical method with regards to the absorbing boundary at zero. For any simulated path we set $F_k(T_{k-1}) = 0$ as soon as $F_k(t)$ becomes negative; we then move on to simulate the next path. More sophisticated and efficient techniques to implement a Monte Carlo scheme with an absorbing boundary have been thoroughly researched by academics as well as by practitioners. We refer the interested reader to Chen et al. (2012) for a deeper discussion on the topic.

The Python code for the Euler scheme applied to the SABR dynamics is reported in Table 5.5.

Table 5.5 Monte Carlo Euler scheme for SABR – Python code

```
import math

def simulateSABRMonteCarloEuler (no_of_sim, no_of_steps,
expiry, F_0, alpha_0, beta, rho, nu):
    '''
    Monte Carlo SABR using Euler scheme.

    @var no_of_sim: Monte Carlo paths
    @var no_of_steps: discretization steps required
    to reach the option expiry date
    @var expiry: option expiry (in years)
    @var F_0: forward interest rate
    @var alpha_0: SABR Alpha at t=0
    @var beta: SABR Beta
    @var rho: SABR Rho
    @var nu: SABR Nu
    '''
    # Step length in years
    dt = float(expiry) / float(no_of_steps)
    dt_sqrt = math.sqrt(dt)
    no_of_sim_counter = 0
    simulated_forwards = []
    while no_of_sim_counter < no_of_sim:
        F_t = F_0
        alpha_t = alpha_0
        no_of_steps_counter = 1
        while no_of_steps_counter <= no_of_steps:
            # Zero absorbing boundary used for all the beta
            # choices except beta = 0 and beta = 1
```

```
if ((beta > 0 and beta < 1) and
     F_t <= 0):
     F_t = 0
     no_of_steps_counter = no_of_steps + 1
else:
     # Generate two correlated
     # random numbers
     rand = drawTwoRandomNumbers(rho)
     # Simulate the forward interest rate using
     # the Euler scheme. Use the absolute for the
     # diffusion to avoid numerical issues
     # if the forward interest rate
     # goes into negative territory
     dW_F = dt_sqrt * rand[0]
     F_b = math.pow(abs(F_t), beta)
     F_t = F_t + alpha_t * F_b * dW_F
     # Simulate the stochastic volatility using
     # the Euler scheme
     dW_a = dt_sqrt * rand[1]
     alpha_t = (alpha_t +
                      nu * alpha_t * dW_a)
no_of_steps_counter += 1
# At the end of each path, we store the forward
# interest rate in a list
simulated_forwards.append(F_t)
no_of_sim_counter = no_of_sim_counter + 1

return simulated_forwards
```

The Euler scheme is prone to oscillatory results depending on the number of simulations n_{sim} and the number of time steps n_{step} used. A thorough analysis is therefore necessary to be able to decide which combination of n_{step} and n_{sim} provides "sufficient" accuracy in an "acceptable" calculation time. We therefore performed several hundred tests with different combinations of time step size, number of paths and SABR parameters. This has been done not because we want to provide a "one size fits all" solution, but to give the reader some guidance on where to focus her or his testing efforts. Among all the tests performed we report in Tables 5.6, 5.7 and 5.8 a distilled sample providing the most significant results. We can classify our tests in three different groups based on ρ_k:

$$\rho_k = 0,$$

$$\rho_k = -0.2,$$

$$\rho_k = -0.8.$$

Table 5.6 Black implied volatilities (%) produced by the Euler scheme for $\rho_k = 0$ and various combinations of β_k. For all cases: $T_{k-1} = 19.5y$, $v_k = 0.25$

		Strike (%)								
	Steps	0.5	1	1.5	2	2.5	3	3.5	4	5
$\beta_k = 0$,	78	52.65	33.64	26.01	21.85	19.31	17.98	17.25	16.85	16.58
$\rho_k = 0$,	468	52.45	33.54	25.93	21.76	19.43	18.06	17.32	16.93	16.63
$v_k = 0.25$	936	52.92	33.77	26.09	21.91	19.59	18.25	17.53	17.15	16.89
	1872	52.98	33.82	26.15	21.94	19.57	18.2	17.47	17.1	16.84
$\beta_k = 0.3$,	78	27.18	20.97	17.53	15.52	14.66	14.26	14.22	14.32	14.68
$\rho_k = 0$,	468	27.2	20.96	17.5	15.47	14.6	14.22	14.21	14.34	14.74
$v_k = 0.25$	936	27.37	21.11	17.62	15.59	14.49	14.14	14.13	14.26	14.65
	1872	27.32	21.07	17.58	15.55	14.62	14.25	14.22	14.35	14.73
$\beta_k = 0.5$,	78	28.18	22.5	19.44	17.76	16.93	16.62	16.59	16.69	17.05
$\rho_k = 0$,	468	28.1	22.4	19.37	17.69	16.75	16.46	16.45	16.57	16.95
$v_k = 0.25$	936	28.27	22.58	19.52	17.82	16.82	16.54	16.53	16.65	17.05
	1872	28.14	22.44	19.39	17.72	16.87	16.58	16.58	16.72	17.15
$\beta_k = 0.7$,	78	33.9	29.05	26.59	25.24	24.35	24.02	23.89	23.88	24.05
$\rho_k = 0$,	468	33.58	28.79	26.4	25.09	24.31	23.98	23.85	23.86	24.07
$v_k = 0.25$	936	33.64	28.89	26.49	25.17	23.86	23.58	23.49	23.51	23.72
	1872	33.56	28.89	26.41	25.13	24.29	23.97	23.87	23.89	24.1
$\beta_k = 1$,	78	18.21	14.02	11.77	10.78	10.76	11.36	12.08	12.77	14
$\rho_k = 0$,	468	17.78	13.79	11.62	10.66	10.56	11.15	11.85	12.51	13.7
$v_k = 0.25$	936	17.92	13.89	11.67	10.72	10.53	11.12	11.83	12.53	13.74
	1872	17.82	13.85	11.65	10.71	10.73	11.34	12.07	12.79	14.03

For each of them we have tested five different sets of β_k:

$$\beta_k = 0,$$
$$\beta_k = 0.3,$$
$$\beta_k = 0.5,$$
$$\beta_k = 0.7,$$
$$\beta_k = 1,$$

and four different sets of time step number:

$$n_{step} = 78,$$
$$n_{step} = 468,$$
$$n_{step} = 936,$$
$$n_{step} = 1872,$$

Table 5.7 Black implied volatilities (%) produced by the Euler scheme for $\rho_k = -0.2$ and various combinations of β_k. For all cases: $T_{k-1} = 19.5y$, $v_k = 0.25$

		Strike (%)								
	Steps	0.5	1	1.5	2	2.5	3	3.5	4	5
$\beta_k = 0$,	78	57.05	35.33	26.78	21.98	18.94	17.24	16.28	15.76	15.39
$\rho_k = -0.2$,	468	56.73	35.18	26.67	21.87	19.05	17.3	16.33	15.81	15.43
$v_k = 0.25$	936	57.37	35.46	26.85	22.03	19.15	17.44	16.51	16.01	15.66
	1872	57.48	35.51	26.91	22.07	19.11	17.38	16.43	15.92	15.58
$\beta_k = 0.3$,	78	27.93	21.43	17.65	15.25	14.11	13.41	13.17	13.16	13.42
$\rho_k = -0.2$,	468	28.12	21.58	17.75	15.31	14.07	13.39	13.17	13.17	13.41
$v_k = 0.25$	936	28.21	21.65	17.82	15.36	14.02	13.35	13.15	13.17	13.44
	1872	28.23	21.67	17.81	15.36	14.01	13.34	13.15	13.17	13.45
$\beta_k = 0.5$,	78	28.79	22.79	19.4	17.3	16.06	15.43	15.17	15.11	15.28
$\rho_k = -0.2$,	468	28.85	22.85	19.43	17.31	16.07	15.44	15.22	15.19	15.39
$v_k = 0.25$	936	28.77	22.85	19.45	17.33	16.1	15.48	15.26	15.26	15.5
	1872	28.94	22.91	19.45	17.33	16.1	15.48	15.26	15.26	15.5
$\beta_k = 0.7$,	78	34.27	28.98	26.1	24.33	23.17	22.5	22.12	21.92	21.83
$\rho_k = -0.2$,	468	33.88	28.66	25.81	24.08	22.94	22.28	21.91	21.72	21.67
$v_k = 0.25$	936	33.89	28.7	25.86	24.13	22.64	22.03	21.68	21.5	21.4
	1872	33.88	28.66	25.81	24.05	23.08	22.42	22.05	21.87	21.82
$\beta_k = 1$,	78	18.62	14.4	11.96	10.58	10.17	10.44	10.96	11.51	12.54
$\rho_k = -0.2$,	468	18.37	14.22	11.83	10.05	10.33	10.3	10.8	11.4	12.4
$v_k = 0.25$	936	18.42	14.27	11.85	10.51	10.05	10.32	10.85	11.41	12.45
	1872	18.34	14.24	11.83	10.5	10.2	10.51	11.07	11.67	12.76

for all cases: $T_{k-1} = 19.5y$ and $v_k = 0.25$. All of the tests reported have been obtained using 10^5 simulation paths as we found this value of n_{sim} to give, generally, a very good convergence. A convergence chart is depicted in Figure 5.18, where a far out of the money option has been priced using a different set of simulation paths (and a fixed random number seed). The results show how increasing the paths n_{sim} affects the option price. Convergence is achieved at $n_{sim} = 100000$, as an increase to $n_{sim} = 200000$ returns an almost identical implied volatility.

A note on the choice of time steps chosen for testing is in order. It is generally considered standard to have 252 trading days in a year. We can consider the number of time steps chosen to be a function of the frequency within which our set of processes is discretized during a trading year (Table 5.9). If we choose $n_{step} = 78$ we are working with discrete steps which are about 60 trading days long; if we choose $n_{step} = 468$ we are working with discrete steps which are about ten trading days long and so on. We put a cap at $n_{step} = 1872$ as we have not seen any considerable improvement in the convergence for higher values. The reader interested in the "philosophical" task (due to its impracticability) of reducing the discrete time step length to a number closer to the amount of times a liquid financial instrument actually ticks during a trading day should choose an n_{step} of the order $1E6-1E7$.

Table 5.8 Black implied volatilities (%) produced by the Euler scheme for $\rho_k = -0.8$ and various combinations of β_k. For all cases: $T_{k-1} = 19.5y$, $v_k = 0.25$

					Strike (%)					
	Steps	0.5	1	1.5	2	2.5	3	3.5	4	5
$\beta_k = 0$,	78	NA	48.48	34.43	26.63	21.17	17.37	14.64	12.85	11.35
$\rho_k = -0.8$,	468	NA	47.9	34.06	26.33	21.21	17.4	14.65	12.91	11.44
$v_k = 0.25$	936	NA	48.29	34.27	26.49	21.18	17.37	14.66	12.91	11.44
	1872	NA	48.4	34.34	26.54	21.14	17.34	14.6	12.83	11.33
$\beta_k = 0.3$,	78	29.7	22.48	17.83	14.32	11.86	9.74	8.47	7.97	7.83
$\rho_k = -0.8$,	468	29.93	22.67	17.98	14.46	11.79	9.67	8.41	7.89	7.84
$v_k = 0.25$	936	30.04	22.75	18.07	14.51	11.77	9.67	8.42	7.91	7.79
	1872	30.09	22.79	18.07	14.51	11.76	9.66	8.42	7.88	7.71
$\beta_k = 0.5$,	78	33.13	26.15	21.74	18.48	16.06	13.96	12.37	11.25	10.19
$\rho_k = -0.8$,	468	33.19	26.25	21.87	18.59	16.03	13.94	12.36	11.28	10.23
$v_k = 0.25$	936	33.29	26.3	21.88	18.59	15.99	13.92	12.33	11.23	10.2
	1872	33.54	26.44	21.98	18.66	16.04	13.96	12.36	11.27	10.25
$\beta_k = 0.7$,	78	30.75	24.62	20.79	17.97	15.76	14	12.65	11.7	10.76
$\rho_k = -0.8$,	468	30.93	24.71	20.85	18.01	15.77	13.98	12.61	11.65	10.73
$v_k = 0.25$	936	30.61	24.57	20.76	17.94	15.72	13.95	12.61	11.66	10.72
	1872	30.45	24.49	20.71	17.9	15.69	13.94	12.6	11.68	10.76
$\beta_k = 1$,	78	19.57	14.99	12.01	9.73	7.93	6.81	6.55	6.79	7.68
$\rho_k = -0.8$,	468	19.85	15.07	12.04	9.72	7.89	6.73	6.41	6.53	6.94
$v_k = 0.25$	936	19.32	14.89	11.96	9.68	7.87	6.74	6.39	6.46	6.87
	1872	19.93	15.05	12.01	9.7	7.89	6.76	6.44	6.5	6.95

Mathematically, there is no reason to bind these steps to the time grid. We require a large amount of time steps to generate the nested behaviour of the two diffusion equations, that is, the stochastic volatility behaviour of the model. Therefore the required time steps n_{step} do not vary dramatically for different T_{k-1}.

It is evident from the results reported that the case $\rho_k = 0$ shows a generally good convergence of the Monte Carlo scheme: the implied volatilities computed with the different choice of time steps n_{step} have a very low variance. The convergence is excellent especially for $\beta_k = 0.5$. For $\rho_k = -0.2$, the results are good for $\beta_k = 0.3$ and really good for $\beta_k = 0.5$. In general $\beta_k = 0$ seems to present the biggest challenge for low values of ρ_k: we had the worst performances for $\rho_k = -0.8$, where we did not manage to have the Monte Carlo simulation providing valid implied volatility values (the option prices produced could not be converted into implied volatility values, as they lay outside the valid solution range), which are reported as NA entries in Table 5.8.

5.7.5 Milstein scheme

Milstein (1974) and Glasserman (2003) proposed to increase the accuracy of a stochastic process discrete approximation by adding higher order terms. The

Table 5.9 Equivalence between the total number of time steps n_{step} needed to reach the option expiry and the number of time steps per year

Time steps n_{step}	Equivalent time steps per year
78	4
468	24
936	48
1872	96

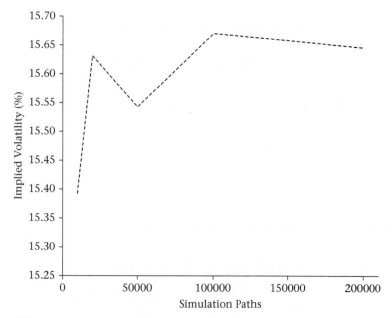

Figure 5.18 Convergence of the SABR Monte Carlo Euler scheme for a varying number of simulation paths n_{sim}. For all cases $n_{step} = 4$ time steps per year

Milstein scheme for a stochastic differential equation of the type

$$dX(t) = aX(t)\,dt + bX(t)\,dW(t)$$

is

$$\widehat{X}(t_{i+1}) = \widehat{X}(t_i) + a\left(t_i, \widehat{X}(t_i)\right)\widehat{X}(t_i)\Delta t + b\left(t_i, \widehat{X}(t_i)\right)\widehat{X}(t_i)\Delta W_{\widehat{X}}(t_{i+1})$$
$$+ \frac{1}{2}b\left(t_i, \widehat{X}(t_i)\right)b'\left(t_i, \widehat{X}(t_i)\right)\left(\left(\Delta W_{\widehat{X}}(t_{i+1})\right)^2 - \Delta t\right),$$

where b' is the first derivative of the term b with respect to x. For the SABR forward process we take $x = \widehat{F}_k(t_i)$ and we have

$$a = 0,$$
$$b = \widehat{a}_k(t_i) x^{\beta_k},$$
$$b' = \widehat{a}_k(t_i) \beta_k x^{(\beta_k - 1)}.$$

Its Milstein discretization is

$$\widehat{F}_k(t_{i+1}) = \widehat{F}_k(t_i) + \widehat{a}_k(t_i) \widehat{F}_k(t_i)^{\beta_k} \Delta W_{\widehat{F}_k}(t_{i+1})$$
$$+ \frac{1}{2} \beta_k \widehat{a}_k(t_i)^2 \widehat{F}_k(t_i)^{(2\beta_k - 1)} \left(\left(\Delta W_{\widehat{F}_k}(t_{i+1}) \right)^2 - \Delta t \right). \quad (5.31)$$

For the SABR volatility process we take $x = \widehat{a}_k(t_i)$ and we have

$$a = 0,$$
$$b = v_k x,$$
$$b' = v_k,$$

which leads to the following Milstein discretization equation

$$\widehat{a}_k(t_{i+1}) = \widehat{a}_k(t_i) + v_k \widehat{a}_k(t_i) \Delta W_{\widehat{a}_k}(t_{i+1})$$
$$+ \frac{1}{2} v_k^2 \widehat{a}_k(t_i) \left(\left(\Delta W_{\widehat{a}_k}(t_{i+1}) \right)^2 - \Delta t \right). \quad (5.32)$$

As we have done in the Euler case, the sample path used to simulate the random process is divided into many steps. For example a path from $t = 0$ to $t = T_{k-1}$ can be divided into n_{step} time steps, generating a time partition $0 = t_0 < t_1 < \cdots < t_{n_{\text{step}}} = T_{k-1}$. We will be drawing, at each time step $i = 0, \ldots, n_{\text{step}}$, two random numbers $Z(t_{i+1}), Y(t_{i+1})$ (with normal distribution $N(0,1)$). By setting

$$\Delta W_{\widehat{F}_k}(t_{i+1}) = Z(t_{i+1}) \sqrt{t_{i+1} - t_i},$$

$$\Delta W_{\widehat{a}_k}(t_{i+1}) = \left(\rho_k Z(t_{i+1}) + \sqrt{1 - \rho_k^2} Y(t_{i+1}) \right) \sqrt{t_{i+1} - t_i},$$

into Equations (5.31) and (5.34) we obtain

$$\widehat{F}_k(t_{i+1}) = \widehat{F}_k(t_i) + \widehat{\alpha}_k(t_i) \widehat{F}_k(t_i)^{\beta_k} Z(t_{i+1}) \sqrt{t_{i+1} - t_i}$$
$$+ \frac{1}{2} \beta_k \widehat{\alpha}_k(t_i)^2 \widehat{F}_k(t_i)^{(2\beta_k - 1)} \left(Z(t_{i+1})^2 - 1 \right) \sqrt{t_{i+1} - t_i},$$

(5.33)

$$\widehat{\alpha}_k(t_{i+1}) = \widehat{\alpha}_k(t_i) + \nu_k \widehat{\alpha}_k(t_i) \left(\rho_k Z(t_{i+1}) + \sqrt{1 - \rho_k^2} Y(t_{i+1}) \right) \sqrt{t_{i+1} - t_i}$$
$$+ \frac{1}{2} \nu_k^2 \widehat{\alpha}_k(t_i) \left(\left(\rho_k Z(t_{i+1}) + \sqrt{1 - \rho_k^2} Y(t_{i+1}) \right)^2 - 1 \right) \sqrt{t_{i+1} - t_i}.$$

(5.34)

We report in Table 5.10 the Python code to simulate the SABR Milstein scheme. Numerical tests for the Milstein scheme are displayed in Table 5.11. We tested various combinations of β_k keeping fixed all the other parameters: $T_{k-1} = 19.5y$, $\nu_k = 0.25$ and $\rho_k = -0.2$. We used 10^5 simulation paths and four annual time steps. These results can be directly compared to the Euler scheme ones reported in Table 5.7. Generally the Milstein scheme does not seem to provide any evident benefit over a simpler Euler scheme. Any gain in accuracy is in any case outweighed by a much slower computation time which for example, on a standard home laptop, increases by a factor in the 70–90% range.

Table 5.10 Monte Carlo Milstein scheme for SABR – Python code

```
import math

def simulateSABRMonteCarloMilstein(no_of_sim, no_of_steps,
expiry, F_0, alpha_0, beta, rho, nu):
    '''
    Monte Carlo SABR using Milstein scheme.

    @var no_of_sim: Monte Carlo paths
    @var no_of_steps: discretization steps required
    to reach the option expiry date
    @var expiry: option expiry date (in years)
    @var F_0: Forward interest rate
    @var alpha_0: SABR Alpha at t=0
    @var beta: SABR Beta
    @var rho: SABR Rho
    @var nu: SABR Nu
    '''
    # Step length in years
```

```
dt = float(expiry) / float(no_of_steps)
dt_sqrt = math.sqrt(dt)
no_of_sim_counter = 0
simulated_forwards = []
while no_of_sim_counter < no_of_sim:
    F_t = F_0
    alpha_t = alpha_0
    no_of_steps_counter = 1
    while no_of_steps_counter <= no_of_steps:
        # Zero absorbing boundary used for all the beta
        # choices except beta = 0 and beta = 1
        if ((beta > 0 and beta < 1) and
            F_t <= 0):
            F_t = 0
            no_of_steps_counter = no_of_steps + 1
        else:
            # Generate two correlated
            # random numbers
            rand = drawTwoRandomNumbers(rho)
            # Simulate the forward interest rate using
            # the Milstein scheme. Use the absolute for
            # the diffusion to avoid numerical issues
            # if the forward interest rate
            # goes into negative territory
            dW_F = dt_sqrt * rand[0]
            F_b = math.pow(abs(F_t), beta)
            exp_F = 2.0 * beta - 1.0
            F_t = (F_t + alpha_t * F_b *
                    dW_F + 0.5 * beta *
                    math.pow(alpha_t, 2.0) *
                    math.pow(abs(F_t), exp_F) *
                    (rand[0] * rand[0] -1.0) * dt)
            # Simulate the stochastic volatility using
            # the Milstein scheme
            dW_a = dt_sqrt * rand[1]
            nu_sqr = math.pow(nu, 2.0)
            alpha_t = (alpha_t + nu *
                        alpha_t * dW_a + 0.5 *
                        nu_sqr * alpha_t *
                        (rand[1] * rand[1] - 1.0) * dt)
        no_of_steps_counter += 1
    # At the end of each path, we store the forward
    # interest rate in a list
    simulated_forwards.append(F_t)
    no_of_sim_counter = no_of_sim_counter + 1

return simulated_forwards
```

Table 5.11 Black implied volatilities (%) produced by the Milstein scheme for various combinations of β_k. For all cases: $T_{k-1} = 19.5y$, $\nu_k = 0.25$ and $\rho_k = -0.2$

	Strike (%)								
	0.5	1	1.5	2	2.5	3	3.5	4	5
$\beta_k = 0$	56.83	35.23	26.72	21.93	18.91	17.21	16.25	15.73	15.37
$\beta_k = 0.3$	27.89	21.4	17.63	15.25	14.09	13.4	13.17	13.18	13.46
$\beta_k = 0.5$	28.76	22.77	19.4	17.32	16.17	15.52	15.25	15.21	15.43
$\beta_k = 0.7$	33.99	28.78	25.97	24.25	23.17	22.52	22.14	21.94	21.84
$\beta_k = 1$	18.71	14.38	11.91	10.56	10.12	10.41	10.94	11.53	12.61

5.7.6 Antithetic sampling

A way to reduce the Monte Carlo standard error (Section 5.7.1), for the schemes presented so far, and therefore improve the accuracy, is to apply a technique known as antithetic sampling. It consists in generating a sample path by drawing two arrays of random variables $Z(t_1), \ldots, Z(t_{n_{step}})$ and $Y(t_1), \ldots, Y(t_{n_{step}})$ and generating its antithetic path using the same, but with opposite sign, arrays of random numbers $-Z(t_1), \ldots, -Z(t_{n_{step}})$ and $-Y(t_1), \ldots, -Y(t_{n_{step}})$ (see, e.g., Glasserman 2003 for a proof). If we want to compute n_{sim} paths, antithetic sampling allows us to draw $\frac{n_{sim}}{2}$ pairs of random variables $Z(t_i), Y(t_i)$, hence halving the number of random variables required. When the process to be simulated is of a simple form (geometric Brownian motion for example), the introduction of antithetic sampling contributes to a reduction of the computation times as well as an improved accuracy.

We have tested and compared the standard Euler scheme with the "enhanced" Euler antithetic sampling scheme. A subset of our tests is reported in Table 5.12 and Table 5.13. Both schemes have been simulated using 10^5 paths and four time steps per year. The peculiarity of the Euler antithetic sampling is that the 100000 paths have been generated using 50000 random number draws (for each of the two stochastic variables) instead of 100000 (for the aforementioned property). For the case $\beta_k = 0$ the results display a slight decrease of the Monte Carlo standard error (Section 5.7.1) across all strikes. For $\beta_k = 1$ the Monte Carlo standard error is higher at very low strikes and then it decreases as the strikes increase. A boost in computational performance is noticeable especially for low betas: for the particular case $\beta_k = 0$ the computation time (on a standard home laptop) decreases by 10% while for $\beta_k = 1$ it improves by a more modest 5%. This is because, in the SABR model case, the time required to compute the forward interest rate and stochastic volatility processes is generally greater than the time required to draw the random numbers $Z(t_i), Y(t_i)$, therefore not providing a substantial reduction of the computation time.

Table 5.12 Monte Carlo standard errors produced by a classic Euler scheme and by an Euler antithetic sampling scheme (Euler AS) for the set of parameters $\beta_k = 0$, $\rho_k = -0.2$, $v_k = 0.25$ and $T_{k-1} = 19.5y$

	Strike (%)					
	0.5	**1**	**2**	**3**	**4**	**5**
Euler	4.15E-05	4.48E-05	5.23E-05	3.69E-05	2.99E-05	2.47E-05
Euler AS	4.11E-05	4.44E-05	5.19E-05	3.63E-05	2.92E-05	2.39E-05

Table 5.13 Monte Carlo standard errors produced by a classic Euler scheme and by an Euler antithetic sampling scheme (Euler AS) for the set of parameters $\beta_k = 1$, $\rho_k = -0.2$, $v_k = 0.25$ and $T_{k-1} = 19.5y$

	Strike (%)					
	0.5	**1**	**2**	**3**	**4**	**5**
Euler	2.33E-06	5.56E-06	1.53E-05	4.59E-05	4.35E-05	4.20E-05
Euler AS	2.37E-06	5.56E-06	1.53E-05	4.40E-05	4.16E-05	4.00E-05

5.8 The limits of Hagan et al. approximations

The approximations presented by Hagan et al. suffer from three major drawbacks:

- For long maturities the risk neutral probability density function (PDF) implied by Equations (5.13) and (5.16) can become negative. This is an undesirable feature, as a negative probability function translates into arbitrageable option prices (i.e., the option prices are no longer convex in the strike dimension).
- Under certain conditions (which we will define later in this section) the Hagan et al. approximations lose accuracy.
- For high β_k values, the approximations have an "explosive" behaviour, returning too high implied volatility values for high strike options.

Being aware of the limits of the model in use is of fundamental importance, as it helps when defining boundaries that delimit where derivative securities can be traded without incurring losses due to mispricing. We will analyse in this section the flaws of the Hagan et al. equations, and in Section 5.9 discuss alternative SABR approximations which have been developed to solve these issues.

5.8.1 Risk neutral probability density function implied by option prices

We present in this section a mathematical tool which can be used to imply the risk neutral PDF from a set of option prices: the Breeden-Litzenberger theorem. We will utilize this tool to provide an overview of the "PDF deficiency" related to the Hagan et al. approximations and we will use empirical results to understand how the SABR parameters influence the behaviour of these equations.

In 1978, Breeden and Litzenberger presented a paper in which they showed how to compute the risk neutral PDF from a set of quoted option prices. We report here the final result without proof, where the considered options are caplets (the result can however be extended to floorlets, swaptions, etc.). The risk neutral PDF $p(y, T_{k-1})$ value at time t, implied by a caplet with strike y and expiring at T_{k-1} is given by

$$p(y, T_{k-1}) = \frac{\partial^2 \mathbf{Cpl}(t, T_{k-1}, T_k, y)}{\partial y^2}. \tag{5.35}$$

The numerical computation of $p(y, T_{k-1})$ can be done trivially using, for example, the Python function reported in Table 4.7. It suffices to have a series of caplet prices

$$\mathbf{Cpl}(t, T_{k-1}, T_k, y_1),$$
$$\mathbf{Cpl}(t, T_{k-1}, T_k, y_2),$$
$$\vdots$$
$$\mathbf{Cpl}(t, T_{k-1}, T_k, y_n),$$

corresponding to a set of options with strikes $y_1, y_2, \ldots, y_n$ and to use Equation (5.35) repeatedly for each pair $(\mathbf{Cpl}(t, T_{k-1}, T_k, y_i), y_i)$. We will use this tool to check the validity of the PDF produced by the Hagan et al. approximations.

5.8.2 Risk neutral probability density function computation for the Hagan et al. approximations

If we are working with the Hagan et al. lognormal approximation, the caplet prices

$$\mathbf{Cpl}^{\mathrm{Blk}}\left(t, T_{k-1}, T_k, y_1, \sigma_k^B(y)\right),$$
$$\mathbf{Cpl}^{\mathrm{Blk}}\left(t, T_{k-1}, T_k, y_2, \sigma_k^B(y)\right),$$
$$\vdots$$
$$\mathbf{Cpl}^{\mathrm{Blk}}\left(t, T_{k-1}, T_k, y_n, \sigma_k^B(y)\right),$$

can be computed by plugging into the Black formula, Equation (4.3), the lognormal Black implied volatility $\sigma_k^B(y)$ obtained by Equation (5.13). Analogously, for the Hagan et al. normal approximation, we will use the caplet prices

$$\mathbf{Cpl}^{\mathrm{Norm}}\left(t, T_{k-1}, T_k, y_1, \sigma_k^N(y)\right),$$

$$\mathbf{Cpl}^{\mathrm{Norm}}\left(t, T_{k-1}, T_k, y_2, \sigma_k^N(y)\right),$$

$$\vdots$$

$$\mathbf{Cpl}^{\mathrm{Norm}}\left(t, T_{k-1}, T_k, y_n, \sigma_k^N(y)\right),$$

computed by plugging into the caplet normal model formula, Equation (4.13), the normal implied volatility $\sigma_k^N(y)$ obtained by Equation (5.16).

5.8.3 Risk neutral probability density function tests for the Hagan et al. approximations

The persistent low level of rates of the last years has led many brokers to start quoting normal volatilities (besides or instead of) Black volatilities (Section 4.2). Many organizations might be tempted to switch from a "Hagan lognormal" based calibration/pricing to a "Hagan normal" one. A PDF analysis of both approximations proposed by Hagan et al. is therefore in order. We can classify our tests in two different groups based on T_{k-1}:

$$T_{k-1} = 10y,$$

$$T_{k-1} = 20y.$$

For each of them we have tested four different sets of β_k:

$$\beta_k = 0,$$

$$\beta_k = 0.5,$$

$$\beta_k = 0.7$$

$$\beta_k = 1,$$

and two different sets of ρ_k:

$$\rho_k = -0.2,$$

$$\rho_k = -0.8.$$

Table 5.14 Risk neutral density function sign generated by the Hagan et al. lognormal (left) and normal (right) approximations for various choices of β_k and ρ_k. For all cases $T_{k-1} = 10y$ and $v_k = 0.25$

	$T_{k-1} = 10y$			$T_{k-1} = 10y$	
	$\rho_k = -0.2$	$\rho_k = -0.8$		$\rho_k = -0.2$	$\rho_k = -0.8$
$\beta_k = 0$	+	-	$\beta_k = 0$	-	-
$\beta_k = 0.5$	+	-	$\beta_k = 0.5$	-	-
$\beta_k = 0.7$	+	+	$\beta_k = 0.7$	-	-
$\beta_k = 1$	+	+	$\beta_k = 1$	+	+

Table 5.15 Risk neutral probability density function sign for the Hagan et al. lognormal (left) and normal (right) approximations for various choices of β_k and ρ_k. For all cases $T_{k-1} = 20y$ and $v_k = 0.25$

	$T_k = 20y$			$T_k = 20y$	
	$\rho_k = -0.2$	$\rho_k = -0.8$		$\rho_k = -0.2$	$\rho_k = -0.8$
$\beta_k = 0$	-	-	$\beta_k = 0$	-	-
$\beta_k = 0.5$	-	-	$\beta_k = 0.5$	-	-
$\beta_k = 0.7$	-	+	$\beta_k = 0.7$	-	-
$\beta_k = 1$	+	+	$\beta_k = 1$	+	+

A (sample) visual representation of our tests is reported in Figures 5.19 and 5.20, and an overall view is given in Tables 5.14 and 5.15. In general the Hagan et al. lognormal approximation performs better than the Hagan et al. normal approximation. The latter is actually providing a positive PDF only when used with $\beta_k = 1$, while for the lognormal approximation, different parameter ranges provides a positive PDF. For the tested parameters we have, for example, a positive PDF for any choice of β_k when $\rho_k = -0.2$ and $T_{k-1} = 10y$. It also provides a positive PDF for $T_{k-1} = 20y$ when $\beta_k = 1$. For both maturities the lognormal approximation is positive also for $\beta_k = 0.7$ when ρ_k is taken particularly low (e.g., $\rho_k = -0.8$). A closer look at the PDF charts shows that the region where this problem manifests itself is very close to zero. In low rate markets (traditionally JPY and more recently CHF and EUR), where the quoted/traded strikes tend to approach zero, the issue cannot be underestimated. This is an undesired feature, which any sell side institution/desk should take into consideration and deal with. We provide in Section 5.9 a possible solution to this problem.

5.8.4 Accuracy tests for the Hagan et al. approximations

The Hagan et al. approximations have been obtained by a small time expansion in the variance $\varepsilon_{var} = v_k^2 T_{k-1}$ (see Hagan et al. 2002). For low values of ε_{var}, the

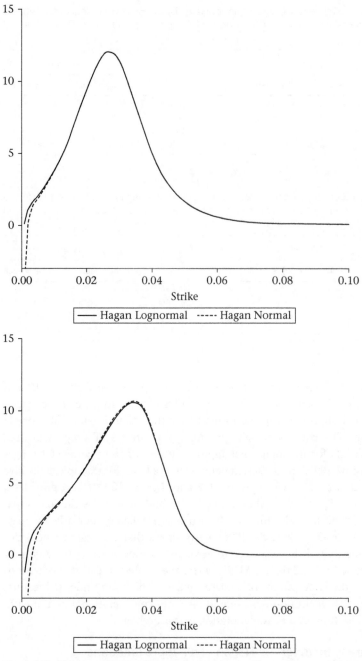

Figure 5.19 Risk neutral probability density function for $T_{k-1} = 10y$, $\beta_k = 0.5$, $v_k = 0.25$, $\rho_k = -0.2$ (top) and $\rho_k = -0.8$ (bottom). The strike is reported as a number, e.g., 0.04 stands for 4%

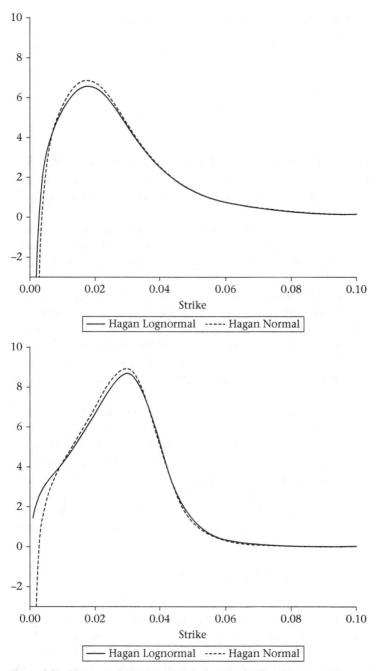

Figure 5.20 Risk neutral probability density function for $T_k = 20y$, $\beta_k = 0.7$, $v_k = 0.25$, $\rho_k = -0.2$ (top) and $\rho_k = -0.8$ (bottom). The strike is reported as a number, e.g., 0.04 stands for 4%

Table 5.16 Test plan for the Hagan et al. approximations

Parameters		$v_k^2 T_{k-1}$
$v_k = 0.2$	$T_{k-1} = 10y$	0.4
$v_k = 0.2$	$T_{k-1} = 20y$	0.8
$v_k = 0.5$	$T_{k-1} = 10y$	2.5
$v_k = 0.5$	$T_{k-1} = 20y$	5

approximations work fine, but as soon as this quantity increases, and in particular when the condition $v_k^2 T_{k-1} \ll 1$ is not attained, they lose accuracy. In other words they are not able anymore to correctly approximate the evolution of the SABR processes, Equations (5.1) and (5.2).

The accuracy tests have been carried out by simulating the SABR processes through a Monte Carlo Euler scheme (Section 5.7.4). We consider the results thus obtained as our benchmarks to which the Hagan et al. approximations should be tested. The set of v_k, T_{k-1} analysed is reported in Table 5.16.

The lognormal approximation test results are reported in Figures 5.21 and 5.22, while for what concerns the normal approximation, the results are reported in Figures 5.23 and 5.24 (we have been analysing the accuracy of both approximations for the same reasons outlined in Section 5.8.3, i.e., the increase in popularity which the normal volatility quotes have recently encountered). The outcomes presented here clearly show how the quality of the approximation is affected by the condition $v_k^2 T_{k-1} \ll 1$.

The practical consequences of this issue manifest themselves when the SABR model is used in a term structure model (such as the SABR LMM) to price exotic interest rate derivatives. As we will see in Chapter 7, the SABR parameters obtained from the calibration of a volatility term structure are then used to simulate (through Monte Carlo schemes) the evolution of the forward rates. From the results presented in this section it is clear that the simulation outcomes would be greatly impacted on every time the condition $v_k^2 T_{k-1} \ll 1$ is not fulfilled. The obvious impacts of this are wrong prices and sensitivities produced by our stochastic volatility term structure model.

5.8.5 Explosive behavior for high strike options

The market standard for pricing CMS products is the replication technique proposed by Hagan (2003). The replication is achieved by integrating swaption prices over a continuum of strikes. As only a limited number of swaptions are actually quoted in the market, it is necessary to adopt a methodology which provides all the needed swaption prices. If we choose to use the Hagan et al. equations[3] to generate these swaption (volatilities which are then turned into) prices, we need to be aware of the "explosive" behaviour which these approximations present at high

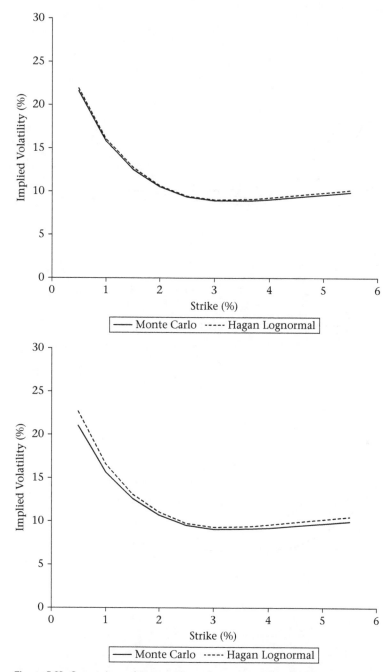

Figure 5.21 Comparison of the volatility smile generated by a SABR Monte Carlo Euler scheme (Monte Carlo) and by the Hagan et al. lognormal approximation (Hagan Lognormal). Numerical tests performed with: $\alpha_k = 0.01$, $\beta_k = 0.4$, $v_k = 0.2$, $\rho_k = -0.1$, $T_{k-1} = 10y$ (top) and $T_{k-1} = 20y$ (bottom)

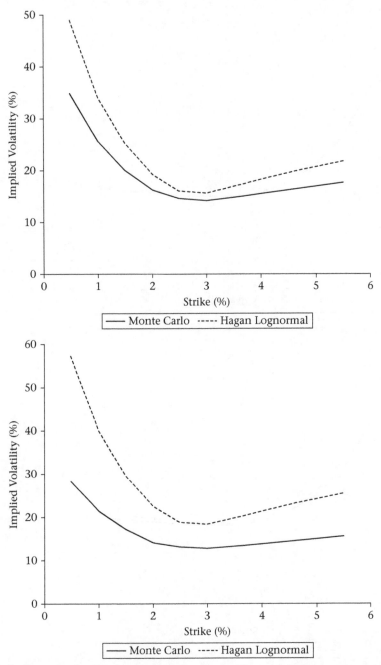

Figure 5.22 Comparison of the volatility smile generated by a SABR Monte Carlo Euler scheme (Monte Carlo) and by the Hagan et al. lognormal approximation (Hagan Lognormal). Numerical tests performed with: $\alpha_k = 0.01$, $\beta_k = 0.3$, $\nu_k = 0.5$, $\rho_k = -0.1$, $T_{k-1} = 10y$ (top) and $T_{k-1} = 20y$ (bottom)

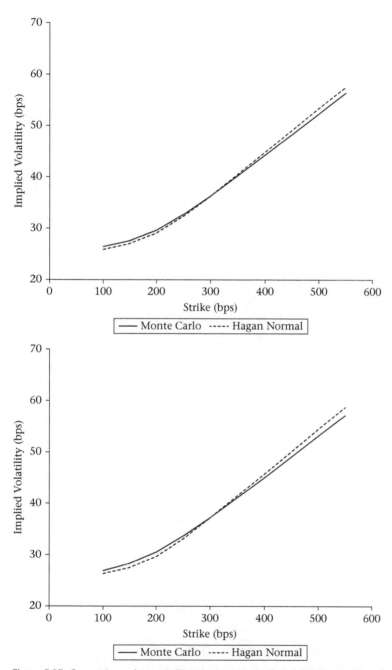

Figure 5.23 Comparison of the volatility smile generated by a SABR Monte Carlo Euler scheme (Monte Carlo) and by the Hagan et al. normal approximation (Hagan Normal). Numerical tests performed with: $\alpha_k = 0.02$, $\beta_k = 0.5$, $\nu_k = 0.2$, $\rho_k = 0.4$, $T_{k-1} = 10y$ (top) and $T_{k-1} = 20y$ (bottom)

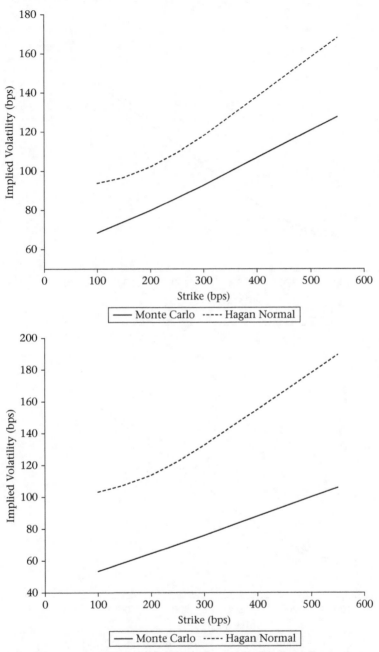

Figure 5.24 Comparison of the volatility smile generated by a SABR Monte Carlo Euler scheme (Monte Carlo) and by the Hagan et al. normal approximation (Hagan Normal). Numerical tests performed with: $a_k = 0.02$, $\beta_k = 0.2$, $v_k = 0.5$, $\rho_k = 0.4$, $T_{k-1} = 10y$ (top) and $T_{k-1} = 20y$ (bottom)

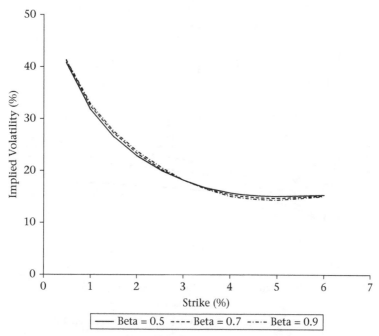

Figure 5.25 Sample calibration, using Hagan et al. lognormal approximation for different β_k, to swaption implied volatilities around the ATM region ($y_{ATM} = 3\%$)

strikes. If we would limit our analysis to the strikes close to the ATM, this problem would not be identified, as different β_k values produce very similar volatility smiles around the ATM region (Figure 5.25). However, if we use the same calibrated parameters (which provide a very good fit near the ATM strike) to compute the implied volatility of high strike options we would obtain results which are very dependent on the β_k value chosen (Figure 5.26). The greater the β_k used, the more pronounced the far right smile wing is. As shown in Mercurio and Pallavicini (2006) this behaviour cannot be underestimated and it has a direct impact on the pricing of CMS products, which might be greatly overpriced.

5.9 Alternative SABR approximations

Over the years, many academics and practitioners have been trying to develop a SABR approximation which would not present the same issues (Section 5.8) characterizing the Hagan et al. approximations and would retain, at the same time, computational ease and pricing/calibration speed. There are several alternative approximations that exist, such as the ones proposed by Henry-Labordere (2008),

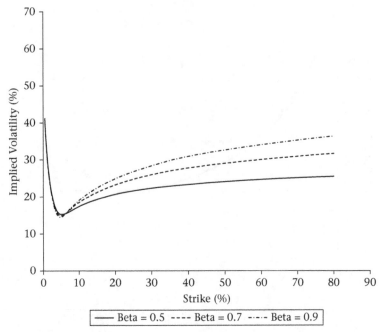

Figure 5.26 Explosive behaviour of the Hagan et al. lognormal approximation in the far right smile wing. The implied volatilities for high strike options are higher, the greater β_k is chosen

Obloj (2008) and Paulot (2009) (see also Appendix A.2). Anyhow, these are all still characterized by a decline in accuracy (i.e., they are not able to approximate correctly the true SABR model defined by Equations (5.1) and (5.2)), although to a lesser extent than that exhibited by the Hagan et al. lognormal approximation (Section 5.8.4).

Much more reliable seem to be the approximations proposed in Antonov and Spector (2012) and Antonov et al. (2013). Their formulas could be used as alternatives to the Hagan et al. lognormal approximation for the case $0 < \beta_k < 1$. They are in fact characterized by an absorbing boundary at zero which prevents it being reliable for $\beta_k = 0$. Also, when $\beta_k = 1$ it is not possible to employ them due to the existence of zero divisors. In the rest of this section we will limit our analysis to the promising work done by Antonov et al.

We would like to mention also a different approach, which can be used to price options under the SABR model, without resulting in the issues described in Section 5.8. Instead of working with an approximation, it is also possible to work with the SABR partial differential equation and price deals by finite difference methods (see, e.g., Sheppard 2007). Although this approach provides exact prices, the major computational difficulties and challenges come when it should be used for calibration purposes. Building a two dimensional PDE solver is a non-trivial task which requires extensive investigation and analysis to avoid numerical instabilities and computational issues.

A yet different, but still PDE based approach, has been proposed by Andreasen and Huge (2011). Their methodology allows us to price and calibrate an approximated SABR model, using a one-dimensional PDE grid. As we will not present here results related to their technique, the interested reader can consult the aforementioned reference for more details.

5.9.1 Antonov et al. approximation, zero correlation case

Antonov and Spector (2012) and Antonov et al. (2013) introduced an approximation for the SABR model for the specific case $\rho_k = 0$. We will refer to this equation as the Antonov et al. zero correlation approximation. Leaving aside for the moment its quality features (which we will analyse later in this chapter), the main difference to the Hagan et al. lognormal approximation is that it returns a caplet Black price $\mathrm{Blk}\left(F_k(t), y_i, \sigma_k^B(y)\sqrt{T_{k-1}-t}, 1\right)$ at time t instead of caplet Black implied volatility $\sigma_k^B(y)$. The Antonov et al. zero correlation approximation is

$$\mathrm{Blk}\left(F_k(t), y_i, \sigma_k^B(y)\sqrt{T_{k-1}-t}, 1\right) = (F_k - y)^+$$
$$+\frac{2}{\pi}\sqrt{yF_k}\left\{\int_{s_-}^{s_+} ds\frac{\sin(\eta\kappa(s))}{\sinh(s)}G(\tau,s)\right.$$
$$\left.+\sin(\eta\pi)\int_{s_+}^{\infty} ds\frac{e^{-\eta\psi(s)}}{\sinh(s)}G(\tau,s)\right\},$$

$$(5.36)$$

where $\tau = (T_{k-1}-t)v_k^2$ and

$$s_- = \mathrm{arcsinh}\left(\frac{v_k|q-q_0|}{\tilde{\alpha}_k}\right), \qquad (5.37)$$

$$s_+ = \mathrm{arcsinh}\left(\frac{v_k|q+q_0|}{\tilde{\alpha}_k}\right), \qquad (5.38)$$

with

$$\kappa(s) = 2\arctan\sqrt{\frac{\sinh^2(s) - \sinh^2(s_-)}{\sinh^2(s_+) - \sinh^2(s)}}, \qquad (5.39)$$

$$\psi(s) = 2\operatorname{arctanh}\sqrt{\frac{\sinh^2(s) - \sinh^2(s_+)}{\sinh^2(s) - \sinh^2(s_-)}},\qquad (5.40)$$

and

$$q = \frac{y^{1-\beta_k}}{1 - \beta_k},$$

$$q_0 = \frac{F_k^{1-\beta_k}}{1 - \beta_k},$$

$$\eta = \left|\frac{1}{2(\beta_k - 1)}\right|. \qquad (5.41)$$

$G(\tau, s)$ is the kernel function

$$G(\tau, s) = 2\sqrt{2}\frac{e^{-\frac{\tau}{8}}}{\tau\sqrt{2\pi\tau}}\int_s^\infty ue^{-\frac{u^2}{\tau}}\sqrt{\cosh(u) - \cosh(s)}\,du, \qquad (5.42)$$

Antonov et al. propose to approximate the kernel function $G(\tau, s)$ to allow Equation (5.36) to involve only single integrals. The approximation follows

$$G(\tau, s) \simeq \sqrt{\frac{\sinh(s)}{s}}e^{-\frac{s^2}{2\tau}-\frac{\tau}{8}}(R(\tau, s) + \delta R(\tau, s)),$$

where

$$R(\tau, s) = 1 + \frac{3\tau g(s)}{8s^2} - \frac{5\tau^2\left(-8s^2 + 3g^2(s) + 24g(s)\right)}{128s^4}$$
$$+ \frac{35\tau^3\left(-40s^2 + 3g^3(s) + 24g^2(s) + 120g(s)\right)}{1024s^6},$$

$$g(s) = s\coth(s) - 1,$$

$$\delta R(\tau, s) = e^{\frac{\tau}{8}} - \frac{3072 + 384\tau + 24\tau^2 + \tau^3}{3072}.$$

5.9.2 Antonov et al. approximation, general correlation case

Using the zero correlation approximation as a mimicking model (the interested reader is referred to Antonov and Spector 2012 and Antonov et al. 2013 for all the technical details), the authors also proposed an approximation for the general correlation case (which we will refer to as the Antonov et al. general correlation approximation):

$$\mathrm{Blk}\left(F_k(t), y_i, \sigma_k^B(y)\sqrt{T_{k-1} - t}, 1\right)$$

$$= (F_k - y)^+ + \frac{2}{\pi}\sqrt{yF_k}\left\{\int_{s_-}^{s_+} ds \frac{\sin(\eta\kappa(s))}{\sinh(s)} G\left((T_{k-1} - t)\tilde{v}_k^2, s\right)\right.$$

$$\left. + \sin(\eta\pi)\int_{s_+}^{\infty} ds \frac{e^{-\eta\psi(s)}}{\sinh(s)} G\left((T_{k-1} - t)\tilde{v}_k^2, s\right)\right\}, \tag{5.43}$$

where

$$s_- = \mathrm{arcsinh}\left(\frac{\tilde{v}_k|q - q_0|}{\tilde{\alpha}_k}\right), \tag{5.44}$$

$$s_+ = \mathrm{arcsinh}\left(\frac{\tilde{v}_k|q + q_0|}{\tilde{\alpha}_k}\right), \tag{5.45}$$

with

$$\kappa(s) = 2\arctan\sqrt{\frac{\sinh^2(s) - \sinh^2(s_-)}{\sinh^2(s_+) - \sinh^2(s)}}, \tag{5.46}$$

$$\psi(s) = 2\mathrm{arctanh}\sqrt{\frac{\sinh^2(s) - \sinh^2(s_+)}{\sinh^2(s) - \sinh^2(s_-)}}, \tag{5.47}$$

and

$$q = \frac{y^{1-\tilde{\beta}_k}}{1 - \tilde{\beta}_k},$$

$$q_0 = \frac{F_k^{1-\tilde{\beta}_k}}{1 - \tilde{\beta}_k},$$

$$\eta = \left|\frac{1}{2(\tilde{\beta}_k - 1)}\right|. \tag{5.48}$$

The kernel function $G(\tau, s)$ is defined as

$$G(\tau, s) = 2\sqrt{2} \frac{e^{-\frac{\tau}{8}}}{\tau\sqrt{2\pi\tau}} \int_s^\infty u e^{-\frac{u^2}{\tau}} \sqrt{\cosh(u) - \cosh(s)}\, du, \tag{5.49}$$

which can be approximated as shown in Section 5.9.1, by simply substituting ν_k with $\tilde{\nu}_k$.

The parameters $\tilde{\alpha}_k$, $\tilde{\beta}_k$, $\tilde{\nu}_k$ relate to the SABR model parameters α_k, β_k, ν_k, ρ_k as follows

$$\tilde{\beta}_k = \beta_k,$$
$$\tilde{\nu}_k = \sqrt{\nu_k^2 - \frac{3}{2}\left\{\nu_k^2\rho_k^2 + \alpha_k\nu_k\rho_k(1 - \beta_k)F_k^{\beta_k-1}\right\}},$$
$$\tilde{\alpha}_k = \tilde{\alpha}_k^{(0)} + T_{k-1}\tilde{\alpha}_k^{(1)} + \cdots, \tag{5.50}$$

where

$$\tilde{\alpha}_k^{(0)} = \frac{2\Phi\delta\tilde{q}\tilde{\nu}_k}{\Phi^2 - 1},$$
$$\delta\tilde{q} = \frac{y^{1-\tilde{\beta}_k} - F_k^{1-\tilde{\beta}_k}}{1 - \tilde{\beta}_k},$$
$$\Phi = \left(\frac{\alpha_k^{min} + \rho_k\alpha_k + \nu_k\rho_k q}{(1 + \rho_k)\alpha_k}\right)^{\frac{\tilde{\nu}_k}{\nu_k}},$$

with

$$\alpha_k^{min} = \sqrt{\nu_k^2\delta q^2 + 2\rho_k\nu_k\delta q\alpha_k + \alpha_k^2},$$

and

$$\delta q = \frac{y^{1-\beta_k} - F_k^{1-\beta_k}}{1 - \beta_k}.$$

The term $\tilde{\alpha}_k^{(1)}$ appearing in Equation (5.50) is given by

$$
\tilde{\alpha}_k^{(1)} = \tilde{\alpha}_k^{(0)} \tilde{v}_k^2 \left[\frac{\frac{1}{2}\left(\beta_k - \tilde{\beta}_k\right)\ln\left(yF_k\right) + \frac{1}{2}\ln\left(\alpha_k \alpha_k^{\min}\right)}{\frac{\Phi^2-1}{\Phi^2+1}\ln\Phi} \right.
$$
$$
\left. - \frac{\frac{1}{2}\ln\left(\tilde{\alpha}_k^{(0)}\sqrt{\delta\tilde{q}\tilde{v}_k^2 + \tilde{\alpha}_k^{(0)^2}}\right) - \mathcal{B}_{\min}}{\frac{\Phi^2-1}{\Phi^2+1}\ln\Phi} \right],
$$

where

$$
\mathcal{B}_{\min} = -\frac{1}{2}\frac{\beta_k}{1-\beta_k}\frac{\rho_k}{\sqrt{1-\rho_k^2}}\left(\pi - \varphi_0 - \arccos\left(\rho_k - I\right)\right),
$$

$$
\varphi_0 = \arccos\left(-\frac{\delta q v_k + \alpha_k \rho_k}{\alpha_k^{\min}}\right),
$$

with

$$
I = \begin{cases} \frac{2}{\sqrt{1-L^2}}\left(\arctan\left(\frac{u_0+L}{\sqrt{1-L^2}}\right) - \arctan\left(\frac{L}{\sqrt{1-L^2}}\right)\right) & \text{for } L < 1 \\ \frac{1}{\sqrt{1-L^2}}\ln\frac{u_0\left(L+\sqrt{L^2-1}\right)+1}{u_0\left(L-\sqrt{L^2-1}\right)+1} & \text{for } L > 1 \end{cases},
$$

and

$$
u_0 = \frac{\delta q v_k \rho_k + \alpha_k - \alpha_k^{\min}}{\delta q v_k \sqrt{1-\rho_k^2}},
$$

$$
L = \frac{\alpha_k^{\min}(1-\beta_k)}{y^{1-\beta_k} v_k \sqrt{1-\rho_k^2}}.
$$

For the special case related to ATM options, for which $y = F_k$, the quantity

$$
u_0 = \frac{\delta q v_k \rho_k + \alpha_k - \alpha_k^{\min}}{\delta q v_k \sqrt{1-\rho_k^2}}
$$

has a singularity due to

$$\delta q = \frac{y^{1-\beta_k} - F_k^{1-\beta_k}}{1 - \beta_k} = 0.$$

It is possible to bypass this issue numerically, calculating the option price for two strikes close enough to the ATM one and then interpolating.

5.9.3 Antonov et al. approximation tests

Although the Antonov et al. approximations proposed in Sections 5.9.1 and 5.9.2 appear quite complicated, their implementation can be done quite easily. The major challenge can be considered the computation of the two integrals, which can be quite easily overcome by employing one of the many functions available in the *scipy.integrate* package (see Jones et al. 2001–). In terms of performances related to pricing and especially calibration, both approximations are fast, with the zero correlation one being faster, as an obvious result of the fewer terms which need to be computed.

A very wide range of tests has been performed by Antonov and Spector in their seminal work (2012). For this reason we will provide only a brief sample of the tests we have performed. However, they are significant enough to show if and how the Antonov et al. (general correlation) approximation can tackle and solve the issues plaguing the Hagan et al. (lognormal) approximation (we omit comparing the normal approximation, which can however be effortlessly done).

There is a general excellent agreement between the results obtained (using the same set of parameters $\alpha_k, \nu_k, \beta_k, \rho_k$) by the Antonov et al. approximation and by simulating the SABR model using a Monte Carlo (Euler) scheme. This finding allows us to conclude that the Antonov et al. approximation can be safely used to obtain (through calibration of multiple implied volatility smiles) a term structure of SABR parameters to be used within a SABR LMM for pricing and hedging exotic interest rate derivatives. We report in Figure 5.27, a comparison of the implied volatility smiles generated by the SABR Monte Carlo, the Antonov et al. approximation as well as the Hagan et al. approximation.

The second issue, affecting the Hagan et al. approximation, that we discussed in Section 5.8, is the presence of arbitrage for low strike options. As we have seen, this is recognizable when the implied risk-neutral PDF turns negative. Such an occurrence appears extremely seldomly when using the Antonov et al. approximation. Even in the rare cases in which this happens (see Figure 5.28), it is of such a small magnitude that it can be neglected.

The last flaw characterizing the Hagan et al. approximation is what we have defined (Section 5.8.5) as "explosive behaviour" for high strike options. This is particularly acute for high β_k values. Our tests indicate (one of them is reported

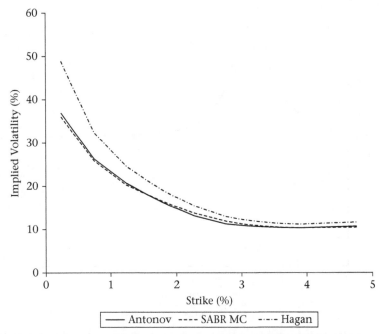

Figure 5.27 Comparison of the volatility smile generated by a SABR Monte Carlo Euler scheme (Monte Carlo), the Hagan et al. lognormal approximation (Hagan) and the Antonov et al. approximation (Antonov). Numerical tests performed with: $\alpha_k = 0.01$, $\beta_k = 0.3$, $v_k = 0.3$, $\rho_k = -0.5$, $T_{k-1} = 19.5y$

in Figure 5.29) that the Antonov et al. approximation has a much smoother behaviour in the far right part of the smile wing. This suggests that it could be safely employed to price CMS products using the replication technique proposed by Hagan (2003).

5.10 Pricing in a negative forward rate regime: shifted SABR approximation

As previously mentioned, the SABR lognormal approximation formula proposed by Hagan et al. (Equation (5.13)) is the market standard to interpolate among liquid caplet/floorlet strikes and produce quotes (in terms of lognormal Black implied volatility) for illiquid strike options.

During a prolonged period of time, starting in 2011, short maturity forward rates, for various currencies (including CHF and EUR), turned negative.

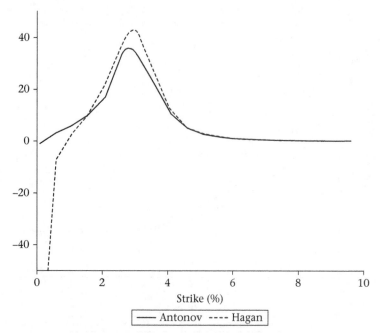

Figure 5.28 Risk neutral probability density function implied by options priced using the Hagan et al. lognormal approximation (Hagan) and the Antonov et al. approximation (Antonov). Numerical tests performed with: $\alpha_k = 0.01$, $\beta_k = 0.3$, $\nu_k = 0.3$, $\rho_k = -0.5$, $T_{k-1} = 19.5y$

A quick look at Equation (5.13) will be enough to tell us that the logarithmic terms $\ln\left(\frac{F_k}{y}\right)$, $\ln^2\left(\frac{F_k}{y}\right)$ and $\ln^4\left(\frac{F_k}{y}\right)$ will not have a solution for negative values of F_k. The problem could be tackled in two fundamentally different ways. The first one would be to switch to a new pricing methodology which can correctly deal with negative values of F_k. Such a route would imply investing time and resources to change the pricing library code to the newly adopted pricing approach. Moreover, it would be quite difficult to find a different pricing technique which yields the same calibration accuracy (Section 5.5.1) as the one provided by the Hagan et al. lognormal approximation.

We would like to clarify that the superiority of the Hagan et al. lognormal approximation comes not only from the excellent fitting of different smile shapes given by Equation (5.13), but also from the fact that this approximation has become the de facto standard in the interest rate market for what concerns caplet/floorlet/swaption smiles interpolation. Hence most (if not all) of the vanilla option prices/implied volatilities quoted have been generated using it. Taking into consideration the drawbacks just mentioned, most of the market participants have reverted to a simpler method to deal with the negativity of F_k: using a *shifted forward*

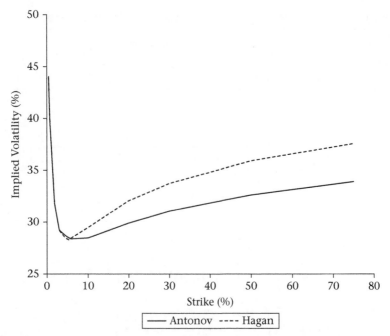

Figure 5.29 Comparison of the volatility smile generated (up to extremely high strike options) by the Hagan et al. lognormal approximation (Hagan) and the Antonov et al. approximation (Antonov). For both cases $\beta_k = 0.8$

version of the Hagan et al. lognormal approximation. The shifted approximation can be derived following the (general) steps provided in Appendix A.3 of Hagan et al. (2002); we report here the final result:

$$
\sigma_k^B(y) = \frac{\alpha_k}{\left((F_k + sf)(y + sf)\right)^{\left(\frac{1-\beta_k}{2}\right)}}
$$

$$
\cdot \frac{1}{\left[1 + \frac{(1-\beta_k)^2}{24} \ln^2\left(\frac{F_k+sf}{y+sf}\right) + \frac{(1-\beta_k)^4}{1920} \ln^4\left(\frac{F_k+sf}{y+sf}\right) + \cdots\right]}
$$

$$
\cdot \left(\frac{z_k}{\xi(z_k)}\right)
$$

$$
\cdot \left[1 + \frac{(1-\beta_k)^2}{24} \frac{\alpha_k^2}{\left((F_k + sf)(y + sf)\right)^{(1-\beta_k)}} T_{k-1} +\right.
$$

Table 5.17 Test plan for *shifted forward* version of the Hagan et al. lognormal approximation

	Parameters			
Case 1	$F_k = 0.1\%$	$sf = 0.2\%$	$\beta_k = 0.5$	$T_{k-1} = 0.5y$
Case 2	$F_k = -0.05\%$	$sf = 0.2\%$	$\beta_k = 0.5$	$T_{k-1} = 0.5y$

$$+ \frac{1}{4} \frac{\alpha_k \beta_k \rho_k v_k}{\left((F_k + sf)(y + sf)\right)^{\left(\frac{1-\beta_k}{2}\right)}} T_{k-1} + \frac{2 - 3\rho_k^2}{24} v_k^2 T_{k-1} + \cdots \bigg],$$

(5.51)

where

$$z_k = \frac{v_k}{\alpha_k} \left((F_k + sf)(y + sf)\right)^{\left(\frac{1-\beta_k}{2}\right)} \ln\left(\frac{F_k + sf}{y + sf}\right),$$

$$\xi(z_k) = \ln\left(\frac{\sqrt{1 - 2\rho_k z_k + z_k^2} + z_k - \rho_k}{1 - \rho_k}\right).$$

The only new term appearing in Equation (5.51) is *sf* which represents the shift factor. It can be arbitrarily chosen as long as it shifts the forward interest rate F_k into positive territory. In practice a buffer is usually applied over the minimum *sf* required to satisfy $F_k > 0$, such that it is not necessary to continuously adjust the shift factor as the forward rate moves further into negative territory. We report in Figures 5.30 and 5.31 how good the calibration fit is for Equation (5.51) in the presence of a shift factor for the two test cases appearing in Table 5.17. Before examining the results we would like to have a brief discussion on the parameters chosen. Negative forward interest rates manifest themselves, usually, at the short end of the curve. As a consequence the expiry $T_{k-1} = 0.5y$ tested is quite representative of the region in which we might see F_k going into negative territory. The value of F_k tested in Case 2 has been taken to reflect the magnitude of negativity that a forward interest rate can take (and that we have observed in the market in the years from 2011 to 2014 for CHF).

Case 1 (Figure 5.30) has been designed as a sanity check for a *shifted forward* version of the Hagan et al. lognormal approximation. We have in fact used a positive forward interest rate; this allowed us first to perform a regular calibration to market data using the *standard* Hagan et al. lognormal approximation, before we used the shifted version of the same approximation. The results show an excellent calibration fit for both. Case 2 (Figure 5.31) deals with a negative forward interest rate. The

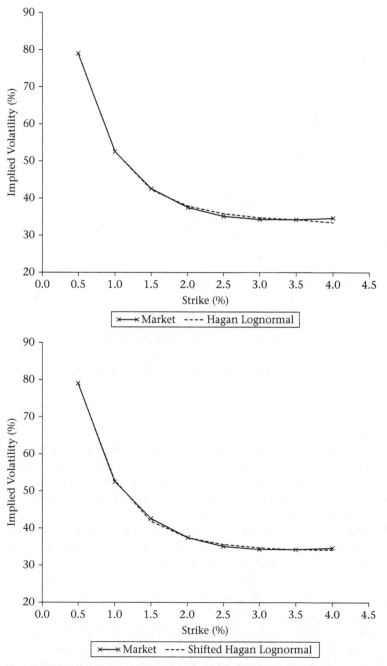

Figure 5.30 Calibration to market quotes (market) for the Hagan et al. lognormal approximation (top) and for its *shifted forward* version (bottom). Numerical tests performed with $F_k = 0.1\%$, $\beta_k = 0.5$ and $T_{k-1} = 0.5y$

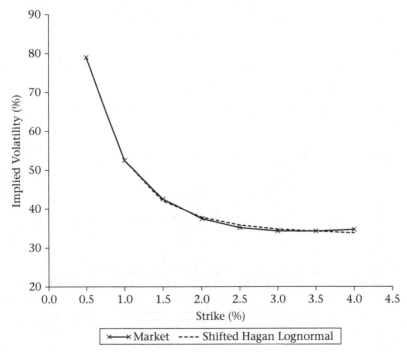

Figure 5.31 Calibration to market quotes for the *shifted forward* version of the Hagan et al. lognormal approximation. Numerical test performed with $F_k = -0.05\%$, $\beta_k = 0.5$ and $T_{k-1} = 0.5y$

calibration fit to market quotes is, also in this instance, outstanding. From a mere pricing point of view, an excellent calibration is all that we need to be able to extract implied volatilities for illiquid strikes. We have however to be careful when the same *modus operandi* is applied to risk managing a pool of deals which have as an underlying a negative forward interest rate F_k.

Extending Case 1 to the calculation of risk sensitivities (we have limited ourselves to delta and vega, but we could have easily broadened our analysis to all the Greeks introduced in Section 5.6) shows that Equation (5.51) provides risk figures which differ from the ones calculated using the *standard* Hagan et al. lognormal approximation (Figure 5.32). These differences could lead to wrong hedges and as a result the trading desk might incur losses.

As the negative forward environment seems to have become customary (at least in some markets) it is very likely that some more sound solutions will be researched and proposed by academics and practitioners. Their effectiveness and implementation might however be a challenging topic.

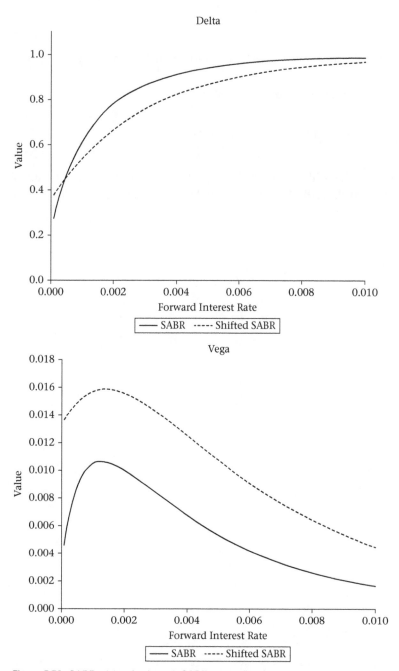

Figure 5.32 SABR delta (top) and SABR vega (bottom) for the Hagan et al. lognormal approximation (SABR) and for its *shifted forward* version (shifted SABR). Numerical tests performed with $F_k = 0.1\%$, $\beta_k = 0.5$ and $T_{k-1} = 0.5y$

Notes

1. In Hagan et al. (2002) a typo is present in formula A.70a. The term $\left(\frac{z_k}{\check{\zeta}(z_k)}\right)$ is in fact missing.
2. Alternatively we could have discretized α_k as

$$\widehat{\alpha}_k(t_{i+1}) = \widehat{\alpha}_k(t_i)e^{\left(v_k \Delta W_{\widehat{\alpha}_k}(t_{i+1}) - \frac{1}{2}v_k^2(t_{i+1}-t_i)\right)}.$$

3. As we are working with swaptions, we would be using the Hagan et al. formulas to approximate the SABR forward swap model reported in Equations (5.4), (5.5) and (5.6).

6 | LIBOR Market Model

6.1 Introduction

In this chapter we draw our attention to the market models. We start by briefly discussing short rate models, with the goal of seeing where they fit in the story of interest rate modelling. We then make a natural transition from the more general short rate models to the Heath-Jarrow-Morton framework, then to the definition of the LIBOR Market Model (LMM).

An analogous formulation for the dynamics of LIBOR rates can be done also for swap rates, resulting in the Swap Market Model (SMM) (see Appendix A.4). LMM and SMM are often referred to as market models since they are defined in terms of parameters which are quoted in the market, rather than being formulated from theoretical constructs, like the spot rate. One immediate benefit of working with these market models is that calibration to market quoted prices of vanilla products is natural and intuitive.

Although we will provide all the basic ingredients for the calibration and implementation of the LIBOR Market Model, our coverage will be somehow limited and focused on providing the necessary material to be able to later introduce the SABR LMM. The reader interested in a broader and more detailed discussion (and analysis) of the LMM is referred to Andersen and Piterbarg (2010) and Brigo and Mercurio (2006).

6.1.1 Short rate models

The short rate models which attempt to capture the dynamics of the short rate $r(t)$ are still used in practice, albeit only for cases where richer modelling dynamics are not necessary. For example, we could have a one-dimensional Itô diffusion process for $r(t)$ as

$$dr(t) = a(r(t))\,dt + b(r(t))\,dW(t).$$

Table 6.1 Different short rate models and their stochastic differential equations

Model	Stochastic Differential Equation
Ho-Lee	$dr(t) = a(t)dt + \sigma dW(t)$
Vasicek	$dr(t) = k(\theta - r(t))dt + \sigma dW(t)$
Hull-White	$dr(t) = k(t)(\theta(t) - r(t))dt + \sigma(t)dW(t)$
CIR	$dr(t) = k(\theta - r(t))dt + \sigma\sqrt{r(t)}dW(t)$
Black-Karasinzki	$d\ln(r(t)) = \left(a(t) + \frac{\sigma'(t)}{\sigma(t)}\ln(r(t))\right)dt + \sigma(t)dW(t)$

Several well known models come under this category, some of them are reported in Table 6.1.

If we use Equation (3.26) to define the price of a zero-coupon bond under the $\mathbb{Q}^B$ measure to be the expectation of 1 unit discounted by the selected numeraire we obtain

$$P(t, T_k) = B(t)\,\mathbb{E}^B\left[\frac{1}{B(T_k)}\right],$$

which, employing Equation (3.5), gives us the value of the stochastic zero-coupon bond $P(t, T_k)$ as

$$P(t, T_k) = \mathbb{E}^B\left[e^{-\int_t^{T_k} r(s)ds}\right]. \tag{6.1}$$

Using the Feynman-Kac theorem (see, e.g., Shreve 2008), one can obtain the diffusion process obeyed by $P(t, T_k)$ as

$$\frac{dP(t, T_k)}{P(t, T_k)} = r(t)\,dt + v(t, T_k)\,dW(t). \tag{6.2}$$

The ability to write the stochastic differential equations (SDEs) for a zero-coupon bond with any maturity for any of the above models means that the short rate is driving the dynamics of the whole curve (we can also rephrase this by saying that such models are arbitrage free along the entire yield curve), leaving no possibility to model its different sections separately hence providing somewhat limited dynamics.

6.1.2 Heath, Jarrow and Morton (HJM) framework

Heath, Jarrow and Morton (see, e.g., 1990, 1992) developed a framework (HJM framework) for modelling the instantaneous continuously compounded forward rates $f(t, T_k)$. We briefly review their work now, since it is a standard part of the interest rate modelling literature and also bridges the gap between the discussion of short rate models and market models. The instantaneous forward rate is the forward rate at time t from maturity T_k to maturity $T_k + \Delta t$

$$f(t, T_k) = -\frac{\partial \ln(P(t, T_k))}{\partial T_k} = \frac{\ln(P(t, T_k - \Delta t)) - \ln(P(t, T_k + \Delta t))}{2\Delta t}, \qquad (6.3)$$

where Δt is an infinitesimal quantity. Using this definition of the instantaneous forward rate we can also reversely find the zero-coupon bond price as

$$P(t, T_k) = e^{-\int_t^{T_k} f(t, u) \, du}. \qquad (6.4)$$

In the limit where T_k approaches t, the forward rate converges to the spot short rate $r(t)$

$$r(t) = f(t, t). \qquad (6.5)$$

Under the spot martingale measure $\mathbb{Q}^B$ the dynamics of the instantaneous forward with maturity T_k is given by

$$df(t, T_k) = \alpha(t, T_k) \, dt + \sigma(t, T_k) \, d\widehat{W}(t), \qquad (6.6)$$

where the volatility $\sigma(t, T_k)$ is a function of time and maturity and $d\widehat{W}(t)$ is the Wiener increment under the spot real world measure $\mathbb{P}$ at time t. By combining Equations (6.4) and (6.6) and differentiating, we obtain

$$
\begin{aligned}
dP(t, T_k) &= de^{-\int_t^{T_k} f(t, u) \, du} \\
&= f(t, t) P(t, T_k) \, dt - P(t, T_k) \int_t^{T_k} df(t, u) \, du \\
&= P(t, T_k) \left\{ f(t, t) \, dt - \int_t^{T_k} \alpha(t, u) \, du \, dt - \int_t^{T_k} \sigma(t, u) \, du \, d\widehat{W}(t) \right\} \\
&\quad + \frac{1}{2} P(t, T_k) \left(\int_t^{T_k} \sigma(t, u) \, du \right)^2 dt \\
&= P(t, T_k) \left\{ r(t) - \left[\int_t^{T_k} \alpha(t, u) \, du - \frac{1}{2} \left(\int_t^{T_k} \sigma(t, u) \, du \right)^2 \right] \right\} dt \\
&\quad - P(t, T_k) \int_t^{T_k} \sigma(t, u) \, du \, d\widehat{W}(t). \qquad (6.7)
\end{aligned}
$$

Musiela and Rutkowski (2005) shows that the zero-coupon bond dynamic is arbitrage free if

$$\int_t^T \alpha\,(t,u)\,du = \frac{1}{2}\left(\int_t^{T_k} \sigma\,(t,u)\,du\right)^2 - \lambda_t \int_t^{T_k} \sigma\,(t,u)\,du,$$

and differentiating with respect to T_k, we find

$$\alpha\,(t,T_k) = \sigma\,(t,T_k) \int_t^{T_k} \sigma\,(t,u)\,du - \lambda_t \sigma\,(t,T_k).$$

Setting $dW(t) = d\widehat{W}(t) - \lambda_t dt$, we obtain, under the risk neutral measure $\mathbb{Q}^B$, the SDE for the instantaneous forward rate

$$df\,(t,T_k) = \sigma\,(t,T_k) \int_t^{T_k} \sigma\,(t,u)\,du\,dt + \sigma\,(t,T_k)\,dW(t). \tag{6.8}$$

HJM applied similar arguments to show that $\alpha\,(t,T_k)$ cannot be chosen arbitrarily but needs to satisfy

$$\alpha\,(t,T_k) = \sigma\,(t,T_k) \int_t^{T_k} \sigma\,(t,u)\,du, \tag{6.9}$$

which is known as the no arbitrage drift condition in the HJM framework. As can be also seen from Equation (6.7), the zero-coupon bond volatility is defined as

$$v\,(t,T_k) = \int_t^{T_k} \sigma\,(t,u)\,du.$$

Now that the ground work has been laid out, we can also infer other properties. The short rate can be rewritten as

$$
\begin{aligned}
r(t) &= f\,(t,t)\\
&= f\,(0,t) + \int_0^t df\,(s,t)\\
&= f\,(0,t) + \int_0^t \sigma\,(s,t) \int_s^t \sigma\,(s,u)\,du\,ds + \int_0^t \sigma\,(s,t)\,dW\,(s).
\end{aligned}
$$

Henrard (2003) obtains the zero-coupon bond value as

$$P(t, T_k) = e^{-\int_t^{T_k} f(t,u)\,du}$$

$$= e^{-\int_t^{T_k}\left(f(0,u)+\int_0^t \sigma(s,u)v(s,u)\,ds+\int_0^t \sigma(s,u)\,dW(s)\right)du}$$

$$= e^{-\int_t^{T_k} f(0,u)\,du}\, e^{-\int_t^{T_k}\int_0^t \sigma(s,u)v(s,u)\,du\,ds}\, e^{-\int_t^{T_k}\int_0^t \sigma(s,u)\,dW(s)\,du}$$

$$= \frac{P(0, T_k)}{P(0, t)}\, e^{-\frac{1}{2}\int_0^t v^2(s,T_k)-v^2(s,t)\,ds-\int_0^t (v(s,T_k)-v(s,t))\,dW(s)}. \qquad (6.10)$$

Assuming now that the volatility of the instantaneous forward rate is split into a time dependent and a maturity dependent part, that is

$$\sigma(t, T_k) = g(t)\, h(T_k),$$

the zero-coupon bond volatility can be written as

$$v(t, T_k) = \int_t^{T_k} g(t)\, h(u)\, du$$

$$= g(t) \int_t^{T_k} h(u)\, du$$

$$= g(t)\,(H(T_k) - H(t)),$$

where H is the integral of h, and the term in the stochastic integral in Equation (6.10) can be further simplified to

$$\int_0^t v(s, T_k) - v(s, t)\, dW(s) = \int_0^t g(s)\,(H(T_k) - H(s)) - g(s)\,(H(t) - H(s))\, dW(s)$$

$$= (H(T_k) - H(t)) \int_0^t g(s)\, dW(s). \qquad (6.11)$$

This is actually an interesting result. When we insert Equation (6.11) into Equation (6.10), we observe that only the quantity $\int_0^t g(s)\, dW(s)$ is stochastic. The factor $\frac{P(0,T_k)}{P(0,t)} e^{-\frac{1}{2}\int_0^t v^2(s,T_k)-v^2(s,t)\,ds}$ and the term $(H(T_k) - H(t))$ can be pre-calculated for each desired maturity. During the simulation these pre-calculated factors are multiplied by the stochastic factor $\int_0^t g(s)\, dW(s)$, leading to an extremely fast simulation. We also observe that the Greeks, Δ and Γ, can be calculated by changing only the zero-coupon bond part of the first pre-factor, that is, $\frac{P(0,T_k)}{P(0,t)}$. The simulation does not have to be repeated and the Greeks therefore become very stable and their evaluation almost instantaneous.

Under the measure $\mathbb{Q}^k$, we can write the SDE for any zero-coupon bond with maturity T_i smaller than T_k as

$$d\frac{P(t,T_i)}{P(t,T_k)} = -\frac{P(t,T_i)}{P(t,T_k)}\left(v\left(t,T_i\right) - v\left(t,T_k\right)\right)dW_k(t),$$

where we have used Girsanov's theorem (see, e.g., Karatzas and Shreve 1988, Brigo and Mercurio 2006) to bring the Brownian motion under the forward measure $\mathbb{Q}^k$ as:

$$dW_k(t) = dW(t) - \int_t^{T_k} \sigma\left(t,u\right)du dt = dW(t) - v\left(t,T_k\right)dt.$$

This will also simplify the price ratio of two zero-coupon bonds under the forward measure to

$$\frac{P(t,T_i)}{P(t,T_k)} = \frac{P(0,T_i)}{P(0,T_k)} e^{-\frac{1}{2}\int_0^t v((s,T_i)-v(s,T_k))^2 ds - \int_0^t (v(s,T_i)-v(s,T_k))dW_k(s)}, \qquad (6.12)$$

which is a martingale (it is a traded asset discounted by the numeraire). The models defined by Equation (6.12) are of a class often referred to as separable volatility (the interested reader is referred to Cheyette 1996). There are plenty of similarities between the LMM and the separable volatility models (see Appendix A.3, where we will briefly review the LMM in the HJM framework). In fact in the former, instead of $\frac{P(t,T_i)}{P(t,T_k)}$, we simulate a forward LIBOR rate, which is nothing more than a linear combination of this ratio and some constant terms.

Another practical application of any HJM framework model is the calculation of the convexity adjustment for Eurodollar futures, which we introduced in Section 3.2.2. The convexity can be calculated (see, e.g., Hull 2000) using a Hull-White model (or any other short rate model from the HJM framework) as

$$\text{convexity}\left(t,T_{k-1},T_k\right) = \frac{B\left(T_{k-1},T_k\right)}{T_k-T_{k-1}}\left(B\left(T_{k-1},T_k\right)\left(1 - e^{-2a^{\text{conv}}T_{k-1}}\right)\right.$$
$$\left. +2a^{\text{conv}}B\left(0,T_{k-1}\right)^2\right) \cdot \frac{(\sigma^{\text{conv}})^2}{4a^{\text{conv}}}, \qquad (6.13)$$

where a^{conv} is the mean reversion speed, σ^{conv} is a constant volatility and $B\left(t,T_{k-1}\right)$ is given by

$$B\left(t,T_{k-1}\right) = \frac{1 - e^{-a^{\text{conv}}\left(T_{k-1}-t\right)}}{a^{\text{conv}}}.$$

6.2 Dynamics of the LIBOR Market Model

6.2.1 Introduction

Up to the late 1990s, the use of short rate models was the only means to value exotic option payoffs in an arbitrage-free framework. These models were calibrated to the option market using complex closed form formulas for plain vanilla caps and floors. However, the market quoted implied Black volatilities and prices were calculated using the Black formula, see Equation 4.6. In 1997 Brace, Gatarek and Musiela came up with their revolutionary paper on a new interest rate pricing model, where the forward LIBOR rates were modelled lognormally. This model was able to simulate the entire term structure of forward rates, under the same measure, using many stochastic drivers, which allowed the obtaining of an arbitrage free price for vanilla as well as exotic instruments. Moreover, due to the lognormality of the forward LIBOR rates, the calibration instruments could be priced consistently with the Black formula for caps and floors used in the markets, such that the volatilities were naturally linked to the market quotes.

6.2.2 Lognormal dynamics under the terminal measure

Let us consider the forward rate $F_k(t)$ at t, relevant for unfunded financing in the time interval $[T_{k-1}, T_k]$, which fixes at time T_{k-1}. At this fixing time T_{k-1}, the forward rate is equal to the simply compounded spot LIBOR rate $L(T_{k-1}, T_k)$. By definition of the forward rate, we see that discounting it under the T_k-forward measure[1] results in a weighted difference of zero-coupon bonds, both of which are tradable assets, and hence the discounted forward rate is also a tradable asset

$$F_k(t)P(t, T_k) = \frac{P(t, T_{k-1}) - P(t, T_k)}{\tau_k}.$$

Furthermore, dividing these tradable assets by the numeraire $P(t, T_k)$, we observe that the forward LIBOR rate F_k is a martingale under the T_k-forward measure. We make here the assumption that the forward LIBOR rate has lognormal dynamics

$$dF_k(t) = \sigma_k(t)F_k(t)dW_k(t), \tag{6.14}$$

where $W_k(t)$ is an N-dimensional Brownian motion column vector. The instantaneous covariance between Brownian motions $W_k(t)$ and $W_k^\dagger(t)$ is given as $\rho = \rho_{i,j}$, with $i, j = 1, \ldots, N$ and

$$dW_k(t)dW_k^\dagger(t) = \rho dt.$$

It is important to realize that only the forward rate $F_k(t)$ is a martingale under the T_k-forward measure. We will now show how to establish arbitrage free dynamics under other measures. In the LMM we want to propagate a series of adjacent forward LIBOR rates under a common measure. The common measures usually employed are the spot or terminal ones (Section 3.3). Once one is chosen, it is used in the simulation of all forward LIBOR rates.

The terminal measure $\mathbb{Q}^{k=N}$ is the equivalent martingale measure associated with the last maturity, and therefore only the last forward LIBOR rate process $F_N(t)$ is a martingale. To transform the forward LIBOR dynamics when we change measure, we use Girsanov's theorem and apply the Radon-Nykodim derivative

$$
\begin{aligned}
M(t) &= \frac{d\mathbb{Q}^k(t)}{d\mathbb{Q}^{k-1}(t)} \\
&= \frac{P(t,T_k)/P(0,T_k)}{P(t,T_{k-1})/P(0,T_{k-1})} \\
&= \frac{P(t,T_k)}{P(0,T_k)}\frac{P(0,T_{k-1})}{P(t,T_{k-1})} \\
&= \frac{P(0,T_{k-1})}{P(0,T_k)}\frac{1}{1+\tau_k F_k(t)}.
\end{aligned}
\tag{6.15}
$$

In order to use Girsanov's theorem we differentiate and obtain

$$
\begin{aligned}
dM^{-1}(t) &= \frac{P(0,T_k)}{P(0,T_{k-1})}\tau_k dF_k(t) \\
&= \frac{P(0,T_k)}{P(0,T_{k-1})}\tau_k F_k(t)\sigma_k(t)dW_k(t) \\
&= \frac{\tau_k F_k(t)\sigma_k(t)}{1+\tau_k F_k(t)}\frac{P(0,T_k)}{P(0,T_{k-1})}(1+\tau_k F_k(t))\,dW_k(t) \\
&= \frac{\tau_k F_k(t)\sigma_k(t)}{1+\tau_k F_k(t)}M^{-1}(t)\,dW_k(t).
\end{aligned}
\tag{6.16}
$$

This can be solved readily to yield a stochastic exponential form. Using Girsanov's theorem, the process for the Brownian motion under the measure associated with the previous maturity (on the time grid) is

$$
\begin{aligned}
dW_{k-1}(t) &= dW_k(t) - \frac{\tau_k F_k(t)\sigma_k(t)}{1+\tau_k F_k(t)}d\left[W_{k-1}(t),W_k(t)\right] \\
&= dW_k(t) - \frac{\tau_k F_k(t)\sigma_k(t)}{1+\tau_k F_k(t)}\rho_{k-1,k}(t)dt.
\end{aligned}
\tag{6.17}
$$

Taking this all together, we obtain the stochastic differential equation for the forward LIBOR rate with maturity previous to the terminal maturity as

$$dF_{k-1}(t) = \sigma_{k-1}(t)F_{k-1}(t)dW_{k-1}(t)$$
$$= -\frac{\tau_k\sigma_k(t)F_k(t)}{1+\tau_k F_k(t)}\rho_{k-1,k}(t)\sigma_{k-1}(t)F_{k-1}(t)dt + \sigma_{k-1}(t)F_{k-1}(t)dW_k(t).$$

(6.18)

This means that under a measure $\mathbb{Q}^i$, the drift coefficients, that is, the $\mu_k(t)$ terms in the SDE for F_k, $dF_k(t) = \mu_k(t)dt + \sigma_k(t)F_k(t)dW_k(t)$, are

$$\mu_k(t) = -\sigma_k(t)F_k(t)\sum_{l=k+1}^{i}\frac{\tau_l\sigma_l(t)F_l(t)}{1+\tau_l F_l(t)}\rho_{k,l}(t) \qquad\qquad k < i,$$

$$\mu_k(t) = 0 \qquad\qquad k = i,$$

$$\mu_k(t) = \sigma_k(t)F_k(t)\sum_{l=i+1}^{k}\frac{\tau_l\sigma_l(t)F_l(t)}{1+\tau_l F_l(t)}\rho_{k,l}(t) \qquad\qquad k > i. \qquad (6.19)$$

To obtain the dynamics of $F_k(t)$ under the terminal measure, we set $i = N$.

Now that we have introduced the model dynamics we are ready to review how to construct a matrix describing the correlation among the simulated forward rates as well as how the instantaneous volatility $\sigma_k(t)$ is calibrated. We will focus in particular on tools and techniques which will be used (or which can be easily extended) when working with the SABR LMM model.

6.3 The forward-forward correlation and its calibration

If we take any two forward rates $F_k(t)$ and $F_l(t)$ described by the following set of LMM processes

$$dF_k(t) = \mu_k(t)\,dt + \sigma_k(t)F_k(t)dW_k(t),$$
$$dF_l(t) = \mu_l(t)\,dt + \sigma_l(t)F_l(t)dW_l(t),$$

the Brownian motions $dW_k(t)$ and $dW_l(t)$ are correlated according to

$$\mathbb{E}^i\left[dW_k(t)dW_l(t)\right] = \rho_{k,l}dt,$$

where $\mathbb{E}^i$ is the expectation associated with the $\mathbb{Q}^i$ measure, under which we are working. The quantity $\rho_{k,l}$ (often referred to instantaneous or forward-forward correlation in the literature) is a fundamental ingredient of the LMM. We will be working with time invariant correlations, where $\rho_{k,l}$ does not depend on the time t but only on the forward rate maturity. All the results can be however extended to adopt a term structure of correlations (i.e., time dependency).

The estimation of the forward-forward correlation is a delicate task which needs to be performed according to our pricing needs. In particular, depending on the type of instruments which we want to price and hedge in our LMM framework, we might opt for two different routes. If the payoff is only slightly correlation dependent, such as in the case of LIBOR in arrears or swaptions, we might consider extracting the correlation matrix from a time series of forward interest rates. However, if the payoff that we want to price has a high correlation sensitivity, as in the case of a spread product, we should try to imply the correlation matrix from market quotes. The latter approach is more challenging, not simply from a *modus operandi* point of view, but mainly due to the lack of liquid quotes for correlation dependent (CMS spread options, for example) instruments.

The approach we describe in what follows is a historical estimation of the correlation matrix. It suits well the pricing of most interest rate derivatives traded nowadays. Moreover, it can be seen as the groundwork on which to build the required knowledge related to forward interest rate correlation matrices and their use in the LMM. Groundwork is needed also by the interested reader which wants to move on and approach the calibration of correlation matrices from market quotes; for whom we reference, for example, Dhamo (2011).

6.3.1 Historical forward-forward correlation estimation

The estimation of the forward-forward correlation from historical data requires a time series of forward interest rates. The length of this time series is very much a subjective choice. Also, the choice of the observation frequency (daily, weekly, etc.) of the time series can be chosen arbitrarily and based on the specific needs of a particular desk/department. Longer time series tend to provide more stable correlation matrices, as the arrival of new data has a lower impact on the covariance; the downside is that the correlation matrix does not respond quickly enough to market shocks and increasing correlations in stressed markets. Moreover, any smoothing procedures, outlier detection mechanisms or data omission needs to undergo thorough analysis, and cannot always be supported by sound mathematical arguments.

For a set of length D of historical dates t_d, we can calculate the forward rates $F_k(t_d)$ for the maturities $T_1, \ldots, T_N$. This results in a time series of forward rates for each maturity T_k.

There are many different ways to calculate returns, depending on the underlying model assumptions. When dealing with a lognormal distribution, consistent with the Black framework, practitioners most often use logarithmic returns

$$\Delta F_k(t_d) = \ln\left(\frac{F_k(t_d)}{F_k(t_{d-1})}\right).$$

Our choice is to use arithmetic returns

$$\Delta F_k(t_d) = \left(\frac{F_k(t_d)}{F_k(t_{d-1})}\right) - 1, \tag{6.20}$$

which can be employed in a more general modelling framework. Anyhow, for small date intervals (hence small changes in returns) the results of both approaches are nearly identical.

From the historical return series, an average historical change in each forward rate can be calculated using the sample average estimator

$$\overline{\Delta F_k} = \frac{1}{D} \sum_{d=1}^{D} \Delta F_k(t_d).$$

Employing $\overline{\Delta F_k}$, we obtain the standard deviation

$$\mathrm{Std}(\Delta F_k) = \sqrt{\frac{1}{D-1} \sum_{d=1}^{D} \left(\Delta F_k(t_d) - \overline{\Delta F_k}\right)^2},$$

and the covariance

$$\mathrm{Cov}(\Delta F_k, \Delta F_l) = \frac{1}{D-1} \sum_{d=1}^{D} \left(\Delta F_k(t_d) - \overline{\Delta F_k}\right)\left(\Delta F_l(t_d) - \overline{\Delta F_l}\right),$$

between two forward rates.

Table 6.2 Properties characterizing a valid forward-forward correlation matrix

- $\rho_{k,l}^{hist}(\Delta F_k, \Delta F_l)$ is positive (semi) definite,
- along a matrix row, the entries $\rho_{k,l}^{hist}(\Delta F_k, \Delta F_l)$ are desired to be monotonically decreasing for $l \geq k$,
- along a matrix column, the entries $\rho_{k,l}^{hist}(\Delta F_k, \Delta F_l)$ are desired to be monotonically decreasing for $k \geq l$.

The historical correlation between the forward interest rate increments ΔF_k, ΔF_l of the forward rates maturing at times T_k and T_l then simply follows

$$\rho_{k,l}^{hist}(\Delta F_k, \Delta F_l) = \frac{\text{Cov}(\Delta F_k, \Delta F_l)}{\text{Std}(\Delta F_k)\,\text{Std}(\Delta F_l)}. \tag{6.21}$$

Unfortunately, a correlation matrix obtained using this simple procedure presents, most of the time, spurious entries and irregularities which need to be smoothed out. Some general properties (see, e.g., Brigo and Mercurio 2006), which help to confine these unwanted features, are reported in Table 6.2. To refine and polish the historical correlation matrix, practitioners usually resort to two simple mechanisms. They smooth the curves used to obtain the time series of forward rates and they calibrate a parametric form (which observe the properties listed in Table 6.2 by construction) to the historical correlation matrix.

6.3.2 Smoothing the historical forward-forward correlation: Svensson, Nelson and Siegel approach

The anomalies in the forward-forward correlations are often linked to the way in which we build, bootstrap and interpolate our forward curves. The curve construction apparatus can be excellent for the trader's needs to price and risk manage their books, but sometimes it becomes problematic when building smooth correlation matrices. Further intervention, in the form of a different forward curve construction methodology, can obviously alleviate the problem. Another approach is the possibility of fitting the forward curves to a more parsimonious parametric function. The disadvantage is a simplification of the shapes that our forward curve can exhibit; however this helps to reduce the variance of the forward rates, and improves the smoothness of the historical correlation matrix.

A reduced parametric form which suits our needs is, for example, the one proposed in Svensson (1994). It is a six-factor parametric form introduced as an extension of Nelson and Siegel (1987), and defined in terms of instantaneous forward rates $f(t, T_k)$ as:

$$f(t, T_k) = \alpha + \beta e^{-\frac{T_k-t}{\lambda_1}} + \gamma\left(\frac{T_k-t}{\lambda_1}\right)e^{-\frac{T_k-t}{\lambda_1}} + \delta\left(\frac{T_k-t}{\lambda_2}\right)e^{-\frac{T_k-t}{\lambda_2}},$$

which yields (using $R(t, T_k) = \frac{1}{T_k-t}\int_t^{T_k} f(t, u)du$) the following result for the spot interest rate $R(t, T_k)$ from t to T_k:

$$R(t, T_k) = \alpha + \beta\left(\frac{1-e^{-\frac{T_k-t}{\lambda_1}}}{\frac{T_k-t}{\lambda_1}}\right) + \gamma\left(\frac{1-e^{-\frac{T_k-t}{\lambda_1}}}{\frac{T_k-t}{\lambda_1}} - e^{-\frac{T_k-t}{\lambda_1}}\right)$$

$$+ \delta\left(\frac{1-e^{-\frac{T_k-t}{\lambda_2}}}{\frac{T_k-t}{\lambda_2}} - e^{-\frac{T_k-t}{\lambda_2}}\right).$$

The parameters α, β, γ, δ, λ_1 and λ_2 need to be calibrated to the spot rates obtained from the projection curve. Once these are calibrated, the forward rates are then calculated using

$$F_k(t) = \frac{1}{\tau_k}\left(\frac{e^{-R(t,T_{k-1})(T_{k-1}-t)}}{e^{-R(t,T_k)(T_k-t)}} - 1\right),$$

where we have substituted the following relationship (Equation (3.5))

$$P(t, T_k) = e^{-R(t,T_k)(T_k-t)},$$

into Equation (3.18).

Using these smoothed forward curves to calculate forwards, forward returns and hence the forward-forward correlation matrix has an enormous potential to increase the smoothness of the matrix, as can be seen in Figure 6.1.

The procedure just described suffers, nevertheless, from two main pitfalls. The first one is related to the reduction of parameters implied by this technique. Although six parameters can generally be considered enough to describe the forward curve evolution there might be instances in which this could be a too simplistic framework (Section 6.5.1). The second pitfall is related to the difficulties of the calibration of the parameters α, β, γ, δ, λ_1 and λ_2. The procedure is quite lengthy and the final result is highly dependent on the starting values chosen for the parameters to be calibrated.

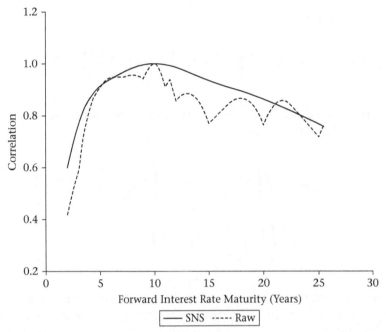

Figure 6.1 Comparison of the correlation generated using daily forward rates extracted from the pricing curve (Raw) and from the Svensson Nelson Siegel reduced parametric form curve (SNS). The correlation values are related to the 10y forward interest rate versus the other forward interest rate maturities

6.3.3 Forward-forward correlation parametrization

To generate a smooth and well-behaved forward-forward correlation matrix, we parametrize it using a low-dimensional functional form. The calibration algorithm consists of minimizing the sum of squared errors

$$\sum_{k,l\in\Omega} \left(\rho_{k,l}^{\text{hist}} (\Delta F_k, \Delta F_l) - \rho_{k,l} \right)^2, \tag{6.22}$$

where Ω represents the set of forward maturities available, $\rho_{k,l}^{\text{hist}} (\Delta F_k, \Delta F_l)$ are the entries of the historical forward-forward correlation matrix and $\rho_{k,l}$ are the elements generated by the chosen parametric form. The minimization procedure can be performed, as we did for the volatility calibration case (Section 5.5), by using the *numpy.optimize* package. The use of a parametric form not only provides a smooth and valid correlation matrix but it also helps to reduce the computational burden, as a full correlation matrix can be built employing a simple equation consisting of very few parameters. Many correlation parametrization forms, which can accommodate various types of calibration needs, have been presented, over the past years, in the literature. We will review three different parametrizations, presented in Rebonato (2004), all part of the same evolutionary pattern, which lead to the form we have chosen for our tests (Section 6.3.4). For an overview of various other approaches used by practitioners, we refer the interested reader to Brigo and Mercurio (2006).

6.3.3.1 Exponential parametrization

The simplest functional form for a correlation matrix decays with increasing distance (where by, distance, we mean the difference in maturities $|T_k - T_l|$); it is defined as

$$\rho_{k,l} = e^{-\beta|T_k - T_l|}, \tag{6.23}$$

where β is a constant.

The matrix diagonals produced by this form are constant, which prevents us from obtaining a good fit to the usual shapes seen in the historical forward-forward correlation matrices. A visual representation of the matrix generated by this parametric form, using $\beta = 0.05$, is reported in Figure 6.2.

6.3.3.2 Exponential parametrization with decay control

A more advanced correlation parametrization has a terminal ρ_∞ which helps to control how the correlation decays:

$$\rho_{k,l} = \rho_\infty + (1 - \rho_\infty) e^{-\beta|T_k - T_l|}. \tag{6.24}$$

The parameter ρ_∞ is usually kept fixed during the calibration routine and can be approximated by the correlation value between the farthest apart forward rates observed in the historical correlation matrix (i.e., for a matrix with N entries: $\rho_\infty = \rho_{1,N}$). If, for example, the first row of our historical correlation matrix appears as in Table 6.3, we will set $\rho_\infty = 0.4$.

A visual representation of the matrix generated by this parametric form, using $\beta = 0.1$ and $\rho_\infty = 0.4$, is reported in Figure 6.3.

Table 6.3 First row entries of a historical forward-forward correlation matrix for semi-annual spanning forward rates

	1y	1.5y	2y	...	30y
1y	1	0.98	0.96	...	0.4

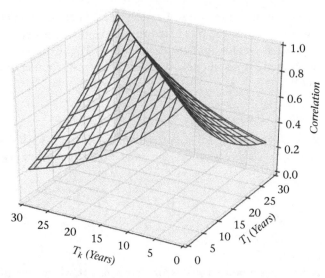

Figure 6.2 Forward-forward correlation matrix generated using the exponential parametrization, Equation (6.23), with $\beta = 0.05$

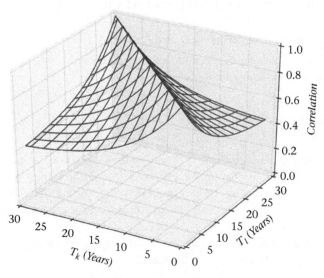

Figure 6.3 Forward-forward correlation matrix generated using the exponential parametrization with decay control, Equation (6.24), with the following set of parameters: $\beta = 0.05$, $\rho_\infty = 0.4$

6.3.3.3 Double exponential parametrization

An extension of the exponential parametrization with decay control is characterized by a 'double exponential' function

$$\rho_{k,l} = \rho_\infty + (1 - \rho_\infty)\, e^{-\beta|T_k - T_l|}\, e^{-\min(T_k, T_l)\alpha}, \tag{6.25}$$

where α and β are constants.

This form allows the long end of the correlation term structure to decrease less strongly. This is a feature typically seen in the historical forward-forward correlation matrix. Its financial interpretation is that the forward rates at the long end of the forward curve tend to be more correlated than the ones at the short end. A visual representation of the matrix generated by this parametric form, using $\alpha = 0.1$, $\beta = 0.1$ and $\rho_\infty = 0.4$, is reported in Figure 6.4. The Python code for this parametrization is presented in Table 6.4.

Table 6.4 Double exponential correlation parametrization – Python code

```
import numpy

def generateParametricCorrelationMatrix(alpha, beta,
rho_inf, maturity_grid):
    '''
    Function which generates a correlation matrix
    using the double exponential parameterization.

    @var alpha: alpha parameter
    @var beta: alpha parameter
    @var rho_inf: alpha parameter
    @var maturity_grid: represents a list containing the
    forward rate maturities which we are going to model.
    For example, if we want to model the semi-annual
    forward rates maturing between 1 and 5 years from now,
    we will set:
    maturity_grid = [1, 1.5, 2, 2.5, 3, 3.5, 4, 4.5, 5]
    '''
    grid = range(maturity_grid)
    # Create a null correlation matrix
    corr_matrix = numpy.zeros((grid, grid))
    for i in grid:
        for j in grid:
            first_e = numpy.exp(-beta * abs(maturity_grid[i]
                                - maturity_grid[j]))
            second_e = numpy.exp(-alpha * min(maturity_grid[i],
                                maturity_grid[j]))
            corr_matrix[i,j] = (rho_inf + (1.0 - rho_inf) *
                                first_e * second_e)
    return corr_matrix
```

6.3.4 Forward-forward correlation calibration tests

Following the steps described in Section 6.3.1, we have generated a historical forward-forward correlation matrix with 60×60 entries. The size of the matrix is determined by the maturities T_k corresponding to the forward rates F_k that we want

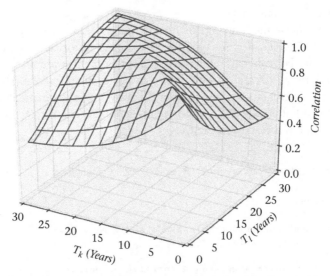

Figure 6.4 Forward-forward correlation matrix generated using the double exponential parametrization, Equation (6.25), with the following set of parameters: $\alpha = 0.1$, $\beta = 0.1$, $\rho_\infty = 0.4$

Table 6.5 Double exponential correlation form parameters obtained from the calibration to CHF and EUR historical forward-forward correlation data

	CHF	EUR
ρ_∞	0.41077	0.094
α	0.20682	0.20725
β	0.19386	0.21193

to model and their tenor. In our tests we have used forward rates with maturities from 0.5y to 30y and tenor $x = 6m$. We have used six months of daily data, spanning from June to December 2013. We have then employed a least square algorithm, such as the one described in Equation (6.22), to find the parameters (of the chosen correlation parametric form) which minimizes the difference between the historical correlation matrix and the parametric one. Among the three parametric forms presented in Section 6.3.3, we have chosen to work with the double exponential one. The fact that it is characterized by features typically seen in the historical correlation matrices (Section 6.3.3.3) gives a substantial amelioration in the fitting exercise when compared to the other parametrizations presented.

For CHF and EUR data, the calibration has produced the set of parameters reported in Table 6.5. The full correlation matrices generated using these parameters are displayed in Figures 6.5 and 6.6, respectively.

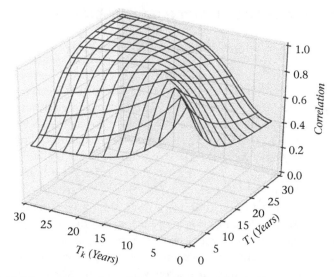

Figure 6.5 CHF forward-forward correlation obtained using the double exponential parametrization with parameters: $\alpha = 0.20682$, $\beta = 0.19386$, $\rho_\infty = 0.41077$

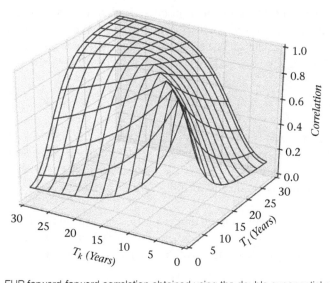

Figure 6.6 EUR forward-forward correlation obtained using the double exponential parametrization with parameters: $\alpha = 0.20725$, $\beta = 0.21193$, $\rho_\infty = 0.094$

6.4 Volatility parametrization and calibration

6.4.1 Calibrating to a term structure of ATM caplet volatilities

The term structure of instantaneous ATM caplet volatilities seen in practice is generally characterized by two forms. The first one is humped, where the instantaneous volatility increases in the short term of the curve, reaches a hump at mid-term expiries (e.g., the peak of the hump can be generally seen between the $2y$ and $5y$ expiry) and then it decreases. The second form is a monotonically decreasing one. The observation of this recurrent structure has led practitioners (see, e.g., Rebonato 1998, Brigo and Mercurio 2006) to think of the instantaneous volatility as a homogeneous function in time. As a result, the instantaneous volatility is generally modelled and dependent only on the time left to expiry $T_{k-1} - t$ rather than through a factor solely depending on the expiry T_{k-1} or time t. An implication of this choice is that the future instantaneous volatility shape is considered to be exactly the same as it is today. In the following we calibrate the instantaneous volatility function to caplet volatilities through a function $g\left(T_{k-1} - t\right)$, hence

$$\sigma_k(t) = g\left(T_{k-1} - t\right).$$

A very vast selection of forms could be assumed by $g\left(T_{k-1} - t\right)$, as many functions can satisfy the requirements just described. Among this variety, one form which has gained widespread popularity amid the practitioners has been presented by Rebonato (see, e.g., 2002). The proposed instantaneous volatility for the forward rate F_k with fixing time T_{k-1} is given by

$$g\left(T_{k-1} - t\right) = \left(a + b\left(T_{k-1} - t\right)\right) e^{-c\left(T_{k-1} - t\right)} + d. \tag{6.26}$$

The term in brackets $a + b\left(T_{k-1} - t\right)$ describes a straight line; this is then multiplied by an exponential decay to give the bump shape which is then shifted up and down accordingly to match the required shape. The Python function which returns the instantaneous volatility defined in Equation (6.26) is reported in Table 6.7.

The Black implied volatility at time t of a caplet expiring at time T_{k-1} and paying at time T_k (hence, whose underlying is F_k) is given by Equation (4.2). This expression can be rewritten in terms of the parametric function $g\left(T_{k-1} - t\right)$ as

$$\sigma_k^B\left(y_{ATM}\right) = \sqrt{\frac{1}{\left(T_{k-1} - t\right)} \int_t^{T_{k-1}} g(u)^2 \, du}. \tag{6.27}$$

If we choose to work with Rebonato's parametrization, the integral $\int_t^{T_{k-1}} g(u)^2 \, du$ has an analytical solution. This feature allows us to compute it without using any numerical approximation.

The calibration of the a, b, c, d parameters appearing in Equation (6.26) is done by minimizing the sum of squared errors between the difference of the ATM caplet volatility $\sigma_k^{B-\text{MKT}}(y_{\text{ATM}})$ seen in the market at time $t=0$ and Equation (6.27)

$$\sum_{k=1}^{N} \left(\sigma_k^{B-\text{MKT}}(y_{\text{ATM}}) - \sqrt{\frac{1}{T_{k-1}} \int_0^{T_{k-1}} g(u)^2 \, du} \right)^2. \tag{6.28}$$

Practically this is done through one of the minimization functions present in *scipy.optimize*, where

$$\sqrt{\frac{1}{T_{k-1}} \int_0^{T_{k-1}} g(u)^2 \, du}$$

is computed using the Python code reported in Table 6.6.

Table 6.6 Compute the Black volatility $\sigma_k^B(y_{\text{ATM}})$ in terms of the instantaneous volatility parametrized using Equation (6.26) – Python code

```
import numpy

def getCapletVolatility(expiry, a, b, c, d):
    '''
    Return the caplet volatility at time t=0,
    computed in terms of the the instantaneous
    volatility function form proposed by Rebonato.

    @var expiry: caplet expiry (in years)
    @var a: parameter a of Rebonato's instant. vol. function
    @var b: parameter b of Rebonato's instant. vol. function
    @var c: parameter c of Rebonato's instant. vol. function
    @var d: parameter d of Rebonato's instant. vol. function
    '''
    a_sqr = a * a
    b_sqr = b * b
    c_sqr = c * c
    d_sqr = d * d
```

```
tau = expiry
exp_term = numpy.exp(-c * tau)
exp_plus_term = numpy.exp(c*tau)
term1 = (-2.0 * c_sqr * (a_sqr + 4.0 * a * d * exp_plus_term -
                         2.0 * c * d_sqr * tau *
                         exp_plus_term * exp_plus_term))
term2 = (2.0 * b * c * (2.0 * a * c * tau + a + 4.0 * d *
                        exp_plus_term * (c * tau + 1.0)))
term3 = (b_sqr * (-(2.0 * c_sqr * tau * tau +
                    2.0 * c * tau + 1.0)))
variance_expiry = ((1.0 / (4.0 * c * c * c)) * exp_term
                   * exp_term * (term1 - term2 + term3))

tau = 0
exp_term = numpy.exp(-c * tau)
exp_plus_term = numpy.exp(c*tau)
term1 = (-2.0 * c_sqr * (a_sqr + 4.0 * a * d * exp_plus_term -
                         2.0 * c * d_sqr * tau *
                         exp_plus_term * exp_plus_term))
term2 = (2.0 * b * c * (2.0 * a * c * tau + a + 4.0 * d *
                        exp_plus_term * (c * tau + 1.0)))
term3 = (b_sqr * (-(2.0 * c_sqr * tau * tau +
                    2.0 * c * tau + 1.0)))
variance_t0 = ((1.0 / (4.0 * c * c * c)) * exp_term
              * exp_term * (term1 - term2 + term3))

variance = variance_expiry - variance_t0
volatility =  numpy.sqrt(variance / expiry)

return volatility
```

Although the parametric form presented in Equation (6.26) can provide a really good fit to the market volatility $\sigma_k^{B-MKT}(y_{ATM})$, it is usually never capable of providing an exact match. Rebonato (2002) proposes to use

$$g\left(T_{k-1} - t\right) s_k, \tag{6.29}$$

where s_k can be considered as correction factors that ensure a perfect match to the volatilities seen in the market (if they are all chosen to be equal to 1, it implies that $g\left(T_{k-1} - t\right)$ has provided an exact match to $\sigma_k^{B-MKT}(y_{ATM})$). Their calibration, at time $t = 0$, is done using the following relationship:

$$s_k = \frac{\sigma_k^{B-MKT}(y_{ATM})}{\sqrt{\frac{1}{T_{k-1}} \int_0^{T_{k-1}} g(u)^2 \, du}}. \tag{6.30}$$

Table 6.7 Compute the instantaneous volatility in terms of the parametric form defined in Equation (6.26) – Python code

```python
import numpy

def getInstantaneousVolatility(t, expiry, a, b, c, d):
    '''
    Return the instantaneous volatility,
    computed in terms of the parametric
    form proposed by Rebonato, at a given time t.

    @var t: time at which we want to compute the
    instantaneous volatility (in years)
    @var expiry: caplet expiry (in years)
    @var a: parameter a of Rebonato's instant. vol. function
    @var b: parameter b of Rebonato's instant. vol. function
    @var c: parameter c of Rebonato's instant. vol. function
    @var d: parameter d of Rebonato's instant. vol. function
    '''
    tau = expiry - t
    instantaneous_vol = (a + b * tau) * numpy.exp(-c * tau) + d

    return instantaneous_vol
```

6.4.2 Swap approximation in the LMM

To compute swaption prices using the LMM, we are able to use some simplifications. Rebonato (1998) shows that the forward swap rates in Equation (3.22) can interpreted as a weighted linear combination of forward rates, according to

$$S_{m,n}(t) = \sum_{k=m+1}^{n} \omega_k(t) F_k(t), \qquad (6.31)$$

where

$$\omega_k(t) = \frac{\tau_k P(t, T_k)}{\sum_{j=m+1}^{n} \tau_j P(t, T_j)}. \qquad (6.32)$$

Rebonato (1998) has found that the variability of the weights is small in comparison with the variability of the forwards and approximated the $\omega_k(t)$ weight terms by their initial values $\omega_k(0)$ (also known as the weight freezing technique). This facilitates the computation of the swap rate, which is approximated as

$$S_{m,n}(t) \approx \sum_{k=m+1}^{n} \omega_k(0) F_k(t), \qquad t \in [0, T_m]. \tag{6.33}$$

6.4.3 Calibrating to the ATM swaption surface

Equation (6.33) can be used to compute the swap rate, hence price swaptions, in a LMM framework, where the forward rates F_k in the formula for $S_{m,n}$ are simulated. It is however necessary to calibrate the implied volatilities, used in this simulation, to the swaption market. Brigo and Morini (2003) proposed an automatic, fast and analytical swaptions calibration called the cascade calibration algorithm (CCA), which consists of solving a cascade of second-order algebraic equations.

Starting from Equation (6.33) we can rewrite the dynamics of the swap rate as follows

$$dS_{m,n}(t) \approx \sum_{k=m+1}^{n} \omega_k(0) dF_k(t)$$

$$= \sum_{k=m+1}^{n} \omega_k(0) \sigma_k(t) F_k(t) dW_k(t).$$

We then further approximate by setting the forward rates to their initial time value, which allows us to calculate the quadratic variation of the logarithm of the swap rate

$$\langle d\ln\left(S_{m,n}(t)\right), d\ln\left(S_{m,n}(t)\right)\rangle$$

$$\approx \sum_{k=m+1}^{n} \sum_{l=m+1}^{n} \frac{\omega_k(0) \omega_l(0) F_k(0) F_l(0) \rho_{k,l}}{S_{m,n}(0)^2} \sigma_k(t) \sigma_l(t) dt.$$

This equation has then simply to be integrated to obtain the Black implied swaption volatility in the LMM:

$$\left(\sigma_{m,n}^B\right)^2 T_m \approx \int_0^{T_m} \langle d\ln\left(S_{m,n}(t)\right), d\ln\left(S_{m,n}(t)\right)\rangle$$

$$= \sum_{k=m+1}^{n} \sum_{l=m+1}^{n} \frac{\omega_k(0) \omega_l(0) F_k(0) F_l(0) \rho_{k,l}}{S_{m,n}(0)^2} \int_0^{T_m} \sigma_k(t) \sigma_l(t) dt. \tag{6.34}$$

Brigo and Mercurio (2006) (who cover in a very detailed fashion how this calibration is done in practice) show how using Equation (6.34) it is straightforward to build a two-dimensional grid of piecewise constant volatilities which are able to reprice the calibrated ATM swaptions in a LMM framework.

6.5 Simulation

In order to price any exotic interest rate derivatives, we need to simulate the underlying forward rates using Monte Carlo methods. In this section we will describe how we can go about this and cover several techniques, often used in practice to improve computational efficiency and reduce the variance of the simulation results.

6.5.1 Factor reduction

Aiming at a fast and computationally viable simulation for our LMM is considerably important. One way to achieve computation speed is by reducing the number of random variables (factors) N.

If we are working with semi-annual forward interest rates, spanning a 30-year period, we would need to use, in our Monte Carlo scheme, $N = 60$ different correlated random shocks $dW(t)$ to simulate the path of the forward interest rates $F_1, \ldots, F_N$. Generating 60 correlated random numbers (using the Cholesky decomposition introduced in Section 5.7.3) at each time step of our simulation is a major bottleneck which we can overcome by employing a factor reduction.

As we can see from the correlation matrices reported in Section 6.3.4, forward rates, especially adjacent ones, are very highly correlated. This gives us the possibility to reduce the number of factors used in our simulation without losing 'too much' explanatory information. We could then reduce the number of random shocks $dW(t)$ needed in the simulation from N to n.

The quantity n to use is very much a subjective choice driven by the right balance between the type of products that we want to price (structures which have a high correlation sensitivity need more factors than low correlation sensitivity ones) and an adequate simulation speed: most practitioners use between 3 and 10 factors. Exhaustive studies on the topic published over the years (see, e.g., Brigo and Mercurio 2006, Rebonato 1998), show mixed results on the number of factors to be adopted so as to capture most of the actual forward curve dynamics seen in the market. These dynamics are generally of three types:

- Parallel Shifts: forward rates move in parallel.
- Twists: long-term forward rates increase while short-term ones decrease (or vice versa).

- Torsions: long-term and short-term forward rates increase while medium-term ones decrease (or vice versa).

An obvious candidate technique to be used to reduce factors is principal component analysis (PCA). This methodology however can be computationally cumbersome. Brigo and Mercurio (2006) propose an approach called eigenvalues zeroing, which borrows directly from PCA, with the advantage of being numerically fast.

A positive (semi) definite matrix ρ, with size $N \times N$, can be expressed as

$$\rho = Q \Lambda Q^{\dagger},$$

where each column of Q contains the eigenvector of ρ and Λ is a diagonal matrix whose elements are the eigenvalues of ρ. Eigenvalues zeroing is obtained by:

- setting to zero the $N - n$ smallest eigenvalues of the correlation matrix ρ,
- take the square root of the eigenvalues which have not been set to zero.

These two operations applied to the matrix Λ generate the matrix Λ^{reduced}. The matrix B is given by

$$B = Q \Lambda^{\text{reduced}}. \tag{6.35}$$

The reduced correlation matrix $\hat{\rho}^{\text{reduced}}$, which can be considered an approximation of ρ, is then given by

$$\hat{\rho}^{\text{reduced}} = BB^{\dagger}. \tag{6.36}$$

The matrix B, which corresponds to the Cholesky decomposition of $\hat{\rho}^{\text{reduced}}$, is then used to generate the correlated random shocks needed to perform our Monte Carlo simulation.

A drawback of this method is that, after zeroing the eigenvalues, the matrix $\hat{\rho}^{\text{reduced}}$ no longer has only ones on the diagonal. Brigo and Mercurio suggest that we consider it a covariance matrix and, in order to restore a proper correlation matrix, apply the following normalization

$$\rho_{k,l}^{\text{reduced}} = \frac{\hat{\rho}_{k,l}^{\text{reduced}}}{\sqrt{\hat{\rho}_{k,k}^{\text{reduced}} \hat{\rho}_{l,l}^{\text{reduced}}}}.$$

The Python code for the eigenvalue zeroing technique is reported in Table 6.8. We have used the NumPy singular value decomposition (SVD) function *numpy.linalg.svd.* We could have also employed the NumPy eigenvalue decomposition function *numpy.eid.* The reason behind our choice lies in the fact that *numpy.linalg.svd* can be applied to singular matrices, making the algorithm more stable.

Table 6.8 Reduce the correlation matrix rank through the eigenvalue zeroing technique – Python code

```python
import numpy

def reduceRank(corr_matrix, no_of_factors):
    '''
    Function which reduces the correlation matrix
    rank by employing the eingenvalue zeroing
    technique.

    @var corr_matrix: input correlation matrix
    containing the forward-forward correlations
    @var no_of_factors: number of factors that we want
    to employ
    '''
    B = None
    reduced_cov_matrix = None
    reduced_corr_matrix = numpy.zeros((corr_matrix.shape[0],
                                       corr_matrix.shape[0]))
    Q, lambda_, Q_inv = numpy.linalg.svd(corr_matrix)
    H = numpy.zeros((corr_matrix.shape[0], no_of_factors))
    for i in range(no_of_factors):
        H[i,i] = numpy.sqrt(lambda_[i])
    B = Q.dot(H)
    reduced_cov_matrix = B.dot(B.T)
    # Transform the covariance matrix into a correlation
    # matrix
    for i in range(corr_matrix.shape[0]):
        for j in range(corr_matrix.shape[0]):
            reduced_corr_matrix[i,j] = (reduced_cov_matrix[i,j]/\
            (numpy.sqrt(reduced_cov_matrix[i,i] * \
            reduced_cov_matrix[j,j])))

    return B, reduced_corr_matrix
```

Correlated Brownian motions using factor reduction: an example

We report here an example on how to use the eigenvalue zeroing to reduce the rank of the forward-forward correlation matrix. We also show how to generate correlated Brownian motions from the outputs given by the *reduceRank* function reported in Table 6.8.

Table 6.9 Portion of the correlation matrix generated using the double exponential parametric form and the parameters reported in Table 6.5

	1y	1.5y	2y	2.5y	3y	3.5y	4y	4.5y	5y
1y	1	0.9553	0.9141	0.8759	0.8407	0.8081	0.7780	0.7501	0.7244
1.5y	0.9553	1	0.9596	0.9219	0.8869	0.8542	0.8238	0.7954	0.7690
2y	0.9141	0.9596	1	0.9634	0.9291	0.8969	0.8667	0.8384	0.8119
2.5y	0.8759	0.9219	0.9634	1	0.9669	0.9357	0.9062	0.8784	0.8521
3y	0.8407	0.8869	0.9291	0.9669	1	0.9701	0.9417	0.9147	0.8891
3.5y	0.8081	0.8542	0.8969	0.9357	0.9701	1	0.9729	0.9471	0.9225
4y	0.7780	0.8238	0.8667	0.9062	0.9417	0.9729	1	0.9755	0.9521
4.5y	0.7501	0.7954	0.8384	0.8784	0.9147	0.9471	0.9755	1	0.9779
5y	0.7244	0.7690	0.8119	0.8521	0.8891	0.9225	0.9521	0.9779	1

Suppose that we want to simulate, under the LMM, the CHF semi-annual forward rates F_k maturing between $1y$ and $5y$, with

$$T_k \in \{1, 1.5, 2, 2.5, 3, 3.5, 4, 4.5, 5\}.$$

After having calibrated the double exponential parametric form, Equation (6.25), to the historical forward-forward correlation matrix, we obtain the parameters reported in Table 6.5. The parametric correlation matrix portion, corresponding to the chosen forward rates, is reported in Table 6.9.

Let us suppose that we have decided to use $n = 2$ factors in our LMM simulation. By passing as inputs to the *reduceRank* function the correlation matrix reported in Table 6.9 as well as

$$no\_of\_factors = 2,$$

we obtain the following result for the matrix B defined in Equation (6.35)

$$B = \begin{bmatrix} -0.9129 & -0.3663 \\ -0.9430 & -0.2719 \\ -0.9622 & -0.1528 \\ -0.9716 & -0.0274 \\ -0.9723 & 0.0898 \\ -0.9656 & 0.1888 \\ -0.9528 & 0.2643 \\ -0.9349 & 0.3145 \\ -0.9132 & 0.3404 \end{bmatrix}.$$

The matrix B corresponds to the Cholesky decomposition (Section 5.7.3) of $\hat{\rho}^{\text{reduced}}$. The sample paths used to simulate the forward rate processes in the LMM need to be divided into many steps. For example, a path from $t = 0$ to $t = T_{k-1}$ can be divided into n_{step} time steps, generating a time partition $0 = t_0 < t_1 < \cdots < t_{n_{step}} = T_{k-1}$. We will be drawing, at each time step $i = 0,\ldots,n_{step}$, an array $Z(t_{i+1})$ of independent random numbers (with normal distribution $N(0,1)$) $Z(t_{i+1}) = \left[Z^1(t_{i+1}),\ldots Z^n(t_{i+1})\right]$, where n is the reduced number of factors that we want to adopt. With a simple matrix multiplication we obtain the correlated Brownian motions required to simulate the forward rates $\widehat{F}_1(t_{i+1}),\ldots,\widehat{F}_N(t_{i+1})$, between t_i and t_{i+1}, as

$$\Delta W_{\widehat{F}_1}(t_{i+1}),\ldots,\Delta W_{\widehat{F}_N}(t_{i+1}) = BZ(t_{i+1})^\dagger \sqrt{t_{i+1} - t_i}.$$

If at the t_i step we have drawn the following array of random numbers

$$Z(t_{i+1}) = [-0.8514, 1.1600],$$

we obtain

$$BZ(t_{i+1})^\dagger = \begin{bmatrix} 0.3523 \\ 0.4875 \\ 0.6420 \\ 0.7954 \\ 0.9322 \\ 1.0425 \\ 1.1128 \\ 1.1556 \\ 1.1719 \end{bmatrix}$$

(the Python code to use to compute $BZ(t_{i+1})^\dagger$ is reported in Table 6.10). We should, at this point, multiply the above array by $\sqrt{t_{i+1} - t_i}$ to obtain $\Delta W_{\widehat{F}_1}(t_{i+1}),\ldots,\Delta W_{\widehat{F}_N}(t_{i+1})$ and use it at the t_{i+1} step of our LMM Monte Carlo simulation.

Table 6.10 Draw correlated random numbers – Python code

```
import numpy
# Seed the random number generator
numpy.random.seed()
```

```
def drawRandomNumbers(no_of_factors, cholesky):
    '''
    Draw a set of random numbers.

    @var no_of_factors: number of factors that we want
    to employ.
    @var cholesky: Cholesky decomposition of the
    correlation matrix describing the correlation
    among the random variables to simulate.
    '''
    if no_of_factors > 1:
        rand = numpy.random.normal(size = no_of_factors)
        return cholesky.dot(rand)
    else:
        return numpy.random.normal()
```

6.5.2 Simulation under two-curve framework

Extending the LIBOR Market Model to a multi-curve framework can be done in many different ways, depending on the desired accuracy and complexity. As suggested by Mercurio (2010) we could choose one of the following approaches:

- simulate the forward LIBOR rates and the OIS rates,
- simulate the forward LIBOR rates and the LIBOR-OIS spread,
- simulate the OIS rates and the LIBOR-OIS spread.

Mercurio adopts the first of these approaches and develops a new LMM set of equations (including drifts), for both the LIBOR as well as the OIS rates. The model proposed is quite involved numerically and poses several computational challenges. The results however lay the required theoretical background on which to base a simplified approach to the problem. Where numerical issues could be greatly reduced.

We propose a framework in which the forward LIBOR rates are stochastic and the LIBOR-OIS spread is fully deterministic (obtained from the $t = T_0 \equiv 0$ discount and forward curves), in order to keep the model simpler and more robust. The LIBOR-OIS spread is defined as

$$\mathfrak{Z}_k = F_k(0) - F_{d,k}(0). \tag{6.37}$$

We should also add that the new set of drift terms proposed by Mercurio (which we don't report here) are characterized by a whole set of new of parameters such as a correlation term between the LIBOR and OIS forward rates, as well as a specific instantaneous volatility and year fraction for $F_{d,k}$. In our framework we make the simplified assumption that the correlation term coincides with the LIBOR forward-forward one and that volatility and year fraction are equal between the LIBOR and OIS forward rates. With this in mind we will now rewrite the LMM drift terms (introduced for the single curve framework case in Section 6.2.2).

In the simplified, with constant $\mathfrak{z}_k$, multi-curve set-up just introduced, the drift coefficients $\mu_k(t)$ under a measure $\mathbb{Q}^i$ become,

$$
\begin{aligned}
\mu_k(t) &= -\sigma_k(t)F_k(t) \sum_{l=k+1}^{i} \frac{\tau_l \sigma_l(t)(F_l(t)-\mathfrak{z}_l)}{1+\tau_l(F_l(t)-\mathfrak{z}_l)} \rho_{k,l}(t) & k &< i, \\
\mu_k(t) &= 0 & k &= i, \\
\mu_k(t) &= \sigma_k(t)F_k(t) \sum_{l=i+1}^{k} \frac{\tau_l \sigma_l(t)(F_l(t)-\mathfrak{z}_l)}{1+\tau_l(F_l(t)-\mathfrak{z}_l)} \rho_{k,l}(t) & k &> i.
\end{aligned}
\tag{6.38}
$$

To obtain the dynamics of $F_k(t)$ under the terminal measure, we set $i = N$.

In a single curve set-up the spread $\mathfrak{z}_k$ is zero. It is straightforward to see that the above drifts correspond to the ones presented in Section (6.2.2).

The ideas, techniques and results related to the calibration of the instantaneous volatility $\sigma_k(t)$ as well of the forward-forward correlation $\rho_{k,l}$ presented in the previous sections are not affected by the particular framework in which we are working. They are equally valid in a single curve as well as in the multi-curve set-up just presented.

For ease of exposition we will now revert back to a single curve framework. This will allow us to present the concepts related to variance reduction as well as of sensitivities calculation, appearing in the next sections, in a leaner way. All the ideas presented could be anyhow extended also to a multi-curve LIBOR Market Model, such as the one just presented.

6.5.3 Variance reduction techniques

When we price an instrument through Monte Carlo simulations we know, from the central limit theorem, that the convergence is slow. The convergence order is one over the square-root of the number of simulations. For example, to increase the accuracy by a factor of two, we need to perform four times the number of simulations. In this section we will review several techniques, focusing on the LMM Monte Carlo, which can be used to reduce its standard error (Section 5.7.1) and improve its convergence.

6.5.3.1 Antithetic sampling

The simplest of this methodologies is to use antithetic sampling, which we have already introduced and analysed for the SABR Monte Carlo in Section 5.7.6. In the LMM, it is straightforward to apply this variance reducing technique. Using the Euler discretization a path from $t = T_0 \equiv 0$ to $t = T_{k-1}$ can be divided into n_{step} time steps, generating a time partition $0 = t_0 < t_1 < \cdots < t_{n_{step}} = T_{k-1}$, with $\Delta t = t_{i+1} - t_i$. We can evolve the forward rate as

$$\widehat{F}_k^+(t_{i+1}) = \widehat{F}_k(t_i) e^{\left(\widehat{\mu_k}(t_i) - \frac{1}{2}\sigma_k^2(t_i)\right)\Delta t + \sigma_k(t_i)\sqrt{\Delta t}W(t_{i+1})},$$

where $W(t_{i+1})$ has been obtained using $BZ(t_{i+1})^\dagger$ (as shown in the example reported in Section 6.5.1) and, at the same time, we compute the reflected path, at each time step, by changing the sign on the Gaussian variable vector $Z(t_{i+1})$, that is

$$\widehat{F}_k^-(t_{i+1}) = \widehat{F}_k(t_i) e^{\left(\widehat{\mu_k}(t_i) - \frac{1}{2}\sigma_k^2(t_i)\right)\Delta t - \sigma_k(t_i)\sqrt{\Delta t}W(t_{i+1})}.$$

We then take the average $\widehat{F}_k(t_{i+1}) = \frac{1}{2}\left(\widehat{F}_k^+(t_{i+1}) + \widehat{F}_k^-(t_{i+1})\right)$. The $Z(t_{i+1})$ are samples from a standard normal distribution with mean zero, though we may have a sample which has a mean slightly different from zero, so taking the average, we guarantee that our Brownian samples are centred at zero.

6.5.3.2 Control variates

Control variates are random variables whose expected value is known and is correlated with the value of the product we are estimating. For example, if we are valuing a complex product and we know a closed form solution for a similar, but simpler product, then the price of the more complex product can be expressed as $v_{complex} = v_{simple} + (v_{complex} - v_{simple})$. Since we know what v_{simple} is, we only need to estimate the difference $(v_{complex} - v_{simple})$ which should in fact be small when the simpler product is similar to the complex one. To be more exact, the simpler product should have a payoff similar to that of the product we are trying to price as well as known expected values in the probability measure we are simulating. For the LMM, it is typical to use a set of zero-coupon bonds and caplets/floorlets and possibly swaptions – the latter could be used, for example, as control variates when pricing Bermudan swaptions.

6.5.3.3 Importance sampling

The idea behind importance sampling is to change the measure under which the expectation is calculated to reduce overall variance. Suppose we have a random variable X, and we wish to estimate its mean under the measure $\mathbb{Q}$, that is, $\mu = \mathbb{E}^q[X]$. Under an equivalent measure $\hat{\mathbb{Q}}$, we have $\mu = \mathbb{E}^{\hat{q}}[X]$, where $\mathbb{E}^q\left[\frac{d\hat{\mathbb{Q}}}{d\mathbb{Q}}\right] = 1$. In both cases μ is valid and should evaluate to be the same; it might however be possible that the variance of $X\frac{d\mathbb{Q}}{d\hat{\mathbb{Q}}}$ under $\hat{\mathbb{Q}}$ is lower than the variance of X under

$\mathbb{Q}$, which could bring potential benefits (a more efficient Monte Carlo evaluation). To see how this could work, consider the extreme example where $\frac{d\hat{\mathbb{Q}}}{d\mathbb{Q}} = \frac{X}{\mathbb{E}^q[X]} = \frac{X}{\mu}$, which means that $\mu = X\frac{d\mathbb{Q}}{d\hat{\mathbb{Q}}}$. In this case we are not taking an expectation, so there is no randomness and no variance. This case would not be possible in practice since we would need to know $\mathbb{E}^q[X]$ which is actually what we would be estimating with simulations, though it should give the reader an idea of how these methods work.

Importance sampling has not been heavily used for simulations in the LMM, except for the case of pricing products with a knock-out barrier. The interested reader can find more details in Andersen and Piterbarg (2010).

6.5.3.4 Moment matching

A very practical and product independent variance reduction technique is moment matching. This technique takes advantage of the martingale property of a simulated process $X(t)$, which is a function of the simulated variables $x_1(t), ..., x_n(t)$, that is, $X(t) = X(x_1(t), ..., x_n(t))$. If we consider the usual discretization $0 = t_0 < t_1 < \cdots < t_{n_{step}}$, when applying the moment matching technique to the Monte Carlo simulation, all paths have to be simulated together, time step by time step. At each time step t_i, the expectation of the process $X(t_i)$ is calculated. The martingale property of $X(t_i)$ infers that the sample average is equal to the value at the initial time t_0, that is

$$E[X(t_i)] \equiv E[X(x_1(t_i), ..., x_n(t_i))] = X(x_1(t_0), ..., x_n(t_0)) \equiv X(t_0).$$

The martingale property is now forced onto the simulation by adjusting the simulated variables $x_1(t_i), ..., x_n(t_i)$ by an additive constant or by a multiplicative factor. In the case of a multiplicative factor f, this reads as

$$x_1(t_i), ..., x_n(t_i) \to f(t_i)x_1(t_i), ..., f(t_i)x_n(t_i)$$
$$\to X(f(t_i)x_1(t_0), ..., f(t_i)x_n(t_0)) = X(t_0).$$

The most obvious application of moment matching is the simulation of a forward process under the corresponding forward measure. The expectation of the forward remains constant through time, and the first moment of the distribution is replicated with no simulation error or bias. Therefore, any product with low vega and high delta is simulated accurately with a low number of simulation paths.

In the LMM, only one forward is a martingale under a specific measure, and therefore we cannot use the directly modelled entities. We can however exploit the general fact that every tradable asset divided by the numeraire is a martingale. The tradable assets are the zero-coupon bonds with future maturities $P(t, T_k)$ and hence for all $t > T_0$ and $T_k > t$ we find that

$$\frac{P(T_0, T_k)}{P(T_0, T_N)} = \mathbb{E}^N \left[\frac{P(t, T_k)}{P(t, T_N)} \right].$$

This is equivalent to saying that the forward LIBOR from T_k to T_N is a martingale. To remove unnecessary terms in the equation above, we employ a more practical approach by subtracting adjacent terms

$$\frac{P(T_0, T_k) - P(T_0, T_{k+1})}{P(T_0, T_N)} = \mathbb{E}^N \left[\frac{P(t, T_k) - P(t, T_{k+1})}{P(t, T_N)} \right]$$

$$= \mathbb{E}^N \left[\tau_k F_k(t) \prod_{j>k} \left(1 + \tau_j F_j(t)\right) \right]. \tag{6.39}$$

As can be seen in Equation (6.39), we now have an expression in terms of the forward rates themselves.

6.6 Risk sensitivities

We have discussed so far how one can obtain a price of an interest rate product using the LMM, but equally important is the ability to calculate the sensitivities of this price with respect to changes in the relevant market parameters (see Section 4.3 for an introduction on risk sensitivities). There are several approaches to calculating these risk sensitivities, and we will turn now our attention to some of the common techniques, and then discuss a relatively recent method brought to the financial community by Giles and Glasserman (2006), known as the adjoint method.

6.6.1 Finite difference methods

The simplest approach to calculating the sensitivity of a price with respect to one of its dependent parameters is to use a finite difference scheme as laid out in Section 4.3.4. The Monte Carlo simulation to calculate the price could then be performed another two times, once with the upshift, and once with the downshift, and we could obtain the first and second order derivatives. This is of course computationally very expensive and may lead to inaccurate results if the increment is too small or too big. We may also observe a large variance if we were calculating the sensitivities for products with a discontinuous payoff when the increment is small.

6.6.2 Pathwise sensitivities and likelihood ratio methods

To calculate sensitivities, we typically shift an underlying parameter by a small amount; the type of this parameter determines whether we are talking about pathwise sensitivities or likelihood ratio methods. Pathwise sensitivities put the dependence of the parameter on the underlying stochastic process, leading, by means of Monte Carlo simulation, to the estimation of sensitivities through the sample paths. For example, suppose we have $V(u) = \mathbb{E}\left[g(X(T))\right]$

$$\frac{\partial}{\partial u}\mathbb{E}\left[g\left(X(T)\right)\right] = \mathbb{E}\left[\frac{\partial g(X(T))}{\partial u}\right] = \mathbb{E}\left[\frac{\partial g}{\partial X}\frac{\partial X(T)}{\partial u}\right],$$

where by $\frac{\partial X(T)}{\partial u}$, we mean differentiating the path evolution.

If we instead put the dependence in the probability measure, sensitivities are computed by differentiating probability densities; such techniques are referred to as likelihood ratio methods. Concretely, suppose we use the definition of an expectation as an integral involving the probability density function $p(X)$ as

$$V(u) = \mathbb{E}\left[g(X(T))\right] = \int g(X)p(X(u))dX,$$

then we have

$$\frac{\partial V}{\partial u} = \int g(X)\frac{\partial p(X)}{\partial u}dX = \int g(X)\frac{\partial \log\left(p(X)\right)}{\partial u}p(X)dX = \mathbb{E}\left[g(X)\frac{\partial \log\left(p(X)\right)}{\partial u}\right].$$

This equation tells us that $g(X)\frac{\partial \log(p(X))}{\partial u}$ is an unbiased estimator of $\frac{\partial V}{\partial u}$. Both of these methods can be used within the context of the LMM. We will review the work of Glasserman and Zhao (1999) on this with emphasis on practical implementation.

6.6.2.1 Glasserman and Zhao's pathwise sensitivities

Consider a payoff g, which is a continuous (in the Lipschitz sense) function of the forward LIBOR rates on the time grid point T_γ. We would like to compute the derivative of this payoff with respect to the initial forward LIBOR rates, that is,

$$\frac{\partial}{\partial F_k(T_0)}\mathbb{E}\left[g\left(F_1\left(T_\gamma\right),\ldots,F_N\left(T_\gamma\right)\right)\right],$$

where the expectation is taken under some appropriate measure, for example, spot or terminal. To obtain a continuous pathwise delta estimator, we could bring the derivative inside the expectation, to obtain via the chain rule

$$
\mathbb{E}\left[\sum_{l=1}^{N}\left\{\frac{\partial}{\partial F_l\left(T_\gamma\right)}g\left(F_1\left(T_\gamma\right),\ldots,F_N\left(T_\gamma\right)\right)\right\}\Delta_{lk}\left(T_\gamma\right)\right],
\tag{6.40}
$$

where $\Delta_{lk}\left(T_\gamma\right)=\frac{\partial F_l(T_\gamma)}{\partial F_k(T_0)}$. We can approximate these continuous expressions (a $\hat{}$ is used to denote an approximation to a continuous expression) by simulating the LIBOR forward rates with their corresponding Euler discretization. With this method a path from $t=T_0\equiv 0$ to $t=T_\gamma$ can be divided into n_{step} time steps, generating a time partition $0=t_0<t_1<\cdots<t_{n_{step}}=T_\gamma$, with $\Delta t=t_{i+1}-t_i$. Using Equation (6.18), the incremental step can be written as

$$
\widehat{F}_l\left(t_{i+1}\right)=\widehat{F}_l\left(t_i\right)e^{\left(\widehat{\mu}_l(t_i)-\frac{1}{2}\sigma_l^2(t_i)\right)\Delta t+\sigma_l(t_i)\sqrt{\Delta t}W(t_{i+1})},
\tag{6.41}
$$

where the W's are correlated Brownian motions and

$$
\widehat{\mu}_l\left(t_i\right)=\sum_{j=\eta(i)}^{l}\frac{\tau_j\sigma_l\left(t_i\right)\sigma_j\left(t_i\right)\rho_{l,j}\widehat{F}_j\left(t_i\right)}{1+\tau_j\widehat{F}_j\left(t_i\right)}.
\tag{6.42}
$$

Note that this last equation doesn't have an $\widehat{F}_l(t_i)$ multiplier on the RHS since we are working with the log Euler discretization. $\eta(i)$ refers to the index of the next tenor date at time t_i. By taking derivatives with respect to F_l, we obtain the pathwise delta algorithm as

$$
\widehat{\Delta}_{lk}\left(t_{i+1}\right)=\widehat{\Delta}_{lk}\left(t_i\right)\frac{\widehat{F}_l\left(t_{i+1}\right)}{\widehat{F}_l\left(t_i\right)}+\widehat{F}_l\left(t_{i+1}\right)\sum_{j=1}^{l}\frac{\partial\widehat{\mu}_l\left(t_i\right)}{\partial\widehat{F}_j\left(t_i\right)}\widehat{\Delta}_{jk}\left(t_i\right)\Delta t,
\tag{6.43}
$$

with initial condition $\widehat{\Delta}_{lk}(t_0)=\mathbf{1}_{l=k}$. We notice that the following relationship holds

$$
\widehat{\Delta}_{lk}\left(t_{n_{step}}\right)=\frac{\partial\widehat{F}_l\left(t_{n_{step}}\right)}{\partial F_k(t_0)},
$$

which is consistent with the continuous definition. We can actually estimate these deltas from a single simulation without having to bump the initial values and recalculate, as would be the case using the finite difference method. These pathwise methods described here though do require a simulation of both Equations (6.41) and (6.43) which is computationally expensive (Glasserman and Zhao 1999). In particular, if we look at Equation (6.43) the first term in the summation needs to be recalculated for each time step. One method to increase the computational performance would be to make the approximation $\frac{\partial \widehat{\mu}_l}{\partial F_j} = 0$, since typically $\widehat{\mu}_l$ will be small, so derivations with respect to the forward rates can essentially be ignored; and at the same time, in the simulation of $\widehat{F}_l$ in Equation (6.41) we can use the initial value of $\widehat{\mu}_l$. However, Glasserman and Zhao found that this 'zero drift pathwise' approximation leads to inaccurate results and instead try to find a compromise: they replace the $\widehat{F}_l\left(t_{n_{\text{step}}}\right)$ with their initial values leading to a simplification of Equation (6.42), which we label with a superscript 0, to signify the use of the t_0 forward rates

$$\widehat{\mu}_l^0\left(t_i\right) = \sum_{j=\eta(i)}^{l} \frac{\tau_j \sigma_l(t_i)\sigma_j(t_i)\rho_{l,j}\widehat{F}_j(t_0)}{1 + \tau_j \widehat{F}_j\left(t_0\right)}. \tag{6.44}$$

This means that Equation (6.43) now becomes

$$\widehat{\Delta}_{lk}\left(t_{i+1}\right) = \frac{\widehat{F}_l\left(t_{i+1}\right)}{F_k\left(t_0\right)} \mathbf{1}_{l=k} + \widehat{F}_l\left(t_{i+1}\right) \sum_{r=1}^{i} \frac{\partial \widehat{\mu}_l^0\left(t_r\right)}{\partial F_k\left(t_0\right)} \Delta t, \tag{6.45}$$

where we have used $\widehat{\Delta}_{lk}(t_0) = \mathbf{1}_{l=k}$ in the summation. This is referred to as the 'forward drift approximation'. The derivatives in the summation can be precomputed improving computational efficiency.

One important step in the above derivation was the interchange of derivative and expectation leading to Equation (6.40), but this is only permitted for continuous payoffs. This means the forward rate approximation will only be valid for computation of Greeks for products with continuous payoffs, so would not work for example for products with a digital type payoff. To overcome this limitation, we can use the aforementioned likelihood ratio methods, which we will now discuss in more detail.

6.6.3 Likelihood ratio methods

When we want to add a drift to a Brownian motion, we can do this by adding a $\mu\,dt$ in the SDE; alternatively we can use Girsanov's theorem to add an equivalent drift by changing the probability measure (i.e., we can move this dependence of $F_k\left(t_0\right)$ from the simulated paths to the probability measure). This opens up the possibility of calculating sensitivities for products with discontinuous payoffs (assuming the probability density function is Lipschitz continuous). We will illustrate these methods in a financial setting by seeing how we could compute Greeks of options with discontinuous payoffs and give an example showing how risk sensitivities can be computed in an LMM setting (Giles and Glasserman 2006).

Suppose we have a process with final state $S(T)$ with a probability density function $p(S)$. Then using standard notation, the value of the contract is given by

$$V = \mathbb{E}\big[g(S(T))\big] = \int g(S)p(S)dS,$$

and the first order derivative of the price with respect to a parameter u is given by

$$\frac{\partial V}{\partial u} = \int g \frac{\partial p}{\partial u} dS = \int g \frac{\partial \log (p)}{\partial u} p dS = \mathbb{E}\left[g \frac{\partial \log (p)}{\partial u} \right].$$

In the literature, the quantity $\frac{\partial \log(p)}{\partial a}$ is called the *score function*. If we take $g = 1$, we get $\frac{\partial}{\partial u}\mathbb{E}[1] = 0$ and therefore $\mathbb{E}\left[\frac{\partial \log(p)}{\partial u}\right] = 0$. Not only can we use this property to check that we have derived it correctly, but it also allows us to use the score function as a control variate, as an aid to reduce variance. To illustrate these methods, we take as an example a payoff $g(S(T))$ where S is a geometric Brownian motion. The final lognormal probability density function is

$$p(S(T)) = \frac{1}{S(T)\sigma \sqrt{2\pi T}} e^{-\frac{1}{2}\left(\frac{\log\left(\frac{S(T)}{S(0)}\right) - \left(r - \frac{1}{2}\sigma^2\right)T}{\sigma\sqrt{T}} \right)^2},$$

and it can be shown that

$$\frac{\partial \log (p)}{\partial S(0)} = \frac{\log\left(\frac{S(T)}{S(0)}\right) - (r - \frac{1}{2}\sigma^2)T}{S(0)\sigma^2 T},$$

giving us a delta of

$$\frac{\partial V}{\partial S(0)} = \mathbb{E}\left[\frac{\log\left(\frac{S(T)}{S(0)}\right) - (r - \frac{1}{2}\sigma^2)T}{S(0)\sigma^2 T} g(S(T)) \right].$$

We observe that we can simplify this expression using the fact that $\log\left(\frac{S(T)}{S(0)}\right) - (r - \frac{1}{2}\sigma^2)T = \sigma W(T)$, yielding

$$\frac{\partial V}{\partial S(0)} = \mathbb{E}\left[\frac{W(T)}{S(0)\sigma T} g(S(T)) \right].$$

Note that this means we can estimate the delta in our Monte Carlo simulation at the same time as estimating the price. For completeness and for the interested reader, it can also be shown that vega in this context (Giles 2012) is given by

$$\frac{\partial V}{\partial \sigma} = \mathbb{E}\left[\left(\frac{1}{\sigma}\left(\frac{W(T)^2}{T} - 1\right) - W(T)\right)g(S(T))\right].$$

We consider now the multivariate case which will lay the foundations for showing how to apply this method to the LMM Greek computations. Suppose we have a multivariate normal X (n-dimensional vector) with mean vector $\mu(\alpha)$ and covariance Σ. Our goal would then be to calculate sensitivities with respect to the scalar variable u. We assume Σ has full rank and let the normal multivariate density of X be given by

$$p(x; \mu(u), \Sigma) = \frac{e^{\left(-\frac{1}{2}(x-\mu(u))^{\dagger}\Sigma^{-1}(x-\mu(u))\right)}}{(2\pi)^{n/2}|\Sigma|^{1/2}},$$

and as usual the expectation of any payoff g is given by

$$\mathbb{E}[g(X)] = \int_{\mathcal{R}^n} g(x)p(x; \mu(u), \Sigma)dx. \tag{6.46}$$

From this it follows that

$$\frac{\partial}{\partial u}\mathbb{E}[g(X)] = \int g(x)\frac{\partial p(x; \mu(u), \Sigma)}{\partial u}dx = \int g(x)\frac{\dot{p}(x; \mu(u), \Sigma)}{p(x; \mu(u), \Sigma)}p(x; \mu(u), \Sigma)dx, \tag{6.47}$$

where $\dot{p}(x; \mu(u), \Sigma) = \frac{\partial p(x;\mu(u),\Sigma)}{\partial u}$ is the derivative in the multivariate case. Glasserman and Zhao show with some simple algebra (differentiating and interchanging the derivative and integral) that the score function can be calculated as

$$\frac{\dot{p}(x; \mu(u), \Sigma)}{p(x; \mu(u), \Sigma)} = (x - \mu(u))^{\dagger}\Sigma^{-1}\frac{\partial \mu(u)}{\partial u}.$$

Note that we require smoothness in the dependence of the probability density function on u but not on the payoff g. If we now substitute this expression into

Equation (6.47), we have

$$\frac{\partial}{\partial u}\mathbb{E}[g(X)] = \int g(x)(x - \mu(u))^\dagger \Sigma^{-1}\frac{\partial \mu(u)}{\partial u}p(x; \mu(u), \Sigma)dx$$

$$= \mathbb{E}\left[g(x)(x - \mu(u))^\dagger \Sigma^{-1}\frac{\partial \mu(u)}{\partial u}\right], \tag{6.48}$$

where to make the last equality, we have used the definition of the expectation (Equation (6.46)). This equation tells us that we can use $g(x)(x - \mu(u))^\dagger \Sigma^{-1}\frac{\partial \mu(u)}{\partial u}$ as an unbiased estimator for the derivative on the left hand side. It is important to observe that we do not need to differentiate the payoff, hence we will not have problems for cases when it is discontinuous.

6.6.3.1 Likelihood ratio method and the LMM

In order to apply these methods to the LMM, we first discretize (on the time partition introduced in Section 6.6.2.1) Equation (6.41) and then take logs of both its sides

$$\log\left(\widehat{F}_l(t_{i+1})\right) = \log\left(\widehat{F}_l(t_i)\right) + \left(\widehat{\mu}_l(t_i) - \frac{1}{2}\sigma_l^2(t_i)\right)\Delta t$$

$$+ \sigma_l(t_i)\sqrt{\Delta t}Z(t_{i+1}), \quad l=1\ldots N, \tag{6.49}$$

where the Z's are independent standard normal random variables. In order to move the dependence of the initial forward LIBOR rates from the sample paths to the probability measure, we differentiate as though the drift were deterministic, while simulating the forward LIBOR rates with the original drift. We are able to use the likelihood ratio methods just discussed, since under the forward-drift approximation (Equation (6.45)) Equation (6.49) represents the evolution of a Gaussian process. More concretely, it describes the evolution of a vector of N rates driven by n normal random variables (factors).

Over a single time step, the covariance matrix B (Equation (6.35)) of the increments in Equation (6.49) has rank n, and if $n < N$, this covariance matrix is singular, rendering this method invalid. To overcome this problem, consider that over multiple time steps, we have

$$\log\left(\widehat{F}_l(t_i)\right) = \log\left(\widehat{F}_l(t_0)\right) + \sum_{j=0}^{i-1}\left(\widehat{\mu}_l(t_j) - \frac{1}{2}\sigma_l^2(t_j)\right)\Delta t$$

$$+ \sqrt{\Delta t}[\sigma_l(t_0)|\sigma_l(t_1)|\ldots|\sigma_l(t_{i-1})][Z(t_1), Z(t_2), \ldots, Z(t_i)]^\dagger,$$

where $[\sigma_l(t_0)|\sigma_l(t_1)|\ldots|\sigma_l(t_{i-1})]$ is a vector composed of the volatilities for different time steps $\sigma_l(t_j)$ concatenated into a single vector of length $n \cdot i$ and where the Z vector has been put into a column of the same length. At the t_i time step, all the $n \cdot i$-dimensional volatility vectors have been brought into the $N \times i \cdot n$ (number of rates by number of time steps times by number of factors) of matrix

$$
\Lambda(i) = \begin{bmatrix}
\sigma_1(t_0)|\sigma_1(t_1)|\ldots|\sigma_1(t_{i-1}) \\
\sigma_2(t_0)|\sigma_2(t_1)|\ldots|\sigma_2(t_{i-1}) \\
\ldots \quad \ldots \quad \ldots \\
\sigma_N(t_0)|\sigma_N(t_1)|\ldots|\sigma_N(t_{i-1})
\end{bmatrix}.
$$

Glasserman and Zhao argue that for sufficiently large i, $\Lambda(i)$ could have rank N, even if $n < N$. This means the covariance matrix $\Lambda(i)\Lambda(i)^\dagger$ of the $\log\left(\widehat{F}_l(t_i)\right)$, $l = 1,\ldots,N$ is invertible and the use of the deterministic forward rate approximation (Equation (6.44)) is possible. The following mappings should clarify how these LMM specific equations correspond to those we have seen in the likelihood ratio method

$$
\alpha \longleftrightarrow \widehat{F}_l(t_0),
$$

$$
X \longleftrightarrow \left(\log\left(\widehat{F}_1(t_i)\right),\ldots,\log\left(\widehat{F}_N(t_i)\right)\right)^\dagger,
$$

$$
\mu_l(\alpha) \longleftrightarrow \log\left(\widehat{F}_l(t_0)\right) + \sum_{j=0}^{i-1}\left(\widehat{\mu}_l(t_j) - \frac{1}{2}\sigma_l^2(t_j)\right)\Delta t, \quad l=1,\ldots,N,
$$

$$
\Sigma \longleftrightarrow \Sigma(i) \equiv \sqrt{\Delta t}\Lambda(i)\Lambda(i)^\dagger,
$$

$$
\dot{\mu}_l \longleftrightarrow \frac{\mathbf{1}_{l=k}}{F_k(t_0)} + \sum_{j=0}^{i-1}\frac{\partial\widehat{\mu}_l^0(t_j)}{\partial F_k(t_0)}\Delta t, \quad l=1,\ldots,N,
$$

where $\dot{\mu}_l$ represents the first derivative of μ_l with respect to $F_k(t_0)$.

With these correspondences, we can readily determine the likelihood ratio method delta estimator for an arbitrary payoff $g\left(\widehat{F}_1\left(t_{n_{\text{step}}}\right),\ldots,\widehat{F}_N\left(t_{n_{\text{step}}}\right)\right)$ as

$$
g\left(\widehat{F}_1\left(t_{n_{\text{step}}}\right),\ldots,\widehat{F}_N\left(t_{n_{\text{step}}}\right)\right)(X-\mu)^\dagger\Sigma^{-1}\dot{\mu}.
$$

Setting $i = n_{\text{step}} = N/n$ to make $\Lambda(i)$ a square matrix, allows us to write

$$
g\left(\widehat{F}_1\left(t_{n_{\text{step}}}\right),\ldots,\widehat{F}_N\left(t_{n_{\text{step}}}\right)\right)(\Delta t)^{-1/2}W^\dagger\Lambda^{-1}(i)\dot{\mu}.
$$

Glasserman and Zhao show further that the likelihood ratio method estimator for gamma

$$\frac{\partial^2}{\partial F_k^2(t_0)} \mathbb{E}\left[g\left(\widehat{F}_1\left(t_{n_{\text{step}}}\right),\ldots,\widehat{F}_N\left(t_{n_{\text{step}}}\right)\right)\right]$$

is given by

$$g\left(\widehat{F}_1\left(t_{n_{\text{step}}}\right),\ldots,\widehat{F}_N\left(t_{n_{\text{step}}}\right)\right)\left(\left[(X-\mu)^\dagger \Sigma^{-1}\dot{\mu}\right]^2 - \dot{\mu}^\dagger \Sigma^{-1}\dot{\mu} + (X-\mu)^\dagger \Sigma^{-1}\ddot{\mu}\right),$$

with

$$\ddot{\mu}_l = -\frac{1_{l=k}}{F_k^2(t_0)} + \sum_{j=0}^{i-1}\frac{\partial^2 \widehat{\mu}_l^0(t_j)}{\partial F_k^2(t_0)}\Delta t, \quad l = 1,\ldots,N,$$

where $\ddot{\mu}_l$ represents the second derivative of μ_l with respect to $F_k(t_0)$.

6.6.4 Adjoint methods

Over recent years, there has been a growing interest in the use of adjoint (also sometimes referred to as dual or backward) methods to compute sensitivities for derivative instruments (see, e.g., Capriotti and Giles 2011, Giles 2012, Giles and Glasserman 2006). The idea is to compute in a much more efficient manner the same quantities as when using the forward pathwise sensitivity approach. Adjoint methods have a long history in applied mathematics and have been successful in fields such as design optimization, optimal control theory and linear programming optimization.

6.6.4.1 Automatic differentiation

We start off by discussing the mathematical background with some simple examples on how this all works. Starting rather abstractly, consider that we would like to differentiate a vector v_i with respect to one particular element of input v_0. The derivative is denoted as $\dot{v}_i$, that is

$$\dot{v}_i = \frac{\partial v_i}{\partial v_0}.$$

Calculating the derivative of v_{i+1} with respect to the input then yields

$$\dot{v}_{i+1} = \frac{\partial v_{i+1}}{\partial v_0} = \frac{\partial v_{i+1}}{\partial v_i}\frac{\partial v_i}{\partial v_0} = D_i \dot{v}_i,$$

where we have introduced the derivative operator

$$D_i \equiv \frac{\partial v_{i+1}}{\partial v_i}.$$

Following on the same lines, this means that

$$\dot{v}_{n_{\text{step}}} = D_{n_{\text{step}}-1} D_{n_{\text{step}}-2} \ldots D_1 D_0 \dot{v}_0.$$

To compute, in the forward mode, we would multiply the matrices D_i from right to left, and for each input v_0, the computational cost would be proportional to the dimension of the input. Now let $\bar{v}_i$ be the adjoint of the derivative of output $v_{n_{\text{step}}}$ with respect to v_i

$$\bar{v}_i \equiv \left(\frac{\partial v_{n_{\text{step}}}}{\partial v_i} \right)^\dagger = \left(\frac{\partial v_{n_{\text{step}}}}{\partial v_{i+1}} \frac{\partial v_{i+1}}{\partial v_i} \right)^\dagger = D_i^\dagger \bar{v}_{i+1},$$

which gives us

$$\bar{v}_0 = D_0^\dagger D_1^\dagger \ldots D_{n_{\text{step}}-2}^\dagger D_{n_{\text{step}}-1}^\dagger \bar{v}_{n_{\text{step}}},$$

where we would start with $\bar{v}_{n_{\text{step}}} = 1$. The term $\bar{v}_0$ would give us the sensitivity of $v_{n_{\text{step}}}$ to all the elements of v_0 at a cost which is not dependent on the dimension of the input. This procedure fits into the realm of what is known as automatic differentiation. To see what this means in more detail, consider a computer calculation which creates a new value

$$v_{i+1} = g_i(v_i) \equiv \left(\begin{array}{c} v_i \\ g_i(v_i) \end{array} \right).$$

We can think of this new value as being stored in memory in the usual way, and we represent this as appending the memory vector each time a computation is done. A computer program can be considered as n_{step} such type of operations

$$v_{n_{\text{step}}} = g_{n_{\text{step}}-1} \circ g_{n_{\text{step}}-2} \circ \cdots \circ g_1 \circ g_0(v_0),$$

where the last element of $v_{n_{\text{step}}}$ would give us the value of interest $g_{n_{\text{step}}-1}(v_{n_{\text{step}}-1})$. In forward mode differentiation, we would have

$$\dot{v}_{i+1} = D_i \dot{v}_i, \quad D_i \equiv \left(\begin{array}{c} I_i \\ \frac{\partial g_i}{\partial v_i} \end{array} \right),$$

where I_i represents some identity vector. We now have

$$\dot{v}_{n_{step}} = D_{n_{step}-1} D_{n_{step}-2} \dots D_1 D_0 \dot{v}_0.$$

In reverse mode differentiation, we would have

$$\bar{v}_i = (D_i)^\dagger \bar{v}_{i+1},$$

giving us

$$\bar{v}_0 = (D_0)^\dagger (D_1)^\dagger \dots \left(D_{n_{step}-2}\right)^\dagger \left(D_{n_{step}-1}\right)^\dagger \bar{v}_{n_{step}},$$

where the last element of $\bar{v}_{n_{step}}$ is one and the other elements are zero. In order to carry out this computation, we would first need to perform the original forward calculation to compute and store the D_i, then go in reverse to compute the $\bar{v}_i$. In order to understand what these $\bar{bar}$ terms are, it is useful to look at the level of a single step computation, for example, consider $c = g(a, b)$, so that a and b are variables already defined and we wish to perform an operation on both of them and store this in a new variable c. Let us keep in mind that the subscripts i and $i+1$ express at which stage of the calculation we are. In forward mode we have

$$\begin{pmatrix} \dot{a} \\ \dot{b} \\ \dot{c} \end{pmatrix}_{i+1} = \begin{pmatrix} 1 & 0 \\ 0 & 1 \\ \frac{\partial g}{\partial a} & \frac{\partial g}{\partial b} \end{pmatrix} \begin{pmatrix} \dot{a} \\ \dot{b} \end{pmatrix}_i, \tag{6.50}$$

and in reverse (adjoint) mode we have

$$\begin{pmatrix} \bar{a} \\ \bar{b} \end{pmatrix}_i = \begin{pmatrix} 1 & 0 & \frac{\partial g}{\partial a} \\ 0 & 1 & \frac{\partial g}{\partial b} \end{pmatrix} \begin{pmatrix} \bar{a} \\ \bar{b} \\ \bar{c} \end{pmatrix}_{i+1}.$$

This gives us an algorithm for reverse mode differentiation

$$\bar{a}_i = \bar{a}_{i+1} + \frac{\partial g}{\partial a} \bar{c}_{i+1}, \tag{6.51}$$

$$\bar{b}_i = \bar{b}_{i+1} + \frac{\partial g}{\partial b} \bar{c}_{i+1}. \tag{6.52}$$

In other words, these equations give us the recipe on how to calculate the adjoint variables at each previous step i, given the adjoint variables at step $i+1$. At the final step n_{step}, these adjoint variables are equal to one for each of the outputs we would like to calculate the sensitivity for and zero for the output variables we are ignoring. On a computer, the notation would be simpler to write, for example, $\bar{a}_i + = \frac{\partial g}{\partial a}\bar{c}_{i+1}$. As a concrete example, suppose we have a multiplication, $c = g(a, b) = a.b$, so in total we have two steps and we would like to calculate the sensitivity of output variable $c = g(a, b)$, we set $\bar{c} = 1$ and the other two adjoint variables at the second step equal to zero, that is, $\bar{a}_2 = \bar{b}_2 = 0$

$$\bar{a}_1 = \bar{a}_2 + \frac{\partial g}{\partial a}\bar{c} = \bar{a}_2 + b.\bar{c} = 0 + b.1 = b, \tag{6.53}$$

$$\bar{b}_1 = \bar{b}_1 + \frac{\partial g}{\partial b}\bar{c} = \bar{b}_1 + a.\bar{c} = 0 + a.1 = a. \tag{6.54}$$

One thing worthy here of mention, and reported by Griewank (2000), is that a single multiply operation in the original calculation turns into two multiply-add operations in reverse mode, so the reverse mode has a cost factor, at most, four times that of the original calculation. Let us take a slightly more complicated example, before moving onto financial examples. Let us start with two variables a and b for which we would like to compute the output $c = f(a, b) = a^2.b^3$, followed by a third step where we calculate $d = g(c, a) = c^2.cos(a)$. Calculating the sensitivities of d with respect to the input variables a and b, in the usual forward way, would give us

$$\frac{\partial d}{\partial a} = 4a^3 b^6 \cos(a) - a^4 b^6 \sin(a),$$

$$\frac{\partial d}{\partial b} = 6a^4 b^5 \cos(a).$$

We could also obtain this result following the matrix multiplications in Equation (6.50), which would give us

$$\begin{pmatrix} \dot{a} \\ \dot{b} \\ \dot{c} \\ \dot{d} \end{pmatrix}_3 = \begin{pmatrix} 1 & 0 & 0 \\ 0 & 1 & 0 \\ 0 & 0 & 1 \\ \frac{\partial g}{\partial a} & \frac{\partial g}{\partial b} & \frac{\partial g}{\partial c} \end{pmatrix} \begin{pmatrix} 1 & 0 \\ 0 & 1 \\ \frac{\partial f}{\partial a} & \frac{\partial g}{\partial b} \end{pmatrix} \begin{pmatrix} \dot{a} \\ \dot{b} \end{pmatrix}_1,$$

$$= \begin{pmatrix} \dot{a}_1 \\ \dot{b}_1 \\ 2ab^3 \dot{a}_1 + 3a^2 b^2 \dot{b}_1 \\ (4a^3 b^6 \cos(a) - a^4 b^6 \sin(a))\dot{a}_1 + 6a^4 b^5 \cos(a)\dot{b}_1 \end{pmatrix}.$$

Reading from the coefficients of $\dot{a}_1$ and $\dot{b}_1$, we obtain the derivatives of the output with respect to the two inputs.

Now using the adjoint approach, we should of course arrive at the same result. We have three steps, and at the final step we have $\bar{a}_3 = \bar{b}_3 = \bar{c}_3 = 0$ and $\bar{d}_3 = 1$, since it is the output variable d whose sensitivities we wish to calculate. Working backwards one step, we have

$$
\begin{pmatrix} \bar{a} \\ \bar{b} \\ \bar{c} \end{pmatrix}_2 = \begin{pmatrix} 1 & 0 & 0 & \frac{\partial g}{\partial a} \\ 0 & 1 & 0 & \frac{\partial g}{\partial b} \\ 0 & 0 & 1 & \frac{\partial g}{\partial c} \end{pmatrix} \begin{pmatrix} \bar{a} \\ \bar{b} \\ \bar{c} \\ \bar{d} \end{pmatrix}_3 = \begin{pmatrix} \frac{\partial g}{\partial a}\bar{d}_3 \\ \frac{\partial g}{\partial b}\bar{d}_3 \\ \frac{\partial g}{\partial c}\bar{d}_3 \end{pmatrix} = \begin{pmatrix} -\sin(a)c^2 \\ 0 \\ 2c.\cos(a) \end{pmatrix},
$$

and going back to the first step we have

$$
\begin{pmatrix} \bar{a} \\ \bar{b} \end{pmatrix}_1 = \begin{pmatrix} 1 & 0 & \frac{\partial f}{\partial a} \\ 0 & 1 & \frac{\partial f}{\partial b} \end{pmatrix} \begin{pmatrix} \bar{a} \\ \bar{b} \\ \bar{c} \end{pmatrix}_2
$$

$$
= \begin{pmatrix} \bar{a}_2 + \frac{\partial f}{\partial a}\bar{c}_2 \\ \bar{b}_2 + \frac{\partial f}{\partial b}\bar{c}_2 \end{pmatrix}
$$

$$
= \begin{pmatrix} -\sin(a)c^2 + 2a.b^3.2c.\cos(a) \\ 0 + 3a^2.b^2.2c.\cos(a) \end{pmatrix}
$$

$$
= \begin{pmatrix} -a^4 b^6 \sin(a) + 4a^3 b^6 \cos(a) \\ 6a^4 b^5 \cos(a) \end{pmatrix}
$$

$$
= \begin{pmatrix} \frac{\partial d}{\partial a} \\ \frac{\partial d}{\partial b} \end{pmatrix}.
$$

Which is in agreement with the sensitivities calculated in the usual, non-adjoint way.

6.6.4.2 Giles-Glasserman method

Turning now to a financial context, Giles and Glasserman (2006) showed how adjoint methods could be applied to calculating Greeks in Monte Carlo simulations. Their method calculates pathwise sensitivities, but in contrast to the 'forward' pathwise calculation introduced earlier, they work backwards recursively using the adjoint method just discussed. We will start by describing a generic example to highlight exactly how and when the method can give us a computational advantage.

6.6.4.3 Cost of calculations

We start with the generic stochastic process

$$dX = a(X)dt + b(X)dW,$$

its Euler discretization scheme (omitting the usual $\hat{}$ notation for simplicity in the remainder of this chapter), on the time partition $0 = t_0 < t_1 < \cdots < t_{n_{\text{step}}}$, which reads as

$$X(t_{i+1}) = f_i(X(t_i)) \equiv X(t_i) + a(X(t_i))\Delta t + b(X(t_i))Z(t_{i+1})\sqrt{\Delta t}, \qquad (6.55)$$

where $\Delta t = t_{i+1} - t_i$ is the spacing on the time partition. In the pathwise sensitivity method, we need to calculate derivatives of the payoff $g\left(X(t_{n_{\text{step}}})\right)$, with respect to the initial values. For example delta is given by

$$\frac{\partial g\left(X(t_{n_{\text{step}}})\right)}{\partial X(t_0)} = \frac{\partial g\left(X(t_{n_{\text{step}}})\right)}{\partial X(t_{n_{\text{step}}})} \frac{\partial X(t_{n_{\text{step}}})}{\partial X(t_0)}.$$

We then observe that $\frac{\partial X(t_{n_{\text{step}}})}{\partial X(t_0)}$, which for simplicity we denote as $\Delta(t_{n_{\text{step}}})$, can be further expanded through a time step with the chain rule

$$
\begin{aligned}
\Delta(t_{i+1}) &= \frac{\partial X(t_{i+1})}{\partial X(t_0)} \\
&= \frac{\partial f_i(X(t_i))}{\partial X(t_0)} \\
&= \frac{\partial f_i(X(t_i))}{\partial X(t_i)} \frac{\partial X(t_i)}{\partial X(t_0)} \\
&= \frac{\partial f_i(X(t_i))}{\partial X(t_i)} \Delta(t_i) \\
&= D(t_i)\Delta(t_i),
\end{aligned}
$$

where $f_i(X(t_i)) = X(t_{i+1})$ and $D(t_i) = \frac{\partial f_i(X(t_i))}{\partial X(t_i)}$. Working iteratively through all time steps, we have

$$
\begin{aligned}
\frac{\partial g\left(X(t_{n_{step}})\right)}{\partial X(t_0)} &= \frac{\partial g\left(X(t_{n_{step}})\right)}{\partial X(t_{n_{step}})} \Delta(t_{n_{step}}) \\
&= \frac{\partial g\left(X(t_{n_{step}})\right)}{\partial X(t_{n_{step}})} D(t_{n_{step}-1}) \Delta(t_{n_{step}-1}) \\
&= \frac{\partial g\left(X(t_{n_{step}})\right)}{\partial X(t_{n_{step}})} D(t_{n_{step}-1}) D(t_{n_{step}-2}) D(t_{n_{step}-3}) \ldots D(t_0) \Delta(t_0),
\end{aligned}
$$

$$(6.56)$$

and $\Delta(t_0)$ is the identity matrix. Now suppose that the process X is in fact N-dimensional, so that the derivatives of the Euler approximation are $N \times N$ matrices. Remembering that the computation cost of multiplying two $N \times N$ matrices is $\mathcal{O}(N^3)$, this means the computational cost using standard methodology above would be $\mathcal{O}(n_{step} N^3)$. Equation (6.56) can be computed in an equivalent way as follows

$$
\begin{aligned}
\frac{\partial g\left(X(t_{n_{step}})\right)}{\partial X(t_0)} &= \frac{\partial g\left(X(t_{n_{step}})\right)}{\partial X(t_{n_{step}})} D(t_{n_{step}-1}) D(t_{n_{step}-2}) D(t_{n_{step}-3}) \ldots D(t_0) \Delta(t_0) \\
&= V(t_0)^\dagger \Delta(t_0),
\end{aligned}
$$

where the adjoint is defined as $V(t_{n_{step}}) = \left(\frac{\partial g\left(X(t_{n_{step}})\right)}{\partial X(t_{n_{step}})} \right)^\dagger$. The adjoint at t_0 is calculated using the relationship

$$
V(t_i) = D(t_i)^\dagger V(t_{i+1}), \tag{6.57}
$$

moving recursively from $t_{n_{step}}$ to t_0. These operations involve matrix and vector multiplications with a computational cost of $\mathcal{O}(n_{step} N^2)$.

6.6.4.4 LMM example

Giles and Glasserman gave as an example the calculation of Greeks in the LMM using the adjoint methods just described. Denson and Joshi (2009) extended their work by using the predictor-corrector method in the Euler discretization of the drifts. Capriotti and Giles (2011) introduced the idea of using 'binning' to obtain confidence intervals for correlation risk sensitivities since a standard automatic differentiation approach would not provide this. Capriotti and Giles also have a strong focus on the practical implementation and provide pseudo-code of example implementations.

In the LMM, we have an SDE which matches the following form

$$dF_k(t) = \mu(F_k(t), t, \theta)dt + \sigma(F_k(t), t, \theta)dW(t),$$

where θ is any parameter entering the dynamics such as the interest rate, for which we would also like to calculate a sensitivity. As discussed, the $F_k(t)$ process could be simulated through an Euler scheme defined as

$$F_k(t_{i+1}) = F_k(t_i) + \mu(F_k(t_i), t_i, \theta)\Delta t + \sigma(F_k(t_i), t_i, \theta)\sqrt{\Delta t}W(t_{i+1}),$$

where W is a vector of correlated unit normal random variables. To implement this, we would first (labelled below as subscripts with 1-2, meaning bringing us from step 1 to step 2 of the calculation) compute the drift vector $\mu(t_i) = \mu(F_k(t_i), t_i, \theta)$, then (labelled below as subscripts 2-3) we would compute the volatility matrix $\sigma(t_i) = \sigma(F_k(t_i), t_i, \theta)$ and we would then (labelled below as subscripts 3-4) use these to compute $F_k(t_{i+1}) = F_k(t_i) + \mu(t_i)\Delta t + \sigma(t_i)\sqrt{\Delta t}W(t_{i+1})$. These three steps constitute the computational stages needed to go from time t_i to t_{i+1}. In order to go from time step t_{i+1} to time step t_i, we need to work backwards through these three stages using the adjoint methods discussed. Using the previously introduced bar notation to denote adjoints, we need to proceed backwards as follows: first we need to go from $(F_k(t_i), \mu(t_i), \sigma(t_i), W(t_{i+1}), \bar{F}_k(t_{i+1})) \to \bar{F}_k(t_i)$. Using Equations (6.51) and (6.52), we can see that this backward propagation can be performed as follows

$$\begin{pmatrix} \bar{\sigma}(t_i) \\ \bar{\mu}(t_i) \\ \bar{W}(t_i) \\ \bar{F}_k(t_i) \end{pmatrix}_3 = \begin{pmatrix} 1 & 0 & 0 & \frac{\partial \bar{F}_k(t_{i+1})}{\partial \sigma(t_i)} \\ 0 & 1 & 0 & \frac{\partial \bar{F}_k(t_{i+1})}{\partial \mu(t_i)} \\ 0 & 0 & 1 & \frac{\partial \bar{F}_k(t_{i+1})}{\partial W(t_i)} \\ 0 & 0 & 0 & \frac{\partial \bar{F}_k(t_{i+1})}{\partial \bar{F}_k(t_i)} \end{pmatrix} \begin{pmatrix} \bar{\sigma}(t_{i+1}) \\ \bar{\mu}(t_{i+1}) \\ \bar{W}(t_{i+1}) \\ \bar{F}_k(t_{i+1}) \end{pmatrix}_4$$

$$= \begin{pmatrix} \sqrt{\Delta t}W(t_{i+1})\bar{F}_k(t_{i+1}) \\ \Delta t \bar{F}_k(t_{i+1}) \\ \sqrt{\Delta t}\sigma(t_i)\bar{F}_k(t_{i+1}) \\ \bar{F}_k(t_{i+1}) \end{pmatrix},$$

where $\bar{\sigma}(t_{n_{step}}) = \bar{\mu}(t_{n_{step}}) = \bar{W}(t_{n_{step}}) = 0$ and $\bar{F}_k(t_{n_{step}}) = 1$ at the last time step since this is the output variable whose sensitivities we wish to compute. The next step is to compute the adjoint of the volatility function $\sigma(t_i) = \sigma(F_k(t_i), t_i, \theta)$. Again, employing the machinery defined in Equations (6.51) and (6.52), we have

$$
\begin{pmatrix} \bar{F}_k(t_i) \\ \bar{\theta} \end{pmatrix}_2 = \begin{pmatrix} 1 & 0 & \frac{\partial \sigma(t_i)}{\partial F_k(t_i)} \\ 0 & 1 & \frac{\partial \sigma(t_i)}{\partial \theta} \end{pmatrix} \begin{pmatrix} \bar{F}_k(t_i) \\ \bar{\theta} \\ \bar{\sigma}(t_i) \end{pmatrix}_3 .
$$

Similarly, for the drift function $\mu(t_i) = \mu(F_k(t_i), t_i, \theta)$, the backward adjoint steps are simply to compute

$$
\begin{pmatrix} \bar{F}_k(t_i) \\ \bar{\theta} \end{pmatrix}_1 = \begin{pmatrix} 1 & 0 & \frac{\partial \mu(t_i)}{\partial F_k(t_i)} \\ 0 & 1 & \frac{\partial \mu(t_i)}{\partial \theta} \end{pmatrix} \begin{pmatrix} \bar{F}_k(t_i) \\ \bar{\theta} \\ \bar{\mu}(t_i) \end{pmatrix}_2 .
$$

Capriotti and Giles (2011) provide pseudo-code for an implementation of this for the case where the predictor corrector method is used.

Note

1. As a simplification, the LMM results presented in this chapter are related to a single curve framework. Ideas on how to extend the LMM to a multi-curve framework are reported in Section (6.5.2).

7 | SABR LIBOR Market Model

7.1 Introduction

The extensive analysis carried out in Chapter 5 has shown how well the SABR model is able to capture the volatility dynamics characterizing the vanilla interest rate markets. Its major limitation is however the impossibility of modelling more than one forward rate at a time. This deficiency makes the SABR model impractical in the valuation of exotic interest rate derivatives, since these have payoffs which depend on a combination of several forward rates. While evaluating these payoffs, it is critical to simulate all relevant forward rates under a single measure to avoid arbitrage in the pricing model. Obviously, we have already achieved this by simulating multiple forward LIBOR rates in a market model as shown in Chapter 6. The market models are calibrated to the hedging vanilla instruments, one per expiry, whose payoff references the LIBOR forward rates or swap rates desired. As some of the complex products, such as range accruals or ratchets, depend on several strikes per expiry, we realize that these models suffer from an important shortcoming – they can only be calibrated to one strike per expiry and therefore cannot model the volatility smile characterizing today's markets. Various attempts to overcome this limitation have been pursued by academics and practitioners, following two main directions.

The first one consists of incorporating local volatility in the LIBOR Market Model, an example is the displaced diffusion LMM (see, e.g., Brigo and Mercurio 2006). Practitioners realized this to be a too rigid solution, which is not actually able to accommodate all the possible variation of volatility smile shapes and forms seen in practice.

The second, and most promising, approach is to extend the forward rate dynamics in the LIBOR Market Model by introducing stochasticity in the volatility process (see, e.g., Andersen and Brotherton-Ratcliffe 2005, Piterbarg 2003, Wu and Zhang 2006). Although stochastic volatility is the common denominator of these models, they all differ in the way in which the volatility process is characterized. This difference leads to more or less cumbersome calibration procedures and or poor calibration results. A natural route to follow is leveraging and combining together the positive aspects, described in the previous chapters, characterizing the SABR model (excellent calibration results, clear interpretation of the model parameters, market standard to price vanilla derivatives, etc.) with the LMM. Obviously the extension to incorporate any shape of the volatility smile into the hedging and risk management of the trading book is a big improvement over the LIBOR Market Model. But what can be very appealing to the quantitative analyst and a definitive edge over the introduction of a brand new modelling alternative is the reuse of available calibration algorithms and code for the simulation. We also highly value the understanding of the model behaviour acquired when trading and risk managing using the LMM and SABR models.

The objective of this chapter is to present and analyse precisely a combined SABR LIBOR Market Model (SABR LMM).

7.2 Dynamics of the SABR LIBOR Market Model

The equations of motion of the SABR LMM are defined as

$$dF_k(t) = \mu_k(t)\,dt + \alpha_k(t)\,F_k(t)^{\beta_k}\,dW_{F_k}(t), \tag{7.1}$$

$$d\alpha_k(t) = \eta_k(t)\,dt + \nu_k(t)\,\alpha_k(t)\,dW_{\alpha_k}(t), \tag{7.2}$$

where the Wiener processes are correlated as

$$\mathbb{E}^i\left[dW_{F_k}(t)\,dW_{F_l}(t)\right] = \rho_{k,l}dt,$$

$$\mathbb{E}^i\left[dW_{\alpha_k}(t)\,dW_{\alpha_l}(t)\right] = \vartheta_{k,l}dt,$$

$$\mathbb{E}^i\left[dW_{F_k}(t)\,dW_{\alpha_l}(t)\right] = \phi_{k,l}dt,$$

where $\mathbb{E}^i$ is the expectation associated with the $\mathbb{Q}^i$ measure, under which we are working.

As we will expand later in this chapter, for the entries $\phi_{k,k}$, we have the following identity

$$\phi_{k,k}dt = \rho_k dt,$$

where ρ_k is the correlation between the Wiener processes governing the SABR model[1] (Section 5.2.4).

Various forms of the drift terms $\mu_k(t)$, $\eta_k(t)$ have been proposed over the years (see, e.g., Hagan and Lesniewski 2008, Henry-Labordere 2007, Mercurio and Morini 2009, Rebonato et al. 2009). In the next sections we will present, for practical reasons, only the drifts proposed by Rebonato et al. (2009) and Hagan and Lesniewski (2008). The interested reader is however referred to the aforementioned works to expand on other possible drift forms.[1]

7.2.1 Rebonato et al. drifts

In this section we will present the SABR LMM drifts (obtained using the general form) proposed in Rebonato et al. (2009). Although what follows was not explicitly presented in their work, we will refer to this drift form as the Rebonato et al. one, as a tribute to the authors we have been following to obtain the results here reported.

For the SABR LMM model dynamics, under the $\mathbb{Q}^i$ measure, defined by Equations (7.1) and (7.2), the forward rate drift $\mu_k(t)$ is given by

$$
\begin{aligned}
\mu_k(t) &= -\alpha_k(t)\, F_k(t)^{\beta_k} \sum_{l=k+1}^{i} \frac{\rho_{k,l} \tau_l \alpha_l(t) F_l(t)^{\beta_l}}{1+\tau_l F_l(t)} && k < i, \\
\mu_k(t) &= 0 && k = i, \\
\mu_k(t) &= \alpha_k(t)\, F_k(t)^{\beta_k} \sum_{l=i+1}^{k} \frac{\rho_{k,l} \tau_l \alpha_l(t) F_l(t)^{\beta_l}}{1+\tau_l F_l(t)} && k > i,
\end{aligned}
\tag{7.3}
$$

and the volatility drift $\eta_k(t)$ is defined as

$$
\begin{aligned}
\eta_k(t) &= -\phi_{k,k} v_k(t) \alpha_k(t) \sum_{l=k+1}^{i} \frac{\rho_{k,l} \tau_l \alpha_l(t) F_l(t)^{\beta_l}}{1+\tau_l F_l(t)} && k < i, \\
\eta_k(t) &= 0 && k = i, \\
\eta_k(t) &= \phi_{k,k} v_k(t) \alpha_k(t) \sum_{l=i+1}^{k} \frac{\rho_{k,l} \tau_l \alpha_l(t) F_l(t)^{\beta_l}}{1+\tau_l F_l(t)} && k > i.
\end{aligned}
\tag{7.4}
$$

To obtain the dynamics of $F_k(t)$ under the terminal measure, we set $i = N$.

7.2.2 Hagan and Lesniewski drifts

For the SABR LMM model dynamics, defined by Equations (7.1) and (7.2), the Hagan and Lesniewski drifts under the $\mathbb{Q}^i$ measure follow. The forward rate drift

$\mu_k(t)$ is given by

$$
\begin{aligned}
\mu_k(t) &= -\alpha_k(t)\,F_k(t)^{\beta_k} \sum_{l=k+1}^{i} \frac{\rho_{k,l}\tau_l a_l(t)F_l(t)^{\beta_l}}{1+\tau_l F_l(t)} && k < i, \\
\mu_k(t) &= 0 && k = i, \\
\mu_k(t) &= \alpha_k(t)\,F_k(t)^{\beta_k} \sum_{l=i+1}^{k} \frac{\rho_{k,l}\tau_l a_l(t)F_l(t)^{\beta_l}}{1+\tau_l F_l(t)} && k > i,
\end{aligned}
\tag{7.5}
$$

and the volatility drift $\eta_k(t)$ is defined as

$$
\begin{aligned}
\eta_k(t) &= -\nu_k(t)\,\alpha_k(t) \sum_{l=k+1}^{i} \frac{\phi_{k,l}\tau_l a_l(t)F_l(t)^{\beta_l}}{1+\tau_l F_l(t)} && k < i, \\
\eta_k(t) &= 0 && k = i, \\
\eta_k(t) &= \nu_k(t)\,\alpha_k(t) \sum_{l=i+1}^{k} \frac{\phi_{k,l}\tau_l a_l(t)F_l(t)^{\beta_l}}{1+\tau_l F_l(t)} && k > i.
\end{aligned}
\tag{7.6}
$$

To obtain the dynamics of $F_k(t)$ under the terminal measure, we set $i = N$.

The only difference between the drift form proposed by Rebonato et al. and the one proposed by Hagan and Lesniewski resides in the $\eta_k(t)$ term.

7.3 The correlation matrix Π and its calibration

Both set of drift expressions presented in Sections 7.2.1 and 7.2.2 share the same correlation terms: $\rho_{k,l}$, $\vartheta_{k,l}$ and $\phi_{k,l}$. If we consider all the k,l occurrences, these terms can be practically and easily accommodated into a matrix Π as follows

$$
\Pi = \begin{bmatrix} \rho & \phi \\ \phi^{\dagger} & \vartheta \end{bmatrix},
\tag{7.7}
$$

where:

- ρ represents the forward-forward correlation sub-matrix,
- ϕ represents the forward-volatility correlation sub-matrix and $\phi^{\dagger}$ its conjugate transpose,
- ϑ represents the volatility-volatility correlation sub-matrix.

The correlation matrix Π has $2N \times 2N$ elements; a visual representation of its entries, for $k \in \{1,\ldots,N\}$, is reported in Table 7.1.

Table 7.1 The correlation matrix Π

	F_1	F_2	$\dots$	F_N	α_1	α_2	$\dots$	α_N
F_1	$\rho_{1,1}$	$\rho_{1,2}$	$\dots$	$\rho_{1,N}$	$\phi_{1,1}$	$\phi_{1,2}$	$\dots$	$\phi_{1,N}$
F_2	$\rho_{2,1}$	$\rho_{2,2}$	$\dots$	$\rho_{2,N}$	$\phi_{2,1}$	$\phi_{2,2}$	$\dots$	$\phi_{2,N}$
$\vdots$	$\vdots$	$\vdots$	$\ddots$	$\vdots$	$\vdots$	$\vdots$	$\ddots$	$\vdots$
F_N	$\rho_{N,1}$	$\rho_{N,2}$	$\dots$	$\rho_{N,N}$	$\phi_{N,1}$	$\phi_{N,2}$	$\dots$	$\phi_{N,N}$
α_1	$\phi_{1,1}$	$\phi_{2,1}$	$\dots$	$\phi_{N,1}$	$\vartheta_{1,1}$	$\vartheta_{1,2}$	$\dots$	$\vartheta_{1,N}$
α_2	$\phi_{1,2}$	$\phi_{2,2}$	$\dots$	$\phi_{N,2}$	$\vartheta_{2,1}$	$\vartheta_{2,2}$	$\dots$	$\vartheta_{2,N}$
$\vdots$	$\vdots$	$\vdots$	$\ddots$	$\vdots$	$\vdots$	$\vdots$	$\ddots$	$\vdots$
α_N	$\phi_{1,N}$	$\phi_{2,N}$	$\dots$	$\phi_{N,N}$	$\vartheta_{N,1}$	$\vartheta_{N,2}$	$\dots$	$\vartheta_{N,N}$

7.3.1 Forward-forward correlation calibration

The SABR LMM correlation sub-matrix ρ coincides with the LMM forward-forward correlation matrix ρ introduced in Section 6.3. Consequently, all the analysis, studies and tests carried out for the LMM can be applied equally to the SABR LMM. An institution which is already pricing and hedging using a LIBOR Market Model can easily expand its productive correlation calibration machinery to the SABR LMM, at virtually no efforts and costs. Furthermore, as we will see in Section 7.3.2, the same tools can also be reused for what concerns the volatility-volatility correlation sub-matrix ϑ.

7.3.2 Volatility-volatility correlation calibration

The lack of traded products from which we could try to imply volatility-volatility correlation values forces us to estimate them from historical data. This translates into having a time series available of at the money caplet volatility values for the forward interest rate maturities T_k, with $k \in \{1, \dots, N\}$. In most markets the quoted volatilities do not usually span the whole range of maturities required (most often we can find quotes up to 20y expiry). Using a parametric approximation of the historical correlations allows us to extrapolate beyond these maturities.

The historical volatility-volatility correlation computation follows the exact same procedure pursued when estimating the historical forward-forward correlation (Section 6.3.1). We will briefly review the most important steps.

As for the forward-forward correlation case, we will be using, for a set of length D of historical dates t_d, arithmetic returns

$$\Delta\alpha_k(t_d) = \frac{\alpha_i(t_d)}{\alpha_i(t_{d-1})} - 1, \tag{7.8}$$

Table 7.2 Properties characterizing a valid volatility-volatility correlation matrix

- $\vartheta_{k,j}^{\text{hist}}(\Delta\alpha_k, \Delta\alpha_l)$ is positive (semi) definite,
- along a matrix row, the entries $\vartheta_{k,j}^{\text{hist}}(\Delta\alpha_k, \Delta\alpha_l)$ are desired to be monotonically decreasing for $l \geq k$,
- along a matrix column, the entries $\vartheta_{k,j}^{\text{hist}}(\Delta\alpha_k, \Delta\alpha_l)$ are desired to be monotonically decreasing for $k \geq l$.

to compute a time series of increments $\Delta\alpha_k$.

The correlation between the increments $\Delta\alpha_k$, $\Delta\alpha_l$ for the volatility process of the forward rates maturing at times T_k and T_l is then

$$\vartheta_{k,l}^{\text{hist}}(\Delta\alpha_i, \Delta\alpha_l) = \frac{\text{Cov}(\Delta\alpha_k, \Delta\alpha_l)}{\text{Std}(\Delta\alpha_k)\,\text{Std}(\Delta\alpha_l)}. \tag{7.9}$$

The correlation matrix obtained using Equation (7.9) has irregularities which need to be smoothed out. Some general properties, which help to confine these unwanted features, are reported in Table 7.2.

In order to smooth the historical correlation matrix, a parametric form (Section 6.3.3) is calibrated to it. The calibration algorithm consists in minimizing the sum of squared errors

$$\sum_{k,l \in \Omega} \left(\vartheta_{k,l}^{\text{hist}}(\Delta\alpha_k, \Delta\alpha_l) - \vartheta_{k,l} \right)^2, \tag{7.10}$$

where Ω represents the set of forward maturities available, $\vartheta_{k,l}^{\text{hist}}(\Delta\alpha_k, \Delta\alpha_l)$ are the entries of the historical volatility-volatility correlation matrix and $\vartheta_{k,l}$ are the elements generated by our chosen parametric form.

For the case in which the entries of the historical volatility-volatility matrix do not cover the whole $T_1, \ldots T_N$ range (due to the lack of quoted volatilities), we will simply calibrate the parametric form to the available data, and use the obtained parameters to generate a complete volatility-volatility sub-matrix ϑ, spanning from T_1 to T_N.

7.3.2.1 *Alternative correlation calibration methodology: correlations from GARCH volatilities*

We sketch here an alternative method for the estimation of the volatility-volatility correlation, which borrows from econometrics. It is in fact possible to approximate the volatility process through the use of GARCH models (see, e.g., Bollerslev 1986). From the time series of forward rates ΔF_k, historical volatilities can be implied by calibrating the parameters a_i and b_i of a GARCH model

$$\alpha_{\text{GARCH}}^2\left(t_{d+1}\right) = a_0 + \sum_{i=1}^{D_a} a_i \Delta F_k^2\left(t_d\right) + \sum_{i=1}^{D_b} b_i \alpha_{\text{GARCH}}^2\left(t_d\right), \tag{7.11}$$

such that the log-likelihood is maximized (cf. Francq and Zakoian 2004). It is often good enough to use an expansion of the first order, that is, $D_a = D_b = 1$. Alternatives to the simple GARCH models can be used, such as EGARCH or AGARCH. The GARCH approach has the advantage of being able to produce a stable time inferred for the $\Delta\alpha_{\text{GARCH}}$ terms. A drawback of this methodology is the use of historical instead of implied (hence forward looking) volatilities.

7.3.3 Volatility-volatility correlation calibration tests

The focus of this section is to run a volatility-volatility correlation calibration to real market data. Our references are, as usual, the CHF and EUR markets.

As we have seen in Section 7.3.2, in order to be able to build a historical volatility-volatility correlation matrix we need a time series of ATM volatilities. The latter has been generated by stripping (see, e.g., Hagan and Konikov 2004), on a daily basis (we could have however chosen a different observation frequency depending upon our needs, cf. Section 6.3.1), caplet volatilities from the end of day cap surfaces.

All the other calibration steps are the same as those followed for the forward-forward correlation case (Section 6.3.4). Using historical data collected between June and December 2013, a 60×60 matrix ϑ is built using Equation (7.9). This historical volatility-volatility correlation matrix is then approximated by a double exponential parametric form. This choice has been driven by the excellent fit to historical data provided by this parametrization. The reader can have a feel for the calibration quality that we have performed by referring to Figure 7.1 for CHF volatilities and Figure 7.2 for EUR volatilities. The obvious advantage of using the same parametrization, for both sub-matrices ρ and ϑ, in a productive environment is a rationalization of the code and procedures employed for the calibration routines.

The calibration produces the set of parameters reported in Table 7.3. The full correlation sub-matrices generated using these parameters are displayed in Figure 7.3 for CHF and in Figure 7.4 for EUR.

7.3.4 Forward-volatility correlation calibration

The forward-volatility correlation sub-matrix ϕ is not characterized by the same shared properties defining the sub-matrices ρ and ϑ (Tables 6.2 and 7.2). Additionally, its elements cannot be calculated from a historical time series as we

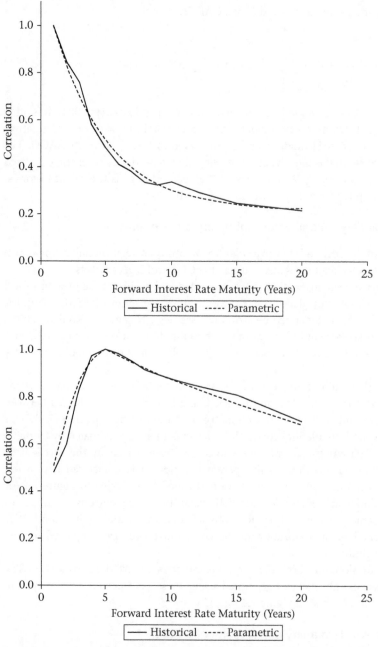

Figure 7.1 Double exponential parametrization calibrated to historical CHF volatility-volatility correlation. The correlation values are related to the 1*y* (top) and to the 5*y* (bottom) forward interest rate volatility versus the other forward interest rate volatilities

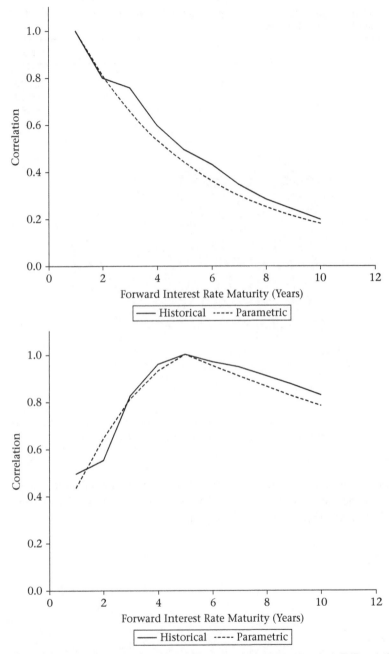

Figure 7.2 Double exponential parametrization calibrated to historical EUR volatility-volatility correlation. The correlation values are related to the 1y (top) and to the 5y (bottom) forward interest rate volatility versus the other forward interest rate volatilities

Table 7.3 Double exponential correlation form parameters obtained from the calibration to CHF and EUR historical volatility-volatility correlation data

	CHF	EUR
ϑ_∞	0.21456	0.05505
α	0.49016	0.36747
β	0.39957	0.32667

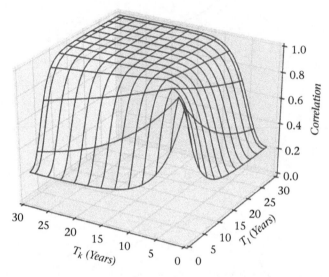

Figure 7.3 CHF volatility-volatility correlation sub-matrix ϑ obtained using the double exponential parametrization with parameters: $\alpha = 0.49016$, $\beta = 0.39957$, $\vartheta_\infty = 0.21456$

cannot directly link this correlation to any traded quantity. The only information pertaining to the sub-matrix ϕ that we have at our disposal are its diagonal elements. For each of them we define a mapping

$$\phi_{1,1} = \rho_1,$$
$$\phi_{2,2} = \rho_2,$$
$$\vdots$$
$$\phi_{N,N} = \rho_N,$$

where $\rho_1, \rho_2, \ldots \rho_N$ correspond to the correlations between the Brownian motions governing the SABR forward rate and volatility processes (Section 5.2.4) for a set of

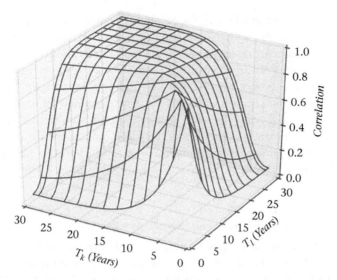

Figure 7.4 EUR volatility-volatility correlation sub-matrix ϑ obtained using the double exponential parametrization with parameters: $\alpha = 0.36747$, $\beta = 0.32667$, $\vartheta_\infty = 0.05505$

maturities T_k, with $k \in \{1, \dots, N\}$. We will present, in the remainder of this section, two ways in which the sub-matrix ϕ can be built.

7.3.4.1 Standard approach: diagonal parameters

This approach consists in fitting the SABR model parameters to the caplet/floorlet smiles for a set of forward rate maturities T_k, with $k \in \{1, \dots, N\}$, by setting each element of the array $\beta_1, \beta_2, \dots \beta_N$ to the desired value within the range 0–1 (Section 5.5.1). The values for $\rho_1, \rho_2, \dots \rho_N$ obtained from the calibration are used to populate the diagonal of the sub-matrix ϕ. We can then reduce the number of factors of the matrices ρ and ϑ from N to n, following for example one of the methods[2] presented in Rebonato et al. (2009), which will yield

$$\rho^{\text{reduced}} = BB^\dagger,$$
$$\vartheta^{\text{reduced}} = CC^\dagger.$$

Finally Rebonato et al. show how a reduced rank version of ϕ is given by

$$\phi^{\text{reduced}} = BC^\dagger.$$

Rebonato et al. show also various ways in which the matrices B and $C^\dagger$ can be calibrated to obtain a ϕ^{reduced} which has, on the diagonal, exactly or almost exactly (depending upon which of the methods presented is followed) the values $\rho_1, \rho_2, \ldots, \rho_N$ obtained by the SABR models calibration (we use the plural to emphasize that each SABR set of parameters calibrated to a particular volatility smile actually represents an independent model where each forward rate lives in its own world, cf. Section 5.1). We will not explore this approach further as it requires a recalibration of the matrices B, C every time a new set of $\rho_1, \rho_2, \ldots, \rho_N$ is obtained. Essentially this approach produces a domino effect: if we feel that we need to perform a new calibration of the SABR models, we are also forced to calibrate B and C. Considering the numerical burden which this entails, we propose in what follows an alternative method which might lead to a faster and leaner solution.

7.3.4.2 *Alternative approach: null foward-volatility correlations*

The idea behind this method is to obtain a null forward-volatility correlation sub-matrix. This can be achieved by fitting the SABR model parameters to the caplet/floorlet smiles for a set of forward rate maturities T_k, with $k \in \{1, \ldots, N\}$, by setting the constraints $\rho_1 = 0, \rho_2 = 0, \ldots \rho_N = 0$. Once the diagonal is set to zero we can safely set all the other elements of ϕ to zero as well. This approach is very appealing for a number of reasons:

- Using a null ϕ sub-matrix translates into a much simpler and faster construction of the matrix Π. The only two sub-matrices which need to be parametrized and calibrated to build Π are ρ and ϑ.
- The tests for the SABR calibration performed keeping ρ_k fixed to zero, have produced excellent fits to market data, for both CHF and EUR (Section 5.5.2). This assures us of the possibility to reprice correctly the quoted caplets/floorlets. This is a desired feature: as our exotic products will be hedged using vanilla instruments, a pricing consistency between the exotic and the vanilla books is of paramount importance. Additionally, setting $\rho_k = 0$ allows us to use the Antonov et al. zero correlation approximation (we will not carry on the calibration using the the Hagan et al. approximations due to the drawbacks presented in Section 5.8.4) to calibrate the SABR models to the caplet/floorlet smiles, which is characterized by a quicker and more stable calibration than the general correlation approximation proposed by the same authors (Section 5.9.3).
- The drift term of the $s(t)$ process in the SABR LMM (Equation 7.16) vanishes by using a null $\phi_{k,k}$, yielding a performance gain.
- As shown in Table 5.6, the SABR Monte Carlo scheme tests for the case $\rho_k = 0$ are characterized by a very low variance in the results. In practical terms this means that the Monte Carlo convergence can be easily achieved. Which in turns translates into a fast and accurate simulation.

A drawback of this approach is that when employed, the swap approximation introduced by Rebonato and White (2009) and presented in Section 7.5.3, does not work. This is however not a problem when the SABR LMM is used, as in the context of this book, for pricing and hedging LIBOR exotics (as this approximation is unecessary). We anyhow believe that also the reader interested in using the SABR LMM to price swap dependent instruments can benefit from the simplifications brought by employing a null forward-volatility correlation sub-matrix. As this set-up can be used to understand the basic model dynamics and would lay the ground for the more complex approach, introduced in Section 7.3.4.1, required to work with Rebonato and White approxmation.

Due to the advantages just described, we will adopt the null forward-volatility correlation approach as our elected working method, which we will be using in the remainder of the book.

7.4 Rebonato et al. SABR LMM parametrization

7.4.1 Volatility and volatility of volatility parametrizations

Rebonato (2007) proposes to define the instantaneous volatility of the forward rate $F_k(t)$ as the product between the parametric form $g(T_{k-1} - t)$ and a correction term $s_k(t)$ as

$$\alpha_k(t) = g(T_{k-1} - t) s_k(t), \tag{7.12}$$

which is consistent with Equation (6.29) specified for the LMM. The function $g(T_{k-1} - t)$ can have multiple forms (e.g., the one introduced in Equation (6.26) for the LIBOR Market Model); it is at the discretion of the department/desk to choose the one more appropriate for its needs.

Moving along the lines followed to obtain a parametrization for the instantaneous volatility, Rebonato (2007) suggests defining the instantaneous volatility of volatility as

$$v_k(t) = h(T_{k-1} - t), \tag{7.13}$$

where $h(T_{k-1} - t)$ is a parametric function which can be chosen, for example, analogous to $g(T_{k-1} - t)$. We will be showing, later in this chapter, how these parametric functions can be chosen, basing our analysis on real market data.

7.4.2 Diffusion processes

With the introduction of Equations (7.12) and (7.13), Rebonato (2007) and Rebonato and White (2009) propose a new parametric form for the SABR LMM

$$dF_k(t) = \mu_k(t)\,dt + \alpha_k(t)\,F_k(t)^{\beta_k}\,dW_{F_k}(t), \tag{7.14}$$

$$d\alpha_k(t) = g\left(T_{k-1} - t\right)ds_k(t), \tag{7.15}$$

$$ds_k(t) = \eta_k(t)\,dt + h\left(T_{k-1} - t\right)s_k(t)\,dW_{s_k}(t), \tag{7.16}$$

where s_k is a stochastic quantity.

The difference between the deterministic volatility LMM and the parametric SABR LMM is precisely in the s_k quantity. In the former we have a term structure of invariant correction terms s_k while in the latter we have a term structure of stochastic $s_k(t)$.

Equations (7.14), (7.15) and (7.16) allow us to rewrite the drift terms presented in Section 7.4. We report here the final results without proof. For more details on the derivation of the parametric form drifts the interested reader is referred to Rebonato et al. (2009).

Under the parametric SABR LMM the forward rate drift $\mu_k(t)$ is given by

$$
\begin{aligned}
\mu_k(t) &= -g\left(T_{k-1} - t\right)s_k(t)\,F_k(t)^{\beta_k}\sum_{l=k+1}^{i}\frac{\rho_{k,l}\tau_l g\left(T_{l-1}-t\right)s_l(t)F_l(t)^{\beta_l}}{1+\tau_l F_l(t)} & k < i, \\
\mu_k(t) &= 0 & k = i, \\
\mu_k(t) &= g\left(T_{k-1} - t\right)s_k(t)\,F_k(t)^{\beta_k}\sum_{l=i+1}^{k}\frac{\rho_{k,l}\tau_l g\left(T_{l-1}-t\right)s_l(t)F_l(t)^{\beta_l}}{1+\tau_l F_l(t)} & k > i,
\end{aligned}
\tag{7.17}
$$

and the drift $\eta_k(t)$ of the stochastic correction term $s_k(t)$ is defined as

$$
\begin{aligned}
\eta_k(t) &= -\phi_{k,k}h\left(T_{k-1} - t\right)s_k(t)\sum_{l=k+1}^{i}\frac{\rho_{k,l}\tau_l g\left(T_{l-1}-t\right)s_l(t)F_l(t)^{\beta_l}}{1+\tau_l F_l(t)} & k < i, \\
\eta_k(t) &= 0 & k = i, \\
\eta_k(t) &= \phi_{k,k}h\left(T_{k-1} - t\right)s_k(t)\sum_{l=i+1}^{k}\frac{\rho_{k,l}\tau_l g\left(T_{l-1}-t\right)s_l(t)F_l(t)^{\beta_l}}{1+\tau_l F_l(t)} & k > i.
\end{aligned}
\tag{7.18}
$$

As usual, to obtain the dynamics of $F_k(t)$ under the terminal measure, we set $i = N$.

In the remainder of the book, we will always use the parametric form of the SABR LMM just presented for our tests and analysis.

7.4.3 Calibrating $g(T_{k-1} - t)$ to a term structure of α_k

We have seen in Section 7.4.1 how to define the instantaneous volatility in terms of the parametric function $g(T_{k-1} - t)$. We are still left with the choice of $g(T_{k-1} - t)$ among the many functions which are suitable for this purpose. We will try to address in this section how to choose $g(T_{k-1} - t)$ based on real market data for CHF and EUR (for consistency with the tests performed in Section 5.5.2 we have chosen to use data from 15 August 2013).

After having obtained, at time $t = 0$, a term structure of volatilities α_k, from the calibration of the SABR models to caplet/floorlet smiles for a set of forward rates with maturities $T_1, \ldots, T_N$, we can calibrate $g(T_{k-1} - t)$ through the following relationship (which follows from Equation (4.2))

$$\alpha_k \approx \sqrt{\frac{1}{T_{k-1}} \int_0^{T_{k-1}} g(u)^2 \, du}, \tag{7.19}$$

by minimizing the sum of squared errors

$$\sum_{k=1}^{N} \left(\alpha_k - \sqrt{\frac{1}{T_{k-1}} \int_0^{T_{k-1}} g(u)^2 \, du} \right)^2. \tag{7.20}$$

Our first candidate for the function $g(T_{k-1} - t)$ is the exponential form already used for the LMM and given by

$$g(T_{k-1} - t) = (a + b(T_{k-1} - t))e^{-c(T_{k-1} - t)} + d. \tag{7.21}$$

The advantage of using the same $g(T_{k-1} - t)$, defined also for the standard LIBOR Market Model, is the computation speed characterizing this functional form. Although being a good candidate for the LMM case (due to a fairly standard and recurrent shape of the ATM caplet volatilities), this function does not seem to be able to accommodate the different shapes of α_k term structure seen in various markets. This is especially true when we are working with a fixed ρ_k (set as in our case to zero) and a varying β_k.

Instead of focusing on a specific form for $g\left(T_{k-1} - t\right)$, a different approach could be to choose a category of functions which can fit a very broad class of α_k term structure shapes and from this one obtain $g\left(T_{k-1} - t\right)$. An excellent candidate is the polynomial

$$a_0 + a_1(T_{k-1} - t) + a_2(T_{k-1} - t)^2 + \cdots + a_{n_{\text{pol}}}(T_{k-1} - t)^{n_{\text{pol}}}.$$

The corresponding $g\left(T_{k-1} - t\right)$ function is given by

$$g\left(T_{k-1} - t\right) = \left(\frac{\partial}{\partial\left(T_{k-1} - t\right)}\left(\left(a_0 + a_1\left(T_{k-1} - t\right) + a_2(T_{k-1} - t)^2\right.\right.\right. \quad (7.22)$$

$$\left.\left.\left. + \cdots + a_{n_{\text{pol}}}(T_{k-1} - t)^{n_{\text{pol}}}\right)^2\left(T_{k-1} - t\right)\right)\right)^{\frac{1}{2}},$$

where the $a_0, a_1, a_2, \ldots, a_{n_{\text{pol}}}$ parameters are chosen by minimizing Equation (7.20).

The order of the polynomial n_{pol} can be chosen differently for each market in which we are working (CHF, EUR, USD, etc.). Its choice has to be driven by the complexity of the α_k term structure shape that we want to fit and the maximum computational effort (hence speed) that we want to allocate to solve Equation (7.22).

A visual comparison of the calibration performances for two choices of $g\left(T_{k-1} - t\right)$ as defined by Equations (7.21) and (7.22), for (a portion of) the CHF and EUR markets as of 15 August 2013, is reported in Figures 7.5 and 7.6. The exponential form defined in Equation (7.21) performs extremely poorly when calibrated to the CHF α_k term structure. Better performances are achieved by reverting to the polynomial form, Equation (7.22), of order $n_{\text{pol}} = 3$ and particularly $n_{\text{pol}} = 4$. The EUR α_k term structure has a convex shape which is easier to calibrate. Although the exponential form is still providing an imperfect fit, we have obtained outstanding results using a polynomial of order $n_{\text{pol}} = 3$. The parameters for the various forms employed in the calibration exercise are reported in Tables 7.4 and 7.5.

Table 7.4 Exponential form parameters obtained from the calibration to 15 August 2013 market data for CHF and EUR

	a	b	c	d
CHF	1E-06	-3.89153	0.07312	18.82591
EUR	30.4296	-7.67966	0.77942	0.04588

Table 7.5 Polynomial form parameters (for various polynomial orders n_{pol}) obtained from the calibration to 15 August 2013 market data for CHF and EUR

$n_{pol} = 2$	a_1	a_2	a_3
EUR	0.05959	-1.83026	18.19524

$n_{pol} = 3$	a_1	a_2	a_3	a_4
CHF	0.0173	-0.54369	3.83366	8.21008
EUR	-0.00228	0.12685	-2.37447	19.20986

$n_{pol} = 4$	a_1	a_2	a_3	a_4	a_5
CHF	-0.00314	0.14824	-2.35722	13.19144	-5.65484

Once the minimization of Equation (7.20) has provided us with the set of parameters for the $g\left(T_{k-1} - t\right)$ form of our choice, we can proceed with the calculation of the $s_k\left(0\right)$ terms as follows

$$s_k\left(0\right) = \frac{\alpha_k}{\sqrt{\frac{1}{T_{k-1}} \int_0^{T_{k-1}} g\left(u\right)^2 du}}.$$

Applying $s_k\left(0\right)$ to $g\left(T_{k-1} - t\right)$ (as defined in Equation (7.12)), allows one to have a perfect fit to the SABR term structure of α_k.

7.4.4 Calibrating $h\left(T_{k-1} - t\right)$ to a term structure of v_k

The function $h\left(T_{k-1} - t\right)$ represents the instantaneous volatility of volatility $v_k\left(t\right)$. As introduced in Section 7.4.1 the relationship among these two functions can be written as

$$v_k\left(t\right) = h\left(T_{k-1} - t\right).$$

Rebonato (2007) proposes to extend it to

$$v_k\left(t\right) = h\left(T_{k-1} - t\right)\varepsilon_k, \tag{7.23}$$

where ε_k can be considered correction terms which will ensure a perfect match to the volatility of volatility v_k term structure obtained by a previous calibration of

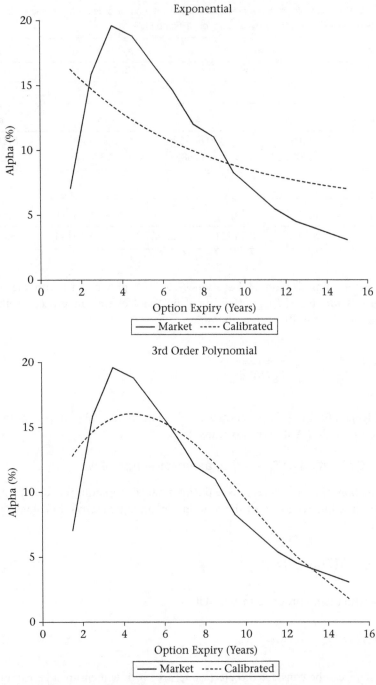

Figure 7.5 Calibration to the CHF term structure of volatilities α_k (Market) as of 15 August 2013. The calibrated curve (Calibrated) has been obtained using the exponential and polynomial (of order $n_{pol} = 3$ and $n_{pol} = 4$) forms for $g\left(T_{k-1} - t\right)$

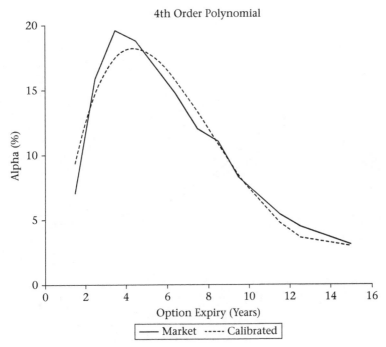

Figure 7.5 Continued

the SABR models to caplet/floorlet smiles for a set of forward rates with maturities $T_1, \ldots, T_N$. If all the ε_k are chosen to be equal to one, this implies that $h(T_{k-1} - t)$ has provided an exact match to the v_k term structure.

The link between the instantaneous volatility of volatility $v_k(t)$ and the volatility of volatility values v_k has been firstly proposed by Rebonato (2007) as

$$v_k = \varepsilon_k \sqrt{\frac{1}{(T_{k-1} - t)} \int_t^{T_{k-1}} h(u)^2 \, du,} \qquad (7.24)$$

and then further refined by Rebonato et al. (2009) as

$$v_k = \frac{s_k(0)}{\alpha_k T_{k-1}} \sqrt{2 \int_t^{T_{k-1}} g(u)^2 \int_0^u h(T_{k-1} - \theta)^2 \frac{u}{T_{k-1}} \, d\theta \, du.} \qquad (7.25)$$

As for the $g(T_{k-1} - t)$ case, the function $h(T_{k-1} - t)$ can also be chosen arbitrarily, and differently, for each market we are working with. A first, natural,

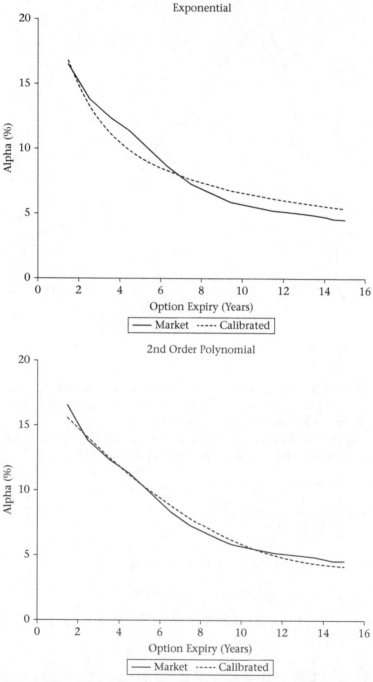

Figure 7.6 Calibration to the EUR term structure of volatilities α_k (Market) as of 15 August 2013. The calibrated curve (Calibrated) has been obtained using the exponential and polynomial (of order $n_{pol} = 2$ and $n_{pol} = 3$) forms for $g(T_{k-1} - t)$

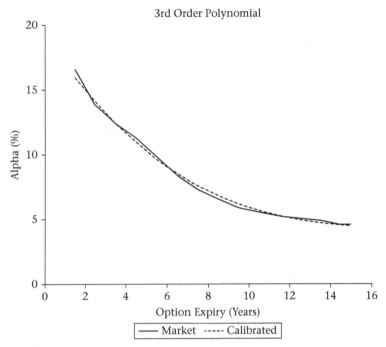

3rd Order Polynomial

Figure 7.6 Continued

candidate would be to define it as

$$h\left(T_{k-1} - t\right) = (a + b(T_{k-1} - t))e^{-c(T_{k-1}-t)} + d. \tag{7.26}$$

This choice has been tested for the CHF and EUR markets, during the period spanning June–December 2013. The results seem to indicate an excellent calibration fit to both aforementioned markets. For this reason we are not exploring other forms of $h(T_{k-1} - t)$, but the interested reader could, for example, use as an alternative, the polynomial form described and tested for $g(T_{k-1} - t)$ in Section 7.4.3.

We report in Figure 7.7 the testing results, using the parametric form of Equation (7.26). The parameters for exponential form employed in the calibration exercise are reported in Table 7.6.

The calibration, at time $t = 0$, has been done using the first of the two relationships between $v_k(t)$ and v_k proposed by Rebonato, and reported in

Equation (7.24). We have proceeded by minimizing the sum of squared errors

$$\sum_{k=1}^{N} \left(v_k - \sqrt{\frac{1}{T_{k-1}} \int_0^{T_{k-1}} h(u)^2 \, du} \right)^2, \tag{7.27}$$

using the Python function reported in Table 6.6, to solve for the terms

$$\sqrt{\frac{1}{T_{k-1}} \int_0^{T_{k-1}} h(u)^2 \, du}.$$

The ε_k terms have been calculated after the minimization exercise as

$$\varepsilon_k = \frac{v_k}{\sqrt{\frac{1}{T_{k-1}} \int_0^{T_{k-1}} h(u)^2 \, du}}. \tag{7.28}$$

7.4.5 Calibrating $\beta_k(t)$

The calibration of the $\beta_k(t)$ function is far less challenging than that which we have presented for the $g(T_{k-1} - t)$ and $h(T_{k-1} - t)$ functions. It is a simple interpolation of the β_k term structure obtained by a previous calibration of the SABR models to the caplet/floorlet smiles, which have as underlying a set of forward rates with maturities T_k, where $k \in \{1,\ldots,N\}$. It is possible to use various type of interpolation, with the most basic one (which we used in our tests) being piecewise constant (the value between two consecutive maturities T_k, T_{k+1} is kept constant). It is however conceivable to adopt more sophisticated interpolation methods by employing, for example, the Python library *scipy.interpolate*. This is recommended especially when the product that we are interested in pricing expires in between two maturities T_k, T_{k+1}, for which our model has been calibrated to the market.

The β_k term structures for (a portion of) the CHF and EUR markets, as of 15 August 2013, are depicted in Figure 7.8.

Table 7.6 Exponential form parameters obtained from the calibration to 15 August 2013 market data for CHF and EUR

	a	b	c	d
CHF	1E-06	32.30698	0.33192	28.50714
EUR	10.72253	−6.7093	0.0585	38.16168

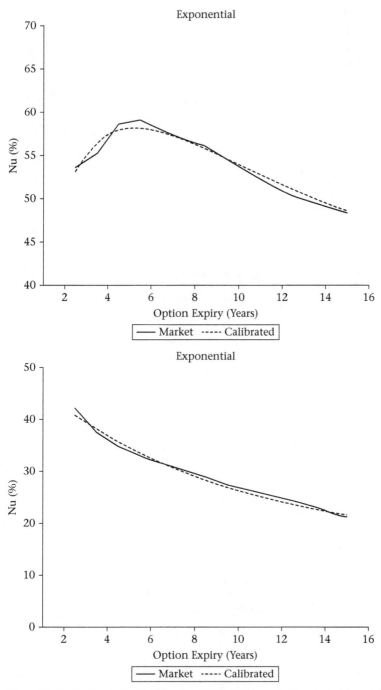

Figure 7.7 Calibration to the CHF (top) and EUR (bottom) volatility of volatility v_k term structure (Market) as of 15 August 2013. The calibrated curve (Calibrated) has been obtained using the exponential form for $h\left(T_{k-1} - t\right)$

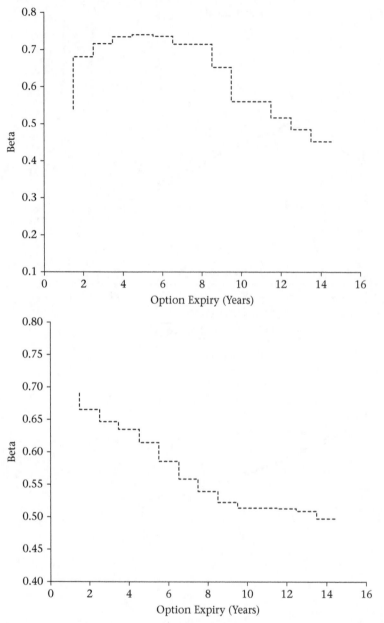

Figure 7.8 The β_k term structure for CHF (top) and EUR (bottom) as of 15 August 2013

7.5 Simulation and pricing

We dedicate this section to the technical details related to the implementation of the SABR LMM. We will present the Python code which can be used to simulate the term structure of forward rates under the terminal measure $\mathbb{Q}^N$.

The code suggested aims to be propaedeutic, and does not represent the best or fastest solution available. It is however, we believe, a good and compact solution which can be used as a starting point to expand towards more sophisticated implementations. In Section 7.5.1, together with the code, we will be also providing some hints and ideas on how the code performances could be improved. In Section 7.5.2 we will show some results obtained using the aforementioned code, on real market data. While in Section 7.5.3 we report a theoretical framework, firstly proposed by Rebonato and White (2009), on which to develop the calibration and pricing of swap dependent instruments.

7.5.1 Simulation of the forward rates under the terminal measure $\mathbb{Q}^N$ – Python code

The Python implementation of SABR LMM simulation (under the terminal measure $\mathbb{Q}^N$) is shown in Table 7.7. To be able to present the code in a compact and legible form, we are providing a specialized version of it, tailored around the null forward-volatility correlation (Section 7.3.4.2) framework. This allows the s_k drift term η_k to be zero. Moreover, our simulation, which starts at $t = T_0 \equiv 0$, spans across all the forward rates, where the first one is maturing at T_1 and the last one at T_N. However, this restriction can be relaxed with a minimal intervention into the code, in case only a subset of the forward rates $F_k(t)$, where $k \in \{1, \ldots, N\}$, is required for our pricing needs.

The Monte Carlo scheme used is a standard Euler. This choice has been based on the extensive analysis carried out in Section 5.7, where we have seen how more sophisticated schemes and techniques add little value to the final results, and are often not worth the additional computational effort required. The interested user is however recommended to modify the proposed code to include the ideas/methodologies introduced in Sections 5.7 and 6.5.3 if she or he feels these could benefit her or his final goals.

In order to achieve faster computation performance, we reduce the rank (employing the *reduceRank* Python function) of the sub-matrices ρ and ϑ. Similarly to $\hat{\rho}^{\text{reduced}}$ (Equation (6.36)) a reduced version of the ϑ sub-matrix is given by

$$\hat{\vartheta}^{\text{reduced}} = CC^\dagger, \tag{7.29}$$

where the matrix C has been obtained using the same steps followed to obtain the B matrix introduced in Section 6.5.1.

The reduced matrices are then used to generate the correlated Brownian motions through the *drawRandomNumbers* Python function, as explained in the example reported in Section 6.5.1.

The performances of the code presented can be greatly improved by pre-computing most of the quantities that are used during the simulation. For example, it is recommended to have readily available, before starting the simulation, the following:

cholesky_fwd_fwd, corr_fwd_fwd, cholesky_vol_vol, corr_vol_vol,

as well as dW_F, dW_s, and g_t, h_t. Those variables are all independent from the simulation in place. Moreover g_t, h_t can be reused multiple times (as long as the number of time steps n_{step} stays the same across the various pricing requests). The only time in which they should be recomputed is after a new calibration of the SABR models, which should however happen quite seldomly (once a day for example).

When dealing with callable products, or for the calculation of the risk sensitivities, it could be useful to store each path of the simulated variable F_t in its whole.

Table 7.7 Simulation of the SABR LIBOR Market Model under the terminal measure Q^N – Python code

```
import math
import numpy

def simulateSABRLMM (no_of_sim , no_of_steps ,
maturity_grid , F_0, s_0, epsilon , corr_fwd_fwd_full_rank ,
corr_vol_vol_full_rank , no_of_factors , beta , tau ,
a_g , b_g , c_g , d_g , a_h , b_h , c_h , d_h):
    '''
    Monte Carlo SABR LMM using Euler scheme .

    @var no_of_sim : Monte Carlo paths
    @var no_of_steps : discretization steps required
    to reach the option expiry date
    @var maturity_grid : list containing the forward
    maturities (in years). For example :
    [0.5 , 1.0 , 1.5 , 2.0 , 2.5 , 3.0 , 3.5 , 4.0 , 4.5 , 5.0]
    @var F_0: list of forward rate values at time t=0
```

```
@var s_0: list of correction terms s
@var epsilon: list of correction terms epsilon
@var corr_fwd_fwd_full_rank: forward-forward full rank
correlation matrix
@var corr_vol_vol_full_rank: volatility-Volatility
full rank correlation matrix
@var no_of_factors: number of factors which we want
to use in the simulation
@var beta: List of beta values
@var tau: forward rate rolling period (in years)
@var a_g: parameter a of the g function
@var b_g: parameter b of the g function
@var c_g: parameter c of the g function
@var d_g: parameter d of the g function
@var a_h: parameter a of the h function
@var b_h: parameter b of the h function
@var c_h: parameter c of the h function
@var d_h: parameter d of the h function
'''
no_of_fwds = len(F_0)
simulated_forwards = numpy.zeros((no_of_fwds, no_of_sim))
# Get the Cholesky decomposition as well as the reduced
# rank matrix from the full rank forward-forward
# correlation matrix
cholesky_fwd_fwd, corr_fwd_fwd = \
reduceRank(corr_fwd_fwd_full_rank, no_of_factors)
# Get the Cholesky decomposition as well as the reduced
# rank matrix from the full rank volatility-volatility
# correlation matrix
cholesky_vol_vol, corr_vol_vol = \
reduceRank(corr_vol_vol_full_rank, no_of_factors)
# Initialize variables
F_t = numpy.array([0.0] * no_of_fwds)
alpha_t = numpy.array([0.0] * no_of_fwds)
s_t = numpy.array([1.0] * no_of_fwds)
ds_t = numpy.array([0.0] * no_of_fwds)
# Get the last LIBOR fixing time.
# It is the next to last element stored in the time grid
last_maturity_index = len(maturity_grid) - 2
last_maturity = maturity_grid[last_maturity_index]
# Step length in years
dt = last_maturity / float(no_of_steps)
dt_sqrt = math.sqrt(dt)
no_sim = 0
while no_sim < no_of_sim:
    t = 0
    no_step = 1
    for fwd_k in range(0, no_of_fwds):
        s_t[fwd_k] = s_0[fwd_k]
        F_t[fwd_k] = F_0[fwd_k]
```

```
        ds_t[fwd_k] = 0.0
# Simulate the processes along the steps composing a
# path
while no_step <= no_of_steps:
    # The t variable will be used to get the parametric
    # vol. and vol. of vol. corresponding to the
    # time step being simulated
    t = no_step * dt
    # Generate the correlated Brownian motions used to
    # simulate dF and ds
    dW_F = drawRandomNumbers(no_of_factors,
                             cholesky_fwd_fwd) * dt_sqrt
    dW_s = drawRandomNumbers(no_of_factors,
                             cholesky_vol_vol) * dt_sqrt
    drift_F = 0.0
    shared_drift_part = [0.0] * no_of_fwds
    drift_correction = [0.0] * no_of_fwds
    # Simulate each forward rate,
    # starting from the last one
    for i in range(1, no_of_fwds):
        fwd_k = no_of_fwds - i
        # The simulation is run only for forward rates
        # which are still alive
        if t < maturity_grid[fwd_k - 1]:
            g_t = getInstantaneousVolatility(t, \
            maturity_grid[fwd_k - 1], a_g, b_g, c_g, d_g)
            h_t = getInstantaneousVolatility(t, \
            maturity_grid[fwd_k - 1], a_h, b_h, c_h, d_h)
            F_beta_t =math.pow(abs(F_t[fwd_k]),
                               beta[fwd_k])
            ds_t[fwd_k] = (h_t * epsilon[fwd_k] *
                          s_t[fwd_k] * dW_s[fwd_k])
            s_t[fwd_k] += ds_t[fwd_k]
            alpha_t[fwd_k] = g_t * s_t[fwd_k]
            # Zero absorbing boundary used for all the
            # beta choices except beta = 0 and beta = 1
            if ((beta[fwd_k] > 0 and beta[fwd_k] < 1)
                and (F_t[fwd_k] <= 0)):
                F_t[fwd_k] = 0.0
            else:
                drift_F = (-g_t * s_t[fwd_k] * F_beta_t *
                          shared_drift_part[fwd_k])
                F_t[fwd_k] += (drift_F * dt +
                              alpha_t[fwd_k] *
                              F_beta_t * dW_F[fwd_k])
                drift_correction[fwd_k - 1] = \
                corr_fwd_fwd[fwd_k - 1, fwd_k] * (tau * \
                g_t * s_t[fwd_k] * F_beta_t) / (1 + \
                tau * F_t[fwd_k])
                # Calculate the drift sum term
```

```
                       # to be used by the next forward which
                       # will be simulated
                       l = fwd_k
                       while l <= (no_of_fwds - 1):
                           shared_drift_part [fwd_k - 1] += \
                           drift_correction [l - 1]
                           l += 1
           no_step += 1
       # Store the forwards simulated in the current
       # Monte Carlo path
       for fwd_k in range(0, no_of_fwds):
           simulated_forwards [fwd_k, no_sim] = F_t [fwd_k]
       no_sim += 1

   return simulated_forwards
```

Table 7.8 SABR LMM Monte Carlo Euler scheme parameters tested

Market	Option Expiry	Time Steps n_{step}	Equivalent Time Steps per Year
CHF	4.5y	432	96
CHF	9.5y	912	96
EUR	4.5y	108	24
EUR	9.5y	228	24

7.5.2 Pricing of forward dependent instruments

7.5.2.1 *Choosing the number of time steps*

The choice of time steps n_{step} to use when simulating the SABR LMM is driven by the Monte Carlo convergence, which in turn is affected by the term structure of α_k , v_k and β_k . It is in particular the v_k term structure which seems to affect the most the number of time steps necessary to obtain a stable scheme. As can be seen in Table 7.8, the CHF market, characterized by a much higher v_k term structure (cf. Figure 7.7) has required considerably more time steps than that employed for the EUR market. The simulation results are reported in Section 7.5.2.2.

7.5.2.2 *Pricing of caplets and floorlets: numerical tests*

The code proposed in Table 7.7 has been tested using 15 August 2013 data for CHF and EUR. We have been pricing caplets/floorlets expiring in 4.5y and 9.5y. The testing benchmark used is a standard SABR Monte Carlo Euler scheme

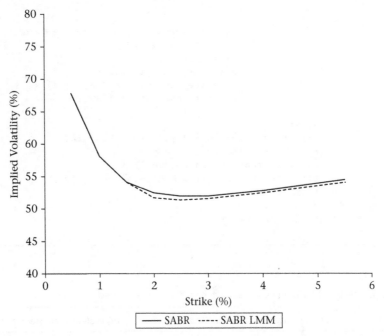

Figure 7.9 Black implied volatilities produced by SABR and SABR LMM for CHF caplets/floorlets expiring in 4.5y. Both SABR and SABR LMM have been simulated using a Monte Carlo Euler scheme with $n_{sim} = 10^5$ and $n_{step} = 432$

(Section 5.7.4). A visual comparison of the results produced by SABR and SABR LMM is reported in Figures 7.9, 7.10, 7.11 and 7.12.

7.5.3 Pricing of swap dependent instruments

7.5.3.1 Swap approximation using the SABR LMM Monte Carlo

Pricing of swap dependent instruments (such as swaptions) can be achieved using the same weight freezing techniques introduced for the LIBOR Market Model (Section 6.4.2). The forward swap rate at T_m is obtained through a weighted sum of forward rates and it can be approximated as

$$S_{m,n}(T_m) \approx \sum_{k=m+1}^{n} \omega_k(0) F_k(T_m).$$

All the forward rates $F_k(t)$ composing the swap rate $S_{m,n}(t)$ can be simultaneously simulated (under the same measure) employing a SABR LMM Monte Carlo code such as the one reported in Table 7.7.

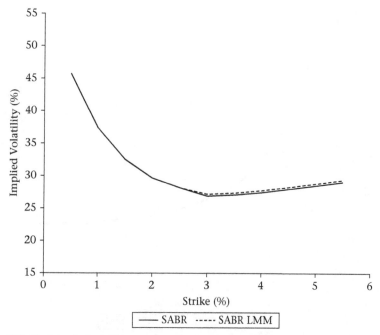

Figure 7.10 Black implied volatilities produced by SABR and SABR LMM for CHF caplets/floorlets expiring in 9.5y. Both SABR and SABR LMM have been simulated using a Monte Carlo Euler scheme with $n_{sim} = 10^5$ and $n_{step} = 912$

As the swap rate is a function of a set of forward rates, one would expect the swaption prices to be directly linked to the cap/floor market. However, various factors such as supply demand as well as different players active in these two markets do not guarantee that this relationship is always respected. As a result, the SABR LMM parameters calibrated to caplets/floorlets are not consistently capable of recovering the swaption quotes seen on the broker screens.

The information contained in the swaption market can be however captured through an approximation[4] proposed by Rebonato and White (2009). We will see in Section 7.5.3.2 how this can be used to adjust, for example, the entries of the correlation matrix Π.

7.5.3.2 *Rebonato and White swaption approximation*

We report for convenience the SABR (swap) model equations previously introduced in Chapter 5

$$dS_{m,n}(t) = \alpha_{m,n}(t) S_{m,n}(t)^{\beta_{m,n}} dW_{S_{m,n}}(t),$$

$$d\alpha_{m,n}(t) = v_{m,n} \alpha_{m,n}(t) dW_{\alpha_{m,n}}(t),$$

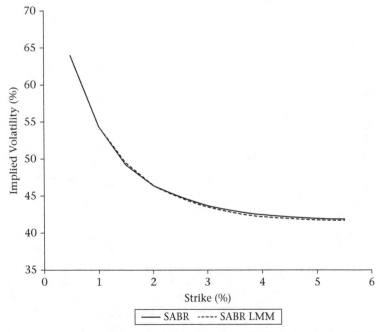

Figure 7.11 Black implied volatilities produced by SABR and SABR LMM for EUR caplets/floorlets expiring in 4.5y. Both SABR and SABR LMM have been simulated using a Monte Carlo Euler scheme with $n_{sim} = 10^5$ and $n_{step} = 108$

with

$$\mathbb{E}^{m,n}\left[dW_{S_{m,n}}(t)dW_{\alpha_{m,n}}(t)\right] = \rho_{m,n}dt.$$

The SABR LMM swaption approximation formulas (see, e.g., Rebonato and White 2009 and Dhamo 2011) give us the parameters $\alpha_{m,n}, v_{m,n}, \beta_{m,n}, \rho_{m,n}$ appearing in the above set of equations. In particular, the parameter $\alpha_{m,n}(t)$ at time $t = 0$ is, as usual, written as $\alpha_{m,n}$ and it is given by

$$\alpha_{m,n} = \sqrt{\frac{1}{T_m}\sum_{k,l=m+1}^{n}\left(\rho_{k,l}\mathbf{W}_k^{m,n}\mathbf{W}_l^{m,n}s_k(0)s_l(0)\int_0^{T_m}g(T_{k-1}-t)g(T_{l-1}-t)\,dt\right)},$$

with

$$\mathbf{W}_k^{m,n} = \omega_k^{m,n}(0)\frac{F_k(0)^{\beta_k}}{S_{m,n}(0)^{\beta_{m,n}}},$$

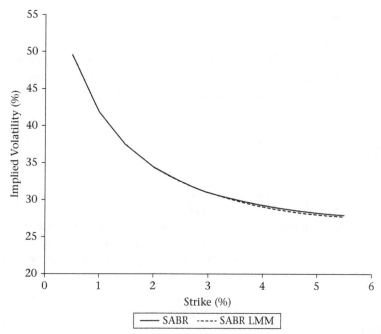

Figure 7.12 Black implied volatilities produced by SABR and SABR LMM for EUR caplets/floorlets expiring in 9.5y. Both SABR and SABR LMM have been simulated using a Monte Carlo Euler scheme with $n_{\text{sim}} = 10^5$ and $n_{\text{step}} = 228$

where $\omega_k^{m,n}(0)$ has been defined in Equation (6.32) and

$$v_{m,n} = \frac{1}{\alpha_{m,n} T_m} \left(2 \sum_{k,l=m+1}^{n} \left(\rho_{k,l} \vartheta_{k,l} \mathbf{W}_k^{m,n} \mathbf{W}_l^{m,n} s_k(0) s_l(0) \right. \right.$$

$$\left. \left. \cdot \int_0^{T_m} g(T_{k-1} - t) g(T_{l-1} - t) \int_0^t h(T_{k-1} - s) h(T_{l-1} - s) \, ds \, dt \right) \right)^{\frac{1}{2}},$$

$$\rho_{m,n} = \sum_{k,l=m+1}^{n} \Omega_{k,l} \phi_{k,l},$$

$$\Omega_{k,l} = \frac{2 \rho_{k,l} \phi_{k,l} \mathbf{W}_k^{m,n} \mathbf{W}_l^{m,n} s_k(0) s_l(0)}{\left(v_{m,n} \alpha_{m,n} T_m \right)^2}$$

$$\cdot \int_0^{T_m} g(T_{k-1} - t) g(T_{l-1} - t) \int_0^t h(T_{k-1} - s) h(T_{l-1} - s) \, ds \, dt,$$

$$\beta_{m.n} = \sum_{k=m+1}^{n} \omega_k^{m,n}(0) \beta_k.$$

These expressions can be employed directly in one of the SABR approximations presented in Chapter 5, to calibrate to the swaption market. The calibration can be performed by adjusting, for example, $\rho_{k,l}$ and $\vartheta_{k,l}$ to minimize

$$\sum_{y \in Y} \left(\sigma_{m,n}^{B-MKT}(y) - \sigma_{m,n}^{B}(y) \right)^2, \tag{7.30}$$

where Y represents the set of strikes to employ in the calibration, $\sigma_{m,n}^{B-MKT}(y)$ is the market implied volatility and $\sigma_{m,n}^{B}(y)$ is the Black implied volatility calculated using a SABR lognormal volatility approximation for a specific strike y, time to expiry T_m and tenor T_n. Performing the calibration by changing the entries of the ρ and ϑ matrices is a way to include (forward looking) market information into data generated using otherwise only historical observations.

Notes

1. The drifts presented in this chapter are related to a single curve framework. This is done as a way to simplify the results. Following the guidelines provided by Mercurio (2010) for the LMM, it is possible to obtain the SABR LMM drifts in a multi-curve framework. This set-up can be simplied in the same ways illustrated for the LIBOR Market Model in Section (6.5.2).
2. Particular care should be taken in discerning between $\rho_{k,l}$ and ρ_k. The former represents the correlation among the Wiener processes driving two forward rates in the (SABR) LIBOR Market Model (Sections 6.3 and 7.3.1), while the latter represents the correlation among the Wiener processes driving the forward rate and volatility in the SABR model.
3. The methods proposed by Rebonato et al. (2009), and reported here, differ from what we have presented in Section 6.5.1, as $BB^\dagger$ and $CC^\dagger$ yield correlation matrices (i.e., with ones on the diagonal) and not covariance matrices.
4. As mentioned in Section 7.3.4.2, this approximation does not work when using the null forward-volatility correlation approach.

A | Appendices

A.1 Time grid and day count conventions

In this appendix we will be reviewing some practical details related to the time grid

$$0 = T_0 < T_1 < \cdots < T_N,$$

introduced in Section 3.1 and used throughout the book. Let us consider the cash flows associated with an interest rate swap and illustrated in Figure 3.3.

Each payment is characterized by a period start and a period end. The year fraction between the period start and the period end is calculated using a leg specific day count convention such as ACT/360 or ACT/365. A CHF or EUR LIBOR leg uses a ACT/360 convention, meaning that each day between period start and period end is counted and then the number of days is divided by 360 (see Python code reported in Table A.1). Additionally, floating leg dates present a gap between the day on which the rate is settled and the day on which it is actually fixed.

A further consideration is related to the possibility that the fixing day or the period start date could fall on a holiday. Usually both the holiday calendar in London and the main financial hub of the currency associated to the rate are considered. For the CHF LIBOR this means that the fixing and period dates need to be business days in both London and in Zurich. The business day convention states what to do when this is not the case. Often LIBOR rates are adjusted according to the "Modified Following" convention. This particular business day convention adjusts the date to the next business date, unless it is the end of the month in which case it would take the previous one. A sample code to implement such an adjustment logic is reported in Table A.2.

We have so far only forgotten one important date, the pay date. The pay date of the cash flow depends strongly on the contract. If the rate is payed in advance, then it is actually payed at the period start date, that is, shortly after it has been fixed. If the cash flow actually settles in arrears, then the payment date is at the end of the period. This has an important implication on the calculation of the cash flow which is called convexity adjustment (see, e.g., Boenkost and Schmidt (2003) and Brigo and Mercurio 2006).

Table A.1 Year fraction between two dates depending on day count convention chosen – Python code

```python
def yearFraction(date1, date2, dcc):
    '''
    Compute the year fraction between two
    dates, for the cases 30/360 and ACT/360.

    @var date1: start date
    @var date1: end date
    @var dcc: string representing the day count convention
    '''
    #30/360
    if dcc == "30/360":
        yearfrac = (360.0 * (date2.year - date1.year)
                    +30.0 * (date2.month - date1.month)
                    + (date2.day - date1.day)) / 360.0
    #ACT/360
    elif dcc == "ACT/360":
        yearfrac=(date2.toordinal() - date1.toordinal()) / 360.0

    return yearfrac
```

Table A.2 Business dates adjustment – Python code

```python
def proceedDays(term, date):
    '''
    @var term: string representing how to move the date on
    the calendar
    @var date: date to adjust
    '''
    if('D' in term.upper()):
        newDate = startDate.toordinal()
        newDate += int(term[:-1])
        newDate = datetime.date.fromordinal(newDate)
    else:
        newDate = datetime.date(date.year, date.month, date.day)

    return newDate

def adjustBDate(date, bdc, ccy):
    '''
    @var date: date to adjust
    @var bdc: business date convention
    @var ccy: currency code
    '''
```

```
# It is a Sunday
if (date.isoweekday()==7):
    if('FOL' in bdc.upper()):
        return adjustBDate(proceedDays("1D", date), bdc, ccy)
    else:
        return adjustBDate(proceedDays("-2D", date),bdc, ccy)
# It is a Saturday
elif(date.isoweekday() == 6):
    if('FOL' in bdc.upper()):
        return adjustBDate(proceedDays("2D", date), bdc, ccy)
    else:
        return adjustBDate(proceedDays("-1D", date),bdc, ccy)
# It is a holiday. We use a HolidayCalendar object (code not
# displayed) which contains all the holidays associated to
# London and the currency main financial hub
elif(HolidayCalendar.isHoliday(date, ccy)):
    if('FOL' in bdc.upper()):
        return adjustBDate(proceedDays("1D", date), bdc, ccy)
    else:
        return adjustBDate(proceedDays("-1D", date),bdc, ccy)

return date
```

Table A.3 Possible constructor for a cash flow object. We introduced unadjusted period start and end dates as well, to see how the dates are adjusted. The year fraction and any time periods on the time grid are calculated using the *yearFraction* Python function

```
class CashFlowData(object):
    def __init__(self, asofdate, pStart, pEnd, payDate, unadEnd,
                 unadStart, dcc):
        self._payDate = payDate
        # Day count convention
        self._dcc = dcc
        # Period end
        self._periodEnd = pEnd
        # Unadjusted period end
        self._unadjustedPeriodEnd = unadEnd
        # Period start
        self._periodStart = pStart
        # Unadjusted period start
        self._unadjustedPeriodStart = unadStart
        self._yf = yearFraction(pStart, pEnd, dcc)
        asOfDate = asofdate
        self._tToPay = yearFraction(asOfDate, payDate, None)
        self._tToStart = yearFraction(asOfDate, pStart, None)
        self._tToEnd = yearFraction(asOfDate, pEnd, None)
```

In practice, we introduce instead of a list of dates a list of cash flow objects. In each of the cash flow objects, all dates associated with the cash flow are given. The object can have a structure similar to what is shown in Table A.3.

A.2 A note on hyperbolic geometry

We provide here a high level overview of the steps followed by Henry-Labordere (2008) and Paulot (2009) to find an alternative SABR approximation.

Their approach is based on solving the forward Kolmogorov equation for the density of the SABR distribution (Section 5.3). Solving the forward Kolmogorov equation as a parabolic PDE with the given boundary conditions is, at best, challenging, and no closed form formula exists. The authors therefore transform the PDE into a heat equation

$$\frac{\partial p}{\partial \theta} = \triangle p,$$

where $\triangle$ is the Laplace operator in the respective geometry. The heat equation is well known in hard sciences and solutions have been searched for decades.

The major difficulty, in the SABR model case, is to transform its Kolmogorov equation into a heat equation. The transformation uses geometry and transforms from the normal Euclidean space (our normal perception of space) into the hyperbolic Poincaré plane $\mathbb{H}^2$, Henry-Labordere (2008). The Poincaré plane can be visualized through the Poincaré disc or the upper half of the complex 2-d plane $\mathbb{C}$.

In order to arrive at the simple form of the heat equation, the authors transform the variables. Naturally for the SABR model, we want to get rid of the beta exponent and the cross terms. The time to expiry $\theta = T - t$ previously introduced in Section 5.3 needs a rescaling to $\theta \to \frac{v_k^2}{2}\theta$ and we obtain in the new variables the heat equation for the density in the hyperbolic Poincaré plane.

Although there is no closed form solution for the heat equation in this geometry available, the best approximation is a short-time asymptotic solution proved by DeWitt, Gilkey, Pleijel and Minakshisundaram, in short the DeWitt theorem, DeWitt (1975). As introduced for stochastic processes in Varadhan (1967a, 1967b), the short-time asymptotic solution can be written as a small time expansion on the heat kernel. The first-order term depends on the geodesic distance, which is the shortest distance between two points on a Riemannian manifold, which the Poincaré plane is. Calculating this geodesic distance between current forward rate and the strike then inserted into the first term of the expansion and integrated yields the implied volatility at zeroth order. A multiplicative factor of the heat kernel expansion provides the first-order (in time) correction to the implied volatility. The first corrective term of the heat kernel is translated into the second-order correction to implied volatility and similarly for higher order corrections, Paulot (2009). The authors usually stop the expansion at the second order in time on the volatility with a reasonable approximation.

These techniques are very powerful and have been applied successfully across different stochastic volatility models (Berestycki et al. (2004)) and different asset classes.

A.3 LIBOR Market Model in the HJM framework

The HJM framework introduced in Section 6.1.2 is a set of equations which should be obeyed by diffusive interest rate models. We recall that HJM models have risk neutral dynamics of the form

$$df(t, T_k) = \sigma(t, T_k) \int_t^{T_k} \sigma(t, u) du + \sigma(t, T_k) dW(t),$$

where $f(t, T_k)$ is the instantaneous forward rate at time t from maturity T_k to maturity $T_k + \Delta t$, and $\sigma(t, T_k)$ is its associated volatility function. From Equation (6.2), we can see that

$$\frac{dP(T_{k-1}, T_k \mid t)}{P(T_{k-1}, T_k \mid t)} = \cdots (dt) - \left(\int_t^{T_k} \sigma(t, s) ds - \int_t^{T_{k-1}} \sigma(t, s) ds \right) dW(t), \tag{A.1}$$

where $P(T_{k-1}, T_k \mid t)$ is a forward starting zero-coupon bond.

Transforming Equation (A.1) into an expression for the forward rate, we have

$$dF_k(t) = \ldots (dt) + \frac{1}{\tau_k} (1 + \tau_k F_k(t)) \int_{T_{k-1}}^{T_k} \sigma(t, u) \, du \, dW(t).$$

From the diffusion invariance principle, it then follows that the volatility of the LMM forward rate $F_k(t)$ is related to the HJM instantaneous forward volatility $\sigma(t, T_k)$ through the relationship

$$\sigma_k(t) = \frac{1}{\tau_k} (1 + \tau_k F_k(t)) \int_{T_{k-1}}^{T_k} \sigma(t, u) \, du.$$

As a sanity check, we can also see that, as the period τ_k tends to zero, the volatilities exactly match, that is, $\sigma_k(t) = \sigma(t, T_k)$. This shows that the LIBOR Market Model is consistent with the HJM framework.

A.4 Swap Market Model

Although it is possible to price swaptions using swaps rates constructed using the forward LIBOR rates we are modelling (Section 6.4.2), it is possible to treat the swap rate itself as the fundamental object to model. This was first developed by Jamshidian (1997) and it is known as the Swap Market Model (SMM).

As introduced in Section 3.3.3, the annuity $A_{d,m,n}$ is a suitable numeraire when working with swap rates since it is the numeraire under which the forward swap rate $S_{m,n}$ is a martingale. The associated measure $\mathbb{Q}^{m,n}$ is the forward swap measure, or swap measure. Under this measure, we can assume that the swap rate follows lognormal dynamics of the form

$$dS_{m,n}(t) = \sigma_{m,n}(t) S_{m,n}(t) dW_{m,n}(t),$$

where the $\sigma_{m,n}(t)$ are deterministic, but can be different for each m, n, and $dW_{m,n}$ is a Brownian motion under $\mathbb{Q}^{m,n}$. The price of a swaption, as calculated using the SMM, agrees with that calculated using the Black formula for swaptions, Equation (4.11). Jamshidian showed that under the assumption of deterministic volatilities, one can construct a self-financing portfolio consisting of zero-coupon bonds. A (payer) swaption at time t has, according to the Black formula, a value

$$A_{d,m,n}(t)\mathbf{Blk}\left(S_{m,n}(t), y, \sigma_{m,n}^{B}(y)\sqrt{T_m - t}, 1\right).$$

This can be rearranged as

$$S_{m,n}(t)\Phi\left(d_{m,n}^{+}\right)A_{d,m,n}(t) - y\Phi\left(d_{m,n}^{-}\right)A_{d,m,n}(t),$$

where

$$d_{m,n}^{\pm} = \frac{\ln\left(\frac{S_{m,n}(t)}{y}\right) \pm \frac{1}{2}\left(\sigma_{m,n}^{B}(y)\right)^{2}(T_m - t)}{\sigma_{m,n}^{B}(y)\sqrt{T_m - t}}. \tag{A.2}$$

There is a trade off one must make when deciding between the LMM and SMM. With the latter, we are able to price swaptions exactly, but we would need to make approximations to price caps, and vice-versa when using the LMM. The swap rate coming from the SMM is lognormally distributed, as is the forward rate coming from the LMM, though we must calculate these two rates under their natural measure for them to be so. However, these differences seem to be rather small (Brace et al. (1998)) in the sense that the swap rate calculated under the LMM is very close to being lognormal, so for practical purposes will suffice. Brigo and Mercurio (2006) apply a change of numeraire techniques to calculate the swap rate $S_{m,n}$ under $\mathbb{Q}^k$, and also the forward rate dynamics F_k under the measure $\mathbb{Q}^{m,n}$, to clarify the inconsistency. When pricing swaptions with the LMM, we are calculating the swap rate through Equation (6.31). From this complex relationship, we cannot expect a lognormally distributed swap rate to emerge from a lognormally distributed forward rate.

Bibliography

L. Andersen and J. Andreasen. Volatility skews and extensions of the Libor market model. *Applied Mathematical Finance*, 7(1):1–32, 2000.

L.B.G. Andersen and R. Brotherton-Ratcliffe. Extended Libor market models with stochastic volatility. *Journal of Computational Finance*, 9(1):1–40, 2005.

L.B.G. Andersen and V.V. Piterbarg. *Interest Rate Modeling I,II,III*. Atlantic Financial Press, 1st edition, 2010.

J. Andreasen and B.N. Huge. ZABR – expansions for the masses. *Working Paper, Danske Bank*, 2011.

A. Antonov, M. Konilov and M. Spector. SABR spreads its wings. *Risk*, 26(8):58–63, 2013.

A. Antonov and M. Spector. Advanced analytics for the SABR model. *Working Paper, Numerix Quantitative Research*, 2012.

L. Bachelier. *Theorie de la speculation*. PhD thesis, 1900.

B. Bartlett. Hedging under SABR model. *Wilmott Magazine*, (July/August):2–4, 2006.

H. Berestycki, J. Busca and I. Florent. Computing the implied volatility in stochastic volatility models. *Comm. Pure Appl. Math.*, 57:1352–1373, 2004.

M. Bianchetti. Two curves, one price. *Risk*, 23(8):66–72, 2010.

M. Bianchetti and M. Carlicchi. Interest rates after the credit crunch: Multiple-curve vanilla derivatives and SABR. *Working Paper, Intesa San Paolo Bank*, 2012.

F. Black. The pricing of commodity contracts. *Journal of Financial Economics*, 3: 167–179, 1976.

W. Boenkost and W.M. Schmidt. Notes on convexity and quanto adjustments for interest rates and related options. *Published by Hochschule fuer Bankwirtschaft/ HfB*, 2003.

T. Bollerslev. Generalized autoregressive conditional heteroskedasticity. *Journal of Econometrics*, 31:307–327, 1986.

A. Brace, D. Gatarek and M. Musiela. The market model of interest rate dynamics. *Mathematical Finance*, 7(2):127–147, 1997.

A. Brace, T. Dunn and G. Barton. Towards a central interest rate model. Option Pricing, Interest Rates and Risk Management: Handbooks in Mathematical Finance, Cambridge University Press, 1998.

D. Breeden and R. Litzenberger. Prices of state-contingent claims implicit in option prices. *The Journal of Business*, 51(4):621–651, 1978.

D. Brigo and F. Mercurio. *Interest Rate Models – Theory and Practice: With Smile, Inflation and Credit*. Springer Finance, 2nd edition, 2006.

D. Brigo and M. Morini. An empirically efficient analytical cascade calibration of the LIBOR market model based only on directly quoted swaptions data. *Working Paper*, 2003.

M. Capinski and T. Zastawniak. *Mathematics for Finance: An Introduction to Financial Engineering*. Springer, 2nd edition, 2011.

L. Capriotti and M.B. Giles. Algorithmic differentiation: Adjoint Greeks made easy. *Available at SSRN: http://ssrn.com/abstract=1801522*, 2011.

G. Cesari, J. Aquilina, N. Charpillon, Z. Filipovic, G. Lee, and I. Manda. *Modelling, Pricing, and Hedging Counterparty Credit Exposure.* Springer, 1st edition, 2009.

B. Chen, C.W. Oosterlee, and H. van der Weide. Efficient unbiased simulation scheme for the SABR stochastic volatility model. *Journal of Theoretical and Applied Finance*, 15(2), 2012.

O. Cheyette. Markov representation of the Heath-Jarrow-Morton model. *Working Paper, BARRA Inc.*, 1996.

M. Choudhry. *The Repo Handbook.* Butterworth-Heinemann, 2nd edition, 2010.

J.C. Cox and S.A. Ross. The valuation of options for alternative stochastic processes. *Journal of Financial Economics*, 3(1–2):145–166, 1976.

J. Crank and P. Nicolson. A practical method for numerical evaluation of solutions of partial differential equations of the heat-conduction type. *Advances in Computational Mathematics*, 6(1):207–226, 1996.

N. Denson and M.S. Joshi. Fast and accurate Greeks for the Libor market model. *Available at SSRN: http://ssrn.com/abstract=1448333*, 2009.

E. Derman and I. Kani. Riding on a smile. *Risk*, 7(2):32–39, 1994.

B.S DeWitt. Quantum field theory in curved space time. *Physics Report*, 19C(6): 295–357, 1975.

E. Dhamo. On the calibration of the SABR-Libor market model correlations. Master's thesis, University of Oxford, 2011.

P. Doust. No-arbitrage SABR. *The Journal of Computational Finance*, 15(3):3–31, 2012.

B. Dupire. Pricing with a smile. *Risk*, 7(1):18–20, 1994.

C. Francq and J.M. Zakoian. Maximum likelihood estimation of pure GARCH and ARMA-GARCH processes. *Bernoulli*, 10(4):605–637, 2004.

M. Giles. Adjoint methods for option pricing, Greeks and calibration using PDEs and SDEs. 12th Winter school on Mathematical Finance, Holland, 2012.

M. Giles and P. Glasserman. Smoking adjoints: fast evaluation of Greeks in Monte Carlo Calculations. *Risk*, 89–92, 2006.

P. Glasserman. *Monte Carlo Methods in Financial Engineering.* Springer, 2003.

P. Glasserman and X. Zhao. Fast Greeks by simulation in forward LIBOR models. *Journal of Computational Finance*, 3:5–39, 1999.

A. Griewank. *Evaluating Derivatives: Principles and Techniques of Algorithmic Differentiation.* Number 19 in Frontiers in Appl. Math. SIAM, Philadelphia, PA, 2000.

P. Hagan. Convexity conundrums: Pricing CMS swaps, caps and floors. *Wilmott Magazine*, (March):38–44, 2003.

P. Hagan and M. Konikov. Interest rate volatility cube: Construction and use. *Working Paper, Bloomberg L.P.*, 2004.

P. Hagan, D. Kumar, A. Lesniewski and D. Woodward. Managing smile risk. *Wilmott Magazine* (September):84–108, 2002.

P. Hagan and A. Lesniewski. LIBOR market model with SABR style stochastic volatility model. *Working Paper*, 2008.

P. Hagan, A. Lesniewski and D. Woodward. Probability distribution in the SABR model of stochastic volatility. *Working Paper*, 2005. Preprint available at http://www.lesniewski.us/papers/working/ProbDistrForSABR.pdf.

D. Heath, R. Jarrow and A. Morton. Bond pricing and the term structure of interest rates: A discrete time approximation. *Journal of Financial and Quantitative Analysis*, 25(4):419–440, 1990.

D. Heath, R. Jarrow and A. Morton. Bond pricing and the term structure of interest rates: A new methodology for contingent claims valuation. *Econometrica*, 60(1): 77–105, 1992.

M. Henrard. Explicit bond option and swaption formula in Heath-Jarrow-Morton one-factor model. *International Journal of Theoretical and Applied Finance*, 6(1): 57–72, 2003.

M. Henrard. *Interest Rate Modelling in the Multi-Curve Framework: Foundations, Evolution and Implementation*. Palgrave Macmillan, 1st edition, 2014.

P. Henry-Labordere. Combining the SABR and LMM models. *Risk*, 20(10):102–107, 2007.

P. Henry-Labordere. *Analysis, Geometry, and Modeling in Finance: Advanced Methods in Option Pricing*. Chapman and Hall, 2008.

J.C. Hull. *Options, Futures, and Other Derivatives*. Prentice Hall, 4th edition, 2000.

John D. Hunter. Matplotlib: A 2d graphics environment. *Computing in Science & Engineering*, 9(3):90–95, 2007.

F. Jamshidian. LIBOR and swap market models and measures. *Finance and Stochastics*, 1(4):293–330, 1997.

E. Jones, T. Oliphant, P. Peterson, et al. SciPy: Open source scientific tools for Python. *Available at http://www.scipy.org/*, 2001–.

I. Karatzas and S Shreve. *Brownian Motion and Stochastic Calculus*. Springer, 1988.

C. Kenyon and R. Stamm. *Discounting, Libor, CVA and Funding: Interest Rate and Credit Pricing*. Palgrave Macmillan, 2012.

J.W. Labuszewski. Understanding Eurodollar futures. *Available at CME: http://www.cme group.com/trading/interest-rates/files/understanding-eurodollar-futures.pdf*, 20, 2013.

A. Lewis. *Option Valuation under Stochastic Volatility*. Finance Press, 1st edition, 2000.

A. Martelli. *Python in a Nutshell*. O'Reilly Media, 2nd edition, 2006.

M. Matsumoto and T. Nishimura. Mersenne twister: a 623-dimensionally equidistributed uniform pseudo-random number generator. *ACM Transactions on Modeling and Computer Simulation (TOMACS) – Special issue on uniform random number generation*, 8(1):3–30, 1998.

F. Mercurio. Cash-settled swaptions and no-arbitrage. *Risk*, 21(2):96–98, 2008.

F. Mercurio. Interest rates and the credit crunch: New formulas and market models. *Working Paper, Bloomberg L.P.*, 2009.

F. Mercurio. LIBOR market models with stochastic basis. *Working Paper, Bloomberg L.P.*, 2010.

F. Mercurio and M. Morini. Joining the SABR and Libor models together. *Risk*, 22(3): 80–85, 2009.

F. Mercurio and A. Pallavicini. Swaption skews and convexity adjustments. *Technical report, Banca IMI*, 2006.

G. N. Milstein. Approximate integration of stochastic differential equations. *Theory of Probability and its Application*, 19(3):557–562, 1974.

M. Musiela and M. Rutkowski. *Martingale Methods in Financial Modelling*. Springer, 2nd edition, 2005.

C.R. Nelson and A.F. Siegel. Parsimonious modeling of yield curves. *The Journal of Business*, 60(4):473–489, 1987.

J. Obloj. Fine-tune your smile: Correction to Hagan et al. *Wilmott Magazine*, 2008.

L. Paulot. Asymptotic implied volatility at the second order with application to the SABR model. *Working Paper, Sophis Technology*, 2009.

V. Piterbarg. A stochastic volatility forward Libor model with a term structure of volatility smiles. *Working Paper, SSRN eLibrary*, 2003.

R. Rebonato. *Interest Rate Option Models*. John Wiley and Sons, 2nd edition, 1998.

R. Rebonato. *Modern Pricing of Interest-Rate Derivatives: The LIBOR Market Model and Beyond*. Princeton University Press, 2002.

R. Rebonato. *Volatility and Correlation: The Perfect Hedger and the Fox*. John Wiley and Sons, 2nd edition, 2004.

R. Rebonato. A time-homogeneous, SABR consistent extension of the LMM. *Risk*, 20 (11):102–106, 2007.

R. Rebonato, K. McKay and R. White. *The SABR/LIBOR Market Model: Pricing, Calibration and Hedging for Complex Interest-Rate Derivatives*. John Wiley and Sons, 2009.

R. Rebonato and R. White. Linking caplets and swaptions prices in the LMM SABR model. *The Journal of Computational Finance*, 13(2):19–45, 2009.

R. Sheppard. Pricing equity derivatives under stochastic volatility: A partial differential equation approach. Master's thesis, University of the Witwatersrand, 2007.

S. Shreve. *Stochastic Calculus for Finance II: Continuous-Time Models*. Springer Finance, 2008.

L.E.O. Svensson. Estimating and interpreting forward interest rates: Sweden 1992–1994. *Working Paper, Institute for International Economic Studies* (579), 1994.

S.R.S Varadhan. Diffusion processes in a small time interval. *Communications on Pure and Applied Mathematics*, 20, 1967a.

S.R.S Varadhan. On the behavior of the fundamental solution of the heat equation with variable coefficients. *Communications on Pure and Applied Mathematics*, 20(2): 431–455, 1967b.

L. Wu and F. Zhang. Libor market model with stochastic volatility. *Journal of Industrial and Management Optimization*, 2(2):199–227, 2006.

Index

annuity, 19
  cash, 27

Bachelier Louis, 34
  formula, 35
bank account, 12
Black model, 29
  delta, 38
  formula, 30
  gamma, 39
  implied volatility, 29, 32
  vega, 39

cap, 25
  Black model, 30
  normal model, 35
caplet, 25
cash account, 12
Cholesky decomposition, 79, 144
CMS, 98
continuously compounded spot rate, 12
control variates, 156
CSA, 6
Curve construction, 13, 15, 17

day count conventions, 203
delta, 38
differential geometry, 206

eurodollar futures, 20
  convexity adjustment, 124

financial crisis, 8
floor, 25
  Black model, 31
floorlet, 25
  Black model, 31
  normal model, 36

Fokker-Planck equation, 51
forward measure, 23
forward rate agreement, 18
FRA rate, 13

gamma, 39
Greeks, 37

Heath, Jarrow and Morton (HJM)
  framework, 120, 207

interest rate swap
  payer, 19
  receiver, 18
ISDA, 6

Kolmogorov equation
  backward, 51
  forward, 51, 206

LIBOR Market Model (LMM), 119
  caplet volatility calibration, 139
  caplet volatility parametrization, 138
  drift, 127
  dynamics, 125
  forward-forward correlation, 127
    calibration, 132, 135
    double exponential parametrization, 134
    exponential parametrization, 133
    exponential parametrization with decay control, 133
  Heath, Jarrow and Morton framework, 207
  Monte Carlo
    antithetic sampling, 149
    control variates, 150
    factor reduction, 143, 145